THE MYTH
OF RESEARCH-
BASED POLICY
& PRACTICE

MARTYN HAMMERSLEY

Los Angeles | London | New Delhi
Singapore | Washington DC

Los Angeles | London | New Delhi
Singapore | Washington DC

SAGE Publications Ltd
1 Oliver's Yard
55 City Road
London EC1Y 1SP

SAGE Publications Inc.
2455 Teller Road
Thousand Oaks, California 91320

SAGE Publications India Pvt Ltd
B 1/I 1 Mohan Cooperative Industrial Area
Mathura Road
New Delhi 110 044

SAGE Publications Asia-Pacific Pte Ltd
3 Church Street
#10-04 Samsung Hub
Singapore 049483

Editor: Katie Metzler
Editorial assistant: Anna Horvai
Production editor: Thea Watson
Copyeditor: Elaine Leek
Proofreader: Emily Ayers
Marketing manager: Ben Griffin-Sherwood
Cover design: Francis Kenney
Typeset by: C&M Digitals (P) Ltd, Chennai, India
Printed by: Replika Press Pvt Ltd, India

© Martyn Hammersley 2013

First published 2013

Library of Congress Control Number: 2012940573

British Library Cataloguing in Publication data

A catalogue record for this book is available from
the British Library

ISBN 978-0-85702-965-2
ISBN 978-0-85702-966-9 (pbk)

ONE WEEK LOAN

This book is due for return on or before the last date shown below.

SAGE has been part of the global academic community since 1965, supporting high quality research and learning that transforms society and our understanding of individuals, groups and cultures. SAGE is the independent, innovative, natural home for authors, editors and societies who share our commitment and passion for the social sciences.

Find out more at: **www.sagepublications.com**

CONTENTS

ACKNOWLEDGEMENTS

An earlier version of Chapter 1 was published in G. Thomas and R. Pring (eds), *Evidence-Based Practice in Education*, Buckingham, Open University Press, 2004.

Chapter 2 was presented in seminars at the Institute of Education (University of London), Westminster College (Oxford Brookes University) and Goldsmiths (University of London). An earlier version was published in the *International Journal of Social Research Methodology*, 8 (4), 2005, pp. 317–30, published by Taylor and Francis (http://www.tandfonline.com).

Chapter 3 was presented at the British Educational Research Association annual conference, University of Warwick, September 2006.

Chapter 4 was given as an invited plenary presentation at the Social Services Research Group Annual Workshop, St Catherine's College, Oxford, March 2006. Earlier versions were published in H.-U. Otto, A. Polutta and H. Ziegler (eds), *Evidence-Based Practice – Modernising the Knowledge Base of Social Work*, Opladen, Verlag Barbara Budrich, 2009 and in R. St Clair (ed.), *Education Science: Critical Perspectives*, Rotterdam, Sense Publishers, 2009.

An earlier version of Chapter 5 was published in G. Walford, E. Tucker and M. Viswanathan (eds), *The Sage Handbook of Measurement: How Social Scientists Generate, Modify, and Validate Indicators and Scales*, London, Sage, 2010.

Chapter 6 was given as a keynote lecture at a conference to celebrate 21 years of the Qualitative Research Unit at the National Centre for Social Research, London, June 2006. An earlier version was published in the *International Journal of Research and Method in Education*, 30 (3), 2007, pp. 287–306, published by Taylor and Francis (http://www.tandfonline.com), and a slightly different version in *Questioning Qualitative Inquiry*, London, Sage, 2008.

Chapter 7 was given as a paper at the British Educational Research Association annual conference, University of Exeter, September 2002. An earlier version was published in the *Oxford Review of Education*, 30 (2), 2004, pp. 165–81, published by Taylor and Francis (http://www.tandfonline.com).

Chapter 8 is a revised version of 'On "systematic" reviews of research literatures: a "narrative" reply to Evans and Benefield', *British Educational Research Journal*, 27 (5), 2001, pp. 543–54.

Chapter 9 was given as a talk to the Public Health Evidence Steering Group of the Health Development Agency, October 2002, and in the Department of Epidemiology and Public Health, University of Leicester, February 2003. An earlier version was published in A. Killoran, C. Swann and M. Kelly (eds), *Public Health Evidence: Changing the Health of the Public*, Oxford, Oxford University Press, 2006, published by Taylor and Francis (http://www.tandfonline.com).

Chapter 10 was given at the British Educational Research Association annual conference, Institute of Education, University of London, September 2007.

Chapter 11 is based on a paper given at a Medical Research Council-sponsored Health Services Research Collaboration Workshop, *Using Meta-ethnography to Synthesise Qualitative Research Findings*, Department of Social Medicine, University of Bristol, July 2003.

ABOUT THE AUTHOR

Martyn Hammersley is Professor of Educational and Social Research at The Open University. He has carried out research in the sociology of education and the sociology of the media. However, much of his work has been concerned with the methodological issues surrounding social enquiry. He has written several books, including: *Reading Ethnographic Research* (Longman 1991); *What's Wrong with Ethnography?* (Routledge 1992); *The Politics of Social Research* (Sage 1995); *Taking Sides in Social Research* (Routledge, 1999); *Educational Research, Policymaking and Practice* (Paul Chapman, 2002); *Questioning Qualitative Inquiry* (Sage 2008); and *Methodology, Who Needs It?* (Sage, 2011) and *Ethics in Qualitative Research* (Sage 2012).

INTRODUCTION

The relationship between research, on the one side, and politics, policymaking and other forms of social practice, on the other, has long been a matter of public concern. Indeed, it has been the site of controversies and crises, with recurrent demands for social science to play a more direct role.[1] The most recent crisis, which is the background to this book, was generated by the rise of the evidence-based practice movement in medicine in the 1980s and 1990s, and its later extension to other fields, notably education, crime, and social welfare (see Gray 1997; Davies et al. 2000; Sackett et al. 2000; Trinder 2000; Welsh and Farrington 2001; McSherry et al. 2002; Sherman et al. 2002; Otto et al. 2009).

The idea that evidence should inform political and social practice can be traced back at least as far as Machiavelli, who believed that wisdom distilled from practical political experience and comparative historical analysis could greatly improve the decisions made by 'princes'. Of course, what has been proposed more recently differs significantly, both in the nature of what counts as knowledge and in the role that it is required to play. For example, in the 1960s, in the United States and elsewhere, the evaluation of new government programmes came to be treated as a central task of social science. This was conceptualised by Donald Campbell under the heading of 'the experimenting society', in which the effectiveness of all new policies and practices was to be scientifically tested.[2] Moreover, as Campbell's slogan makes clear, initially the proposal was that this should be done via experimental method (Cronbach 1979).

---

[1] For a recent discussion of this issue in the context of criminology, see Loader and Sparks (2010). Nisbet and Broadfoot (1980) provide a history of recurrent debates in the field of education. Of course, the socio-political background to this issue has not been not unchanging. Maasen and Weingart (2005) sketch broad shifts that they label 'the democratisation of politics' and 'the politicisation of science'. These refer, respectively, to the growth in influence of political movements outside of the governmental system and governments' attempts to incorporate these, and to the ways in which researchers have been caught up in these developments and have also come to be involved in diverse institutions offering expert advice to governments and other audiences. In part, the second of these changes reflects a significant shift in the 'contract' between researchers and society, from a patronage model of funding to an investment model (see Guston and Keniston 1994; Demeritt 2000; Hammersley 2011).

[2] For his papers on this topic, see Campbell 1988b. See also Dunn 1998.

Later, methodological prescriptions were modified to allow quasi-experimental and other forms of quantitative evaluation. And subsequently all these forms of evaluation came to be criticised, on the grounds that they failed to measure key variables accurately, and did not take sufficient account of the unintended effects of policies and practices, both positive and negative. In the wake of this, various forms of qualitative evaluation were advocated, as providing a better understanding of policies, their implementation, and their results.[3]

In the 1990s the rise of the evidence-based practice movement involved renewed demands for experimental research that would directly inform policymaking and practice. The repercussions of this latest crisis are still being felt, and it has raised some important, albeit perennial, issues:

- How closely can and should social research be directed towards serving policymaking and practice, and of what kinds? What are the limits to the contribution it can make, in principle and in practice?
- Is there a hierarchy of research designs or methods as regards the likely validity of the findings they produce? If not, how are judgements to be made about what are better or worse methods for particular purposes?
- Is it possible to control and measure social variables? Is this a requirement in all kinds of research, at least if they are designed to inform policymaking and practice?
- Is the cumulative development of knowledge possible in the social sciences? Is it desirable? If so, what forms does it and could it take?
- What purposes do reviews of research literatures serve, and what character should they have? Is 'synthesis' the task, and if so what does this mean?

These are issues I will address in this book.

EVIDENCE-BASED MEDICINE

At the core of the evidence-based medicine movement of the late 1980s and 1990s was the argument that the effectiveness of much clinical practice is unknown, and that in some cases standard treatments have been shown by research to be ineffective, and occasionally even damaging to patients (Cochrane 1972; Chalmers 2003). Given this, it was insisted that more research on clinical treatments was required (see Daly 2005), and that medical practitioners must make themselves familiar with the latest research evidence, and only employ those treatments whose effectiveness has been demonstrated.

The main model for the kind of research required to supply this evidence was the randomised controlled trials (RCTs) introduced to check the efficacy and side effects of new drugs (Marks 1997). The argument was that this kind of research – involving random allocation of patients to treatment or control groups, or to groups

---

[3]For outlines of these developments, see Shadish et al. 1991 and Pawson and Tilley 1997: ch. 1.

receiving different treatments, plus measurement of outcome variables across these groups – could be extended to other kinds of clinical treatment. The evidence-based medicine movement stimulated a considerable increase in the amount of research carried out on the effects of a wide variety of clinical practices.

Another important feature of evidence-based medicine was the argument that the results of single studies, even RCTs, are unreliable. Effective practice must be based upon systematic appraisal of *all* the relevant research evidence about the treatment concerned. This stimulated the development of a large body of 'systematic reviews', often involving statistical meta-analysis (see Chalmers et al. 2002). Many of these were developed and made available via the Cochrane Collaboration, an internationally funded network devoted to this task.[4] The rise of online databases was seen as greatly facilitating access to evidence by clinical practitioners and others.

Within medicine, evidence-based practice was presented as an enhanced form of professionalism, one that ensured that clinical interventions were based upon the latest and best scientific results. At the same time, it was also sometimes lauded as playing a 'democratising' role. One aspect of this was the idea that it subverted the dominant medical hierarchy, in which younger, more recently trained staff deferred to their elders, whose knowledge of the relevant scientific evidence was probably outdated, and who were less able to use modern forms of ICT to access the latest findings. Another, perhaps even more important, aspect of democratisation was that the latest scientific evidence would become available to patients, via the Internet, who could therefore evaluate the basis on which decisions about their treatment were being made (Oakley 2000). Here, the shift to evidence-based practice was presented as empowering patients in their dealings with doctors.

In summary, then, in its original or classic version, what counted as evidence was restricted to that coming from 'scientific research', this being treated as trumping all other sources of information, and especially that from practical experience. Furthermore, such research was defined as experimental in design and involved the rigorous measurement of variables, with RCTs as the 'gold standard'. And the findings of multiple studies of this kind were to be synthesised via systematic review.

Another central assumption built into this classic model was that scientific evidence carries direct implications for practice that demand 'implementation'. Thus, experimental research findings synthesised through systematic reviews were seen as producing information about effect sizes that demonstrates 'what works' (and what does not). And it came to be argued that all professional practice, and policymaking too, must operate solely upon this type of evidence.

A final key assumption was that when policymaking and practice are evidence-based in this manner, outcomes will be significantly improved. It is important to note that what is meant by 'improved' here is 'made more effective'. The wider question of what are and are not desirable practical goals and means for policymaking and practice was largely taken for granted. This reflects a predominantly technical or instrumental orientation on the part of advocates of evidence-based practice.

---

[4]For information about the Cochrane Collaboration, see www.cochrane.org/.

THE SPREAD OF 'EVIDENCE-BASED PRACTICE' TO OTHER AREAS

As noted earlier, the influence of the evidence-based practice movement spread out from medicine into other fields, notably social welfare, crime and justice, and education; though the main initial effect was, of course, on social scientific work in the area of health. One of the significant developments here was establishment of the Campbell Collaboration, which like the Cochrane Collaboration was devoted to generating systematic reviews.

The main focus of the evidence-based *medicine* movement had been upon changing the attitudes and practices of clinicians, encouraging them to make use of the increasing amount of scientific evidence about clinical effectiveness available. However, when the notion of evidence-based practice was extended to other areas, the focus often shifted significantly: there were challenges to what was seen as the inadequacy of existing research in serving evidence-based practice. In particular, it was pointed out that much social scientific work is not directly concerned with determining 'what works' in terms of policy or practice. Furthermore, it was claimed that much of it is insufficiently rigorous when judged against the standard of the RCT.

Literature reviews in social science were also criticised as falling short of the requirements of systematic review. For example, Oakley (2007: 96) declared that 'most literature reviews in social science are selective, opinionated and discursive rampages through literature which the reviewer happens to know about or can easily lay his or her hands on'. She also complains that, even when less haphazard than this, reviews do not usually indicate what search procedures have been used to find relevant literature, and that there is frequently a lack of clarity about how studies were judged to be relevant and how the validity of their findings has been assessed. A further complaint was that traditional reviews tend to go 'no further than a narrative synthesis' (p. 96), the contrast here being with what is offered by statistical meta-analysis. Oakley also argued that different reviews on the same topic have often covered different ranges of literature, with little overlap. She claims that this is the reason why, currently, reviews of research literature in social science often produce conflicting findings, which of course causes major problems for any policymaker or practitioner attempting to act in an evidence-based fashion.

Within many fields of social research, in the UK especially, the impact of the evidence-based practice movement occurred against the background of an earlier shift away from the use of quantitative method and towards reliance upon qualitative approaches. Not surprisingly, therefore, it was usually qualitative work that came to be subjected to most criticism by the proponents of research-for-evidence-based practice – though quantitative work that does not involve random allocation to treatment and control groups was also sometimes challenged (Chalmers 2003).

These criticisms of the deficiencies of existing research were often framed not just in methodological terms but also as complaints about an inadequate 'return' on public 'investment'. And there were sometimes appeals for external, government intervention to rectify the situation (see, for example, Hargreaves 1996). This reflected the fact that, in influential quarters, the notion of evidence-based practice had quickly become entangled with 'the new public management', a set of ideas about how the public sector must be reorganised. This was a major influence on politicians and other policymakers, and on the media, in many Western societies from the 1990s onwards (Ferlie et al. 1996; Pollitt 1990; Clarke and Newman 1997; Mayne and Zapico-Goni 1997; Pollitt 1998; Lane 2000; Levy 2010). What was involved here was a demand for 'transparent' accountability on the part of those professional occupations that formed part of the public sector, from doctors and nurses to teachers, social workers and probation officers. It was believed that requiring the work of these professionals to be explicitly based upon research evidence about 'what works' would make them accountable, and thereby increase their effectiveness – with 'cost-effectiveness' increasingly being brought into the calculation.

THE CRITICAL CASE OF EDUCATION

While the evidence-based practice movement affected several social science areas, the one where it probably had the most dramatic impact was education. In the UK, the first major sign of what was to come was a lecture by David Hargreaves in 1996, sponsored by the Teacher Training Agency, in which he criticised educational research for failing to provide the kind of evidence that is needed for evidence-based practice. The requirement he laid down was that it should demonstrate 'conclusively' that some change in practice leads to a 'significant and enduring improvement in teaching and learning' (Hargreaves 1996: 5). In making this critique, Hargreaves held up as a model what he saw as the very different situation in medicine.[5]

Subsequent to Hargreaves' lecture, both the Office for Standards in Education (Ofsted) and what was then the Department for Education and Employment (DfEE) set up inquiries into educational research, and both these reported in 1998. In a brief introduction to the first of these reports, Chris Woodhead, then Chief Inspector of Schools, declared that much educational research is 'on this analysis, at best no more than an irrelevance and a distraction' (Tooley 1998: 1). Furthermore, in the press release for the report (which was headed 'Majority of academic educational research is second-rate') he suggested that 'considerable sums of public money are being pumped into research of dubious quality and little value'. The DfEE-sponsored Hillage Report also raised questions about the quality, and especially about the usefulness, of much educational research, suggesting both that it should be more policy- and practice-relevant and that government ministers and policymakers needed to take more notice of research evidence (Hillage et al. 1998). These two critical reports on educational research were followed by a government statement about what needed to be done to remedy the situation. In the words of Charles Clarke, then Parliamentary Under-Secretary of State at the DfEE, the aim was to '*resurrect* educational research in order to raise standards' (Clarke 1998; emphasis added).

In the wake of these developments, the UK government instituted various policies designed to reform this field of inquiry. One was the establishment of a National Forum for Educational Research, whose task was to facilitate the identification of

---

[5]For a detailed assessment of Hargreaves' argument, see Hammersley 2002: ch 1.

research priorities, to specify quality standards in the field, and to maximise the impact of research on policymaking and practice. Another initiative was the creation of the Economic and Social Research Council's (ESRC) Teaching and Learning Research Programme, which for several years became the conduit for the bulk of external funding for research on education (see Christie and Pollard 2009). A 'research capacity building' arm of this programme was also set up, designed to up-skill education researchers, particularly in the area of quantitative techniques. Equally important, the Evidence for Policy and Practice Information Co-ordinating Centre (EPPI-Centre) was established at the Institute for Education, University of London, in order to facilitate the production of systematic reviews of available research. These reviews were aimed at policymakers and practitioners, so that they could determine which school policies or pedagogical techniques are effective, and thereby improve the performance of the British education system. Equally important was the hope that the production of systematic reviews would reshape the form and character of educational research in the future, so that it would more closely meet the require-ments of policymaking and practice.[6] There were also some schemes designed to facilitate schoolteachers doing research (this had been one of Hargreaves' recom-mendations) and to disseminate research findings across the profession.[7]

The connection with the 'new public management' was important here. This pro-moted the view that the primary role of the education system is to facilitate national economic growth and competitiveness. As Alison Wolf points out in her book *Does Education Matter?*:

> Politicians' faith in education is fuelled by a set of clichés about the nature of the twenty-first-century world: globalized, competitive, experiencing ever faster rates of technical change. In this world, it seems, education is to be a precondition of economic success, and indeed survival, to an even greater degree than in the cen-tury before. (Wolf 2002: xi)[8]

And these ideas were extended beyond schooling to universities and the research that takes place within them. In the words of one of the politicians centrally involved in the crisis, universities should be aiming to 'turn ideas into successful businesses' (Clarke, in Department for Education and Skills 2003). Along with this came the demand that university researchers maximise the 'impact' of their work, this being *measured* in order to document the 'return' on the investment made by funding bodies.

---

[6]On what is required from research syntheses in the context of policymaking, see Davies 2006.

[7]This continues today, for example via the Centre for the Use of Research and Evidence in Education: see www.curee.co.uk/home. See also Evidence-Based Education UK (EBE Network). See http://www.cemcentre.org. For a similar venture in the United States, see the What Works Clearinghouse: http://ies.ed.gov/ncee/wwc. See Foster 1999 for an assessment of the quality of some of the research stimulated by some of these schemes. In fact, there had been practitioners of action research movements within the field of education preceding the rise of evidence-based practice. See Chapter 7.

[8]Wolf mounts a cogent challenge to these assumptions.

The field of education also took the brunt of the criticism in the United States. An early signal there was the publication of a book by the then Secretary of Education which purported to determine 'what works' in teaching and learning (Bennett 1986; see Glass 1987). In 1999, the Reading Excellence Act was passed, specifying the sort of 'scientifically-based' research upon which recommendations for teaching reading should be based. In 2000 there was a request from the National Educational Research Policy and Priorities Board to the National Research Council to set up a committee to examine what constitutes 'scientifically-based education research'. Its report was published in 2000, defining this primarily from within the methodological framework of quantitative method – though it recognised the value of qualitative work under this heading, as well as acknowledging that of 'non-scientific' forms of inquiry in the field of education (see Feuer et al. 2002 and National Research Council 2002).

Subsequently, however, the reauthorisation of the Elementary and Secondary Education Act ('No Child Left Behind') defined 'scientifically-based research', in other words that which could receive Federal funding, more narrowly as involving hypothesis-testing through experimental and quasi-experimental designs, with a preference for random allocation to treatment and control groups. Furthermore, the Department of Education's 2002–7 strategic plan was published, which specified the goal that 75% of its funded research addressing causal hypotheses should use random assignment by 2004. There was also an Education Sciences Reform Act in 2002, designed to set up an institutional framework aimed at ensuring that research serves evidence-based policymaking and practice; here, however, a slightly broader definition of what counts as 'scientific' educational research was adopted than that of the 2001 Act (Eisenhart and Towne 2003).

In this political climate, some members of the educational research community sought to promote randomised controlled trials and systematic reviews (Mosteller and Boruch 2002; Slavin 2002, 2004). Others, especially qualitative researchers, mounted a vigorous critique.[9] Many denounced what they saw as a 'new orthodoxy' (Hodkinson 2004) and dismissed not just its definition of what counts as scientific research, and the priority given to this, but also its conception of the contribution that research can and should make to policymaking and practice.

LIBERALISATION WITHIN LIMITS

Over time, and not least as a result of the move into social science, the notion of research for evidence-based practice came to be liberalised in important respects. One of these concerned what counts as scientific evidence. It was acknowledged that other kinds of research besides RCTs can be of value, though sometimes the

---

[9]For examples, see Erickson and Gutierrez 2002; St Pierre 2002; Atkinson 2004; Lather 2004; Lincoln and Cannella 2004; Maxwell 2004; MacLure 2005; Ryan and Hood 2004; Denzin and Giardina 2006; Eisenhart 2006; St. Pierre 2006. See also Cook 2001, Biesta 2007, Donaldson et al. 2009, and St Clair 2009.

relaxation was quite limited and grudging. For example, addressing the issue of what types of research should be included in systematic reviews, Farrington and Welsh (2001: 9) state that:

> In the case of criminology and criminal justice, this means experimental (random-ized and nonrandomized) and quasi-experimental designs. Ideally we would have been able to limit studies in systematic reviews to only those that used random-ized experimental designs, as this is the most convincing method of evaluating crime prevention programs (Farrington 1983). However, for systematic reviews of criminological interventions, this is rarely feasible …

A more liberal approach was generally adopted in the field of education, with qualitative work increasingly being included as a source of evidence. Nevertheless, it was often seen as playing a subordinate role, for example providing information about the perspectives of those on the receiving end of policies or programmes (see Harden 2006). Furthermore, the narrow conception of the purpose of research characteristic of the evidence-based practice movement – as being con-cerned with 'what works' – was retained. This first aspect of liberalisation prompted various efforts to specify criteria by which qualitative research should be judged, for inclusion in systematic reviews and more generally (Spencer et al. 2003; see Chapter 7), and also the development of procedures for qualitative syn-thesis (see Chapter 10).

A second area of liberalisation involved increasingly explicit recognition that any form of practice necessarily involves the exercise of interpretation and judgement, rather than simply the 'application' of research findings. This was reflected in a shift in terminology from evidence-*based* to evidence-*informed* practice. Once again, though, this was a slackening of the constraints imposed by the original, classical model, rather than a substantial change in its character. Indeed, sometimes this liberalisation was not much more than window-dressing, with advocates oscillating between classic and more liberal versions.[10] Furthermore, within policy circles, some research evidence continued to be treated as if it were demonstrably valid and carried direct instructions to practitioners. Thus, in the field of education it came to be accepted as conventional wisdom that teaching reading via phonics had been demonstrated by RCTs to be the most effective pedagogical strategy, even though the evidence does not support this: it shows that 'systematic phonics' increases 'reading accuracy' but tells us little about its effect on reading comprehension. Moreover, there are important caveats about the reliability of this evidence (Torgerson et al. 2006: 46–7).

Liberalisation reduced the areas of disagreement between advocates of evidence-informed practice and many of their opponents. In doing this, however, it drained the original idea of its radical distinctiveness: the resulting position does not differ significantly from earlier calls for social research to be more policy- and practice-relevant, or indeed from the commitment of many social scientists to maximise the

---

[10]Pawson (2006: viii) describes the phrase 'evidence-informed' as 'thin-lipped, prissy and politically correct'.

impact of their work. A further important consequence of this was that liberalisation reduced the visibility of important issues that the classic model had highlighted.

One of these concerned whether there is a sharp, and hierarchical, distinction to be drawn between the knowledge produced by research (of some specified kind) and 'spontaneous' understandings generated by practical engagement with the world. The classic model of evidence-based practice treats research as providing definitive knowledge whereas practical experience is portrayed as thoroughly unreliable. A second issue raised by this model is whether the knowledge produced by research is limited to factual knowledge about some delimited realm, or can provide a comprehensive basis for action that can replace unreliable lay understandings, and lead to the improvement or even transformation of policymaking and practice. Here questions about the relationship between expertise, technique and values are involved.

It is worth noting that these two issues relate to central themes of Enlightenment thought, and in broad terms can be traced even further back, for example to Plato's *Republic*. In the nineteenth century they were developed into 'grand' conceptions of the role of social science, along divergent lines initially mapped out by Comte and Marx, and these continued to be influential well into the twentieth century (Hammersley 1999). From this perspective, the social scientist should be a public or organic intellectual (Hammersley 2011: ch. 2), if not a 'legislator' (Bauman 1987).

Such views, at least implicitly, underpin social scientists' frequent complaints that their research findings have been ignored by policymakers or practitioners, or that current policies or practices fly in the face of these findings. Indeed, those views often motivate even the strongest opponents of the sort of positivist conception of social science that characterises the evidence-based practice movement. Thus, most varieties of 'critical' research – whether influenced by Marxism, feminism, or anti-racism – present themselves as supplying conclusions about what is wrong, and what should be done, that are superior to those of 'commonsense'; in fact, the latter is frequently dismissed as ideological. In these terms, researchers may be portrayed as dispensing reason, where others are preoccupied with instrumental concerns, values, emotions, and political imperatives (Garland and Sparks 2000: 19). Of course, there is a major difference here in what is taken to be the source of knowledge and how its validity is grounded (systematic theory or a critical perspective rather than 'scientific' research design), as well as in the character of the implications drawn (major social change rather than 'piecemeal social engineering'). Nevertheless, in its fundamentals, a grand conception of research is widely shared among social scientists: it is often assumed that the knowledge they produce can generate conclusions that should replace or correct the practical knowledge of actors, and that this will bring about substantial improvement in the world. At this most fundamental level, there is continuity between arguments for evidence-based practice and much of the rest of social science, despite other important differences.[11]

---

[11]Of course, in the last decades of the twentieth century the contrasts between reason and unreason, knowledge and opinion, etc., came under challenge from that heterogeneous range of ideas labelled 'post-structuralism' or 'postmodernism'. It is important to point out, though, that this involved re-inscribing the distinction between knowledge and opinion in sceptical terms, so that now the contrast was between a select intellectual elite who know that all value, meaning and knowledge are arbitrary and uncertain, and the rest of us who do not.

In many ways it is this grand conception of the role of social science that is being challenged in the chapters that follow. One of my central concerns is limits on the capabilities of research: what is it able to produce, and what is the relationship between this and the demands of policymaking and practice? I argue that the evidence-based practice model greatly exaggerates the current capacities of research, and involves naïve assumptions about the nature of policymaking and practice. But it is not alone in this.

DIVERSITY IN RESEARCH AND PRACTICE

Both social research and policymaking/practice can take diverse forms, whose character and requirements may differ significantly. In the case of research, we need to distinguish between academic and practical forms, the first being geared to building knowledge in a disciplinary field, the second to addressing some specific issue with a view to supplying relevant information to lay audiences concerned with it (Hammersley 2002: ch. 6). And both these types of research must be differentiated from what I refer to in Chapter 7 as inquiry-subordinated-to-another-activity.

The status and value of *academic* research has come under severe challenge as a result of the rise of the evidence-based practice movement, with its prioritising of a particular kind of applied work. This has been exacerbated by the emergence of the 'new public management', and the way that this has shaped research funding and the internal organisation of universities (Collini 2012). Despite recurrent acknowledgement of the importance of 'blue skies' research, the predominant emphasis has been on the need for research that assesses the 'effectiveness' of policies and practices.[12] Given this, it is very important to emphasise the distinctive character and value of academic research (Hammersley 2011), and this requires us to challenge the economistic rhetoric that currently dominates policy talk, and even infuses discussions about the 'strategic planning of research' within universities.

Just as there are different kinds of research, so too there are many forms of practice, and these can vary considerably in how they use research findings. They include:

1   Individual consumers or service users who are faced with personal decisions to which social science findings might be relevant.
2   Occupational practitioners and organisational managers who, in the course of their work, must make decisions, adopt or devise strategies for dealing with problems etc., and may turn to social science for help. The issue here could be the effectiveness of strategies available to them, but research can supply other specific kinds of information, offer a new perspective on the situation faced, or provide background information that allows for better decisions to be made.

---

[12]There are, in any case, important differences between blue skies research and academic inquiry. Furthermore, while the first is almost always a low priority for policymakers in practical terms, the second is either off the radar or is itself a target of abuse: see Hammersley 2000a.

3   Policymakers in governments, and politicians, may draw on social science in the two ways already mentioned. However, they may also be interested in using social science as a source of ammunition for promoting, protecting, or challenging particular policies.

4   Citizens within polities that provide some scope for public participation in policy formation may draw on research findings relevant to the issues in which they are interested. They may be concerned with coming to an informed judgement about what is wrong and what should be done, but they may also often seek to use research as ammunition.

5   Interest groups involved in the policy process will also have diverse attitudes towards research evidence, and like politicians they may be locked into particular positions that they feel compelled to promote or defend.

It is also of significance that any use made of social science findings takes place not only in the context of the availability of information from other sources, but also within fields where ideological viewpoints of various kinds are in play, under the influence of conflicting interests. These viewpoints may not only represent particular issues as having the highest priority but also carry frameworks for understanding them that favour accepting the validity of some research findings while discouraging acceptance of others (Weiss 1983). In other words, in late modern Western societies the contexts within which individuals, citizens, practitioners, policymakers and others operate are often ones in which a diverse range of agents is promoting particular views about what are important problems, how they should be understood, how they ought to be dealt with, and so on. And many of these agents label what they offer as the products of research.

So, all use of social science findings today operates in very 'noisy' and conflictual environments.[13] The discourse that takes place in these is, almost always, very different from the sort of rational dialogue that has often been seen as the ideal in academic discussion, and that some proponents of deliberative democracy believe could operate within the public sphere. What this highlights is the importance of being realistic about the nature of the world in which research, policymaking and practice now operate (Geuss 2008; Swift and White 2008). Such realism is not, I suggest, commonly found in advocacy of evidence-based policymaking and practice, or for that matter in much discussion by social scientists of the political or practical implications of their work.

We should also recognise that policymaking, while itself a form of practice, is institutionally distinct from the various kinds of occupational practice to which it relates. Thus, there are important differences, and complex relationships and tensions, between them. A striking feature of the last couple of decades is the way that research has often come to be entangled in these relationships. Thus, in the context of the 'new public management', research has frequently been used as a means of challenging practitioner claims to expertise, thereby extending policymakers' control, and

---

[13]Loader and Sparks (2010: 3) note how policymaking in crime and justice has 'heated up', coming to be dominated by 'punitive passions and short-term political calculation'. There has also been a heating of some other policy areas, including those of social work and education.

subjecting various occupations in the public sector to new regimes of monitoring purportedly based upon research knowledge. In this manner, many researchers have become implicated in the currently dominant neoliberal model of policymaking (see Steger and Roy 2010). Whatever one's political assessment of this, it is not hard to recognise that it has been consequential for social science.

OVERVIEW OF CHAPTERS

Each essay in this book is designed to stand on its own, despite the interconnections among the issues discussed. As a result, there is occasionally some overlap, but generally the chapters traverse the terrain via different routes, so that where the same ground is covered it will usually be viewed from a somewhat different angle.

The first chapter outlines the key assumptions underpinning the notion of evidence-based practice in its classical form, and the role that research is required to play in enabling it. I begin by noting the radical claims advocates of this notion frequently made, and their reliance upon rhetorical ploys: the very name 'evidence-based practice' seems to dismiss what it excludes, treating this as irrational – who would deny the legitimate role of evidence in policymaking and practice? The chapter goes on to examine how certain kinds of research are privileged – those employing randomised control trials or quantitative methods more generally – and how research evidence is valued above other sources of knowledge, notably professional experience. I argue that there are features of research-based knowledge that count against the role that the notion of evidence-based practice requires it to play. Equally important, I show that the transmission of research evidence to policymakers and practitioners, and their use of it, are much more difficult and complex processes than is typically assumed. Finally, I examine the rise of the 'new public management' and its role in fuelling the influence of 'evidence-based practice'. I spell out why the claims to 'transparency' on which managerialism relies are false, noting the distortions that an overemphasis on 'objective' indicators introduces into policymaking and forms of occupational practice.

Chapter 2 explores how arguments about research for evidence-based practice relate to recurrent debates about both the 'failure' of research to serve policymaking and practice *and* the 'failure' of policymakers and practitioners to make proper use of research findings. The assumptions underpinning the idea of research-based practice are spelt out in more detailed terms here, and doubts about them identified. Central are the widely held ideas that research can supply all the knowledge required by practitioners and policymakers, and that research-based policies and practices will greatly improve outcomes.

The next chapter focuses upon the way in which a particular image of scientific research is central to arguments about evidence-based practice. The claim is not just that policymaking and practice should rely primarily or exclusively upon the best scientific evidence, but also that they should adopt a mode of rationality that is taken to be characteristic of science, in which conclusions are derived from evidence, via some highly determinate means, such as deduction or calculation. I examine the assumptions involved here, noting that they derive from a simplified version of the kind of positivism influential in the philosophy of science in the first half of the twentieth century. I argue that one does not need to adopt the more extreme arguments within the philosophy and sociology of science to recognise that scientific work necessarily relies upon tacit knowledge and judgment, and is therefore very similar in form to the kind of occupational practice that advocates of evidence-based practice criticise and seek to reform.

Chapter 4 begins by looking at the nature of evidence, and in particular at how what counts as evidence is dependent upon the particular question being addressed, as well as on the level of reliability required. I then examine the arguments proposing the superiority of the evidence from randomised controlled trials, suggesting that this relies upon erroneous methodological assumptions. The second half of the chapter points out that policymaking and practice cannot be 'based on' research evidence, that they necessarily involve experience and judgment and therefore demand expertise that has the character of phronesis.

A central assumption of the evidence-based practice model is that, in order to provide sound evidence, research must *measure* outcome variables. This has not usually been given the attention it deserves by advocates of evidence-based practice. Critics of the evidence-based practice model have, of course, often denied that the sort of measurement claimed is possible, and many qualitative researchers typically dismiss the whole concern with measurement as relying upon a false positivism. In Chapter 5 I argue that achieving accurate social measurement is a very demanding task, and I explore the reasons for this. At the same time, I point out that, interpreted in broad terms as 'linking concepts to data', measurement is a problem that arises for qualitative inquiry just as much as it does for quantitative research.

Chapter 6 is concerned with an issue that has been given a great deal of attention in the wake of the evidence-based practice movement: the question of the criteria by which qualitative research should be judged. I examine whether such criteria are possible or desirable. I also explore how the application of any criteria necessarily relies upon background knowledge and expertise, and the problems that this generates for policymakers and practitioners making use of research evidence. Finally, I suggest that there are fundamental divisions within qualitative research today, centred on notions of rigour and also deriving from constructionism and what I call activism, that need to be resolved before there could be any agreement about what would be relevant criteria of assessment; and it is unclear how these can be overcome.

As I noted earlier, the idea that research should have a direct relationship to practical or political activities is by no means restricted to the evidence-based practice movement. In Chapter 7 I consider one of the most prominent examples of this idea, action research, which has been presented by some as a component of evidence-based practice (Hargreaves 1999) but by others as an alternative to it (Elliott 2001). I explore its rationale against the background of older views that tended to privilege *theoria* over *praxis*. I accept the pragmatist notion that all inquiry arises out of human activity, but not the instrumentalism frequently associated with it. I suggest that, even in everyday life, inquiry is often prompted not by some practical problem but by intellectual puzzlement. I propose that inquiry must be treated as operating on the same plane as any other activity, but that the relationship between it and other activities will always be less than isomorphic, and that this creates the prospect of severe tensions. These can be managed contextually in two ways: either by subordinating inquiry to the other activity, or by making it primary and insulating it to a considerable degree from external demands. Both strategies are legitimate, but any attempt simultaneously to treat inquiry and some other activity as equal priorities, as in the case of much action research and some forms of research for evidence-based practice, faces contradiction.

As we saw, the production of 'systematic' reviews of research findings was integral to the demands made on researchers by the evidence-based practice movement. Such reviews synthesise the findings from multiple research studies, relying upon exhaustive search procedures and explicit evaluation of the 'quality' of the evidence provided. Chapter 8 examines the assumptions about research, and about the task of reviewing, which are built into the concept of systematic review, suggesting that these are, in important respects, false.

This theme is continued in the next chapter, which focuses on what it means for a review to be 'systematic': that it involves synthesis, is issue- or remedy-focused, and is 'comprehensive' and 'transparent'. I argue that these features are far from straightforward, and not always of value. Moreover, the attempt to achieve them can have negative effects on the quality of the review produced. Furthermore, I suggest that the currently influential contrast between systematic and traditional reviews obscures important issues, in particular the art and politics of producing reviews for lay audiences. My conclusion is that we need a more complex typology: one that takes into account the various functions, and kinds of audience, that can be served by literature reviews; and one that does not carry an obfuscating evaluative load, in the way that 'systematic/unsystematic' does.

In Chapter 10 I evaluate a very different critique of 'traditional' reviews from that presented by advocates of evidence-based practice, and one that leads to contrasting recommendations. This comes from some qualitative researchers, leading to advocacy of various forms of 'interpretive review'. They treat traditional forms of reviewing as incompatible with the principles of qualitative research. It is suggested that the *aim* of research should be to 'surprise' the reader, to 'challenge' perceptual habits, or to 'recast' social relations. These critics abandon any idea that reviews should be designed to contribute to the cumulative development of knowledge. The chapter begins by outlining the arguments behind this critique, and then subjects them to critical assessment.

In the final chapter I examine the idea of qualitative synthesis, which was stimulated, in large part, by the development of meta-analysis and systematic reviewing. I explore a number of issues here: what 'synthesis' means in this context, and how qualitative synthesis differs from primary research and from traditional reviewing. A range of methods have been proposed for qualitative synthesis, and I look at two basic forms: that which seeks to apply the techniques of grounded theorising; and meta-ethnography, as proposed by Noblit and Hare (1988) and developed by others. I conclude that what is done under these headings does not differ significantly from many traditional reviews. Nevertheless, there are benefits to be gained from the idea of qualitative synthesis, in so far as it encourages careful, comparative reading and assessment of the literature, with a view to clarifying and developing the current state of research knowledge.

1

SOME QUESTIONS ABOUT EVIDENCE-BASED PRACTICE

There is an initial problem with the notion of evidence-based practice which needs to be dealt with. This is that its name is a slogan whose rhetorical effect is to discredit opposition. After all, who would argue that practice should not be based on evidence (Shahar 1997: 110)? In the context of medicine, Fowler commented that the implication of the term seems to be that in the past, practice was based 'on a direct communication with God or the tossing of a coin' (Fowler 1995: 838). So there is an implication built into the phrase 'evidence-based practice' that opposition to it can only be irrational.[1]

Over time, critics did manage to counter the rhetoric by denying that practice can be based *solely* upon research evidence, forcing advocates to change 'evidence-based' to 'evidence-*informed*' practice.[2] At face value, this suggests a more reasonable view of the relationship between research and practice. Yet it is at odds with the radical role initially ascribed to research by the evidence-based practice movement. As a result, albeit in a different way, we have a label that systematically obscures the grounds on which there might be reasonable disagreement with what is proposed. Given this, I will retain the 'evidence-based' label here.

In political terms, as a way of mobilising support, the use of such opposition-excluding labels is no doubt highly effective. But it is a poor basis for rational discussion about the major issues that the notion of evidence-based practice raises. Against this background, it is very important to emphasise that one can believe that research evidence is of value for practice without accepting much of what travels under the heading of

---

[1]Charlton (1997: 169) returns the compliment by describing evidence-based medicine as a 'fundamentalist cult', comparing it with Mao's communists and the Moonies.

[2]Davies et al. (2000: 11) have added two even weaker formulations: 'evidence-influenced' and 'evidence-aware' practice. Chalmers (2005) claims always to have used the label 'evidence-informed', aside from one lapse.

'evidence-based practice', indeed while rejecting substantial parts of it. So, I take it as given that, on the whole and in the long run, practice would be improved if practitioners were more familiar with the results of research. And there is also, no doubt, scope for more directly policy- and practice-relevant social research. Nevertheless, I believe that there are serious problems with the ideas put forward by the evidence-based practice movement in their initial radical form.

The problems I will discuss here include its privileging of research evidence over other considerations in the decisions of policymakers and practitioners, and of a particular kind of research evidence at that; the assumptions made about the nature of professional practice and about the 'transmission' of evidence to practitioners; and the connections between calls for evidence-based practice and managerialism in the public sector.

THE PRIVILEGING OF RESEARCH EVIDENCE

The central claim of the evidence-based practice movement was that research, of a particular kind, can make a very significant contribution to improving the effectiveness of policymaking and practice across many fields. Thus, the term 'evidence' was interpreted in a highly restricted way. In their introduction to *What Works? Evidence-Based Policy and Practice in the Public Services*, Davies et al. comment: 'the presumption in this book is that evidence takes the form of "research", broadly defined. That is, evidence comprises the results of "systematic investigation towards increasing the sum of knowledge"' (Davies et al. 2000: 3). From this point of view, evidence can only come from research, and certainly not from practice itself. Furthermore, as we saw, in the original, classical version of evidence-based practice, only one particular kind of research was trusted as a valid source of evidence: that produced by randomised controlled trials (RCTs) and systematic reviews of their findings.

The transfer of this approach from medicine to the field of social policy and practice largely ignored the history of evaluation research in social science. This had begun, in the 1960s, with advocacy of methods that were similar to the RCT. However, the weaknesses of such an approach soon came to be recognised, and a variety of alternative strategies were developed (Norris 1990; Pawson and Tilley 1997: ch. 1). These included qualitative approaches, which were promoted on the grounds that they could take account of the negotiated trajectory of implementation and the diverse interpretations of policies and programmes among stakeholders, as well as of the unanticipated consequences that more focused quantitative evaluations often missed.

The idea that RCTs can make a major contribution to improving practice stems to a large extent from the assumption that they are systematic, rigorous, and objective in character. By contrast, any 'evidence' derived from professional experience is portrayed as unsystematic – since it reflects the idiosyncratic set of 'cases' with which a practitioner has happened to come into contact – and also as lacking in rigour – in that it is not built up in an explicit, methodical way but rather through an at least partially unreflective process of sedimentation. Indeed, frequently this contrast is presented in the form of caricature. Thus Oakley (2000: 17) claims that the generalisations of 'well-intentioned and skilful doctors ... may be fanciful rather than factual ...'; while Greenhalgh (1997: 4) draws a contrast between evidence-based decision-making and 'decision-making by anecdote'; and Evans and Benefield (2001: 531) suggest that previously, even when health practitioners used research evidence, they relied upon 'idiosyncratic interpretations of idiosyncratic selections of the available evidence (rather than objective interpretation of all the evidence) ...'. Others have portrayed practice as relying upon 'tradition, prejudice, dogma, and ideology' (Cox quoted in Hargreaves 1996: 7–8), 'fad and fashion' (Slavin 2002: 16) or 'theory' (Chalmers 2005). These caricatures complement the already-mentioned rhetorical sleight-of-hand built into the very name of evidence-based practice, and further undermine the scope for reasonable discussion of the important issues involved.

The view of the role of research characteristic of the evidence-based practice movement fits with an Enlightenment-inspired political philosophy that portrays itself as opposing 'forces of conservatism', forces that are taken to represent entrenched interests. For example, Oakley claims that the medical profession, along with the pharmaceutical industry, have 'a vested interest in women's ill-health – in defining women as sick when they may not be, and in prescribing medical remedies when they may not be needed' (Oakley 2000: 51). These interests are seen as disguised and protected by the claim of professionals to a kind of expertise that cannot be communicated or shared with lay people, but which instead demands professional autonomy and public trust.

What all this makes clear is that, in some significant respects, the evidence-based practice movement is anti-professional: it challenges the claims of professional practitioners – whether doctors, teachers, social workers, police officers etc. – to be able to make expert judgements on the basis of their experience and local knowledge. Instead, it is argued that what is good practice can only be determined through research.

Of course, it has long been argued that a distinctive feature of professions is that they operate on the basis of a body of scientific knowledge. In the case of medicine this was taken to be the corpus of knowledge made up of anatomy, physiology etc.; and one of the reasons why schoolteaching and social work were regarded as, at best, 'semi-professions' (Etzioni 1969) was that they did not have any equivalent 'knowledge base' produced by research.[3] However, the evidence-based medicine movement argued that even medical practice was not sufficiently research-based because clinical decision-making remained heavily dependent upon the experience and judgement of the individual practitioner. In the case of the semi-professions, of course, the notion of evidence-based practice identifies a type of scientific knowledge on which they can base practice, but it does so in a way that undermines claims to autonomous conduct grounded in the need for experienced practitioners to exercise judgement about what it is best to do in particular cases. Indeed, it appears to presage a routinisation of occupational work that parallels that which has already taken place in manufacturing and lower-level white collar work (Braverman 1974; Holbeche 2012).

---

[3] In an important sense this was equally true of law, but its status as a profession nevertheless went largely unchallenged.

We need to look much more carefully both at the features of research-based knowledge, as compared to those of knowledge deriving from practical experience, and at how research findings relate to professional practice. It is important to recognise that research knowledge is always fallible, even if it is more likely to be valid than knowledge from other sources. Thus, we are not faced with a contrast between Knowledge, whose epistemic status is certain, and mere Opinion, whose validity is zero or totally unknown.[4] Furthermore, research knowledge usually takes the form of generalisations, of one sort or another, and interpreting the implications of these for dealing with particular cases is rarely straightforward.

Another important point is that factual knowledge is not a sufficient determinant of good practice. One reason for this is that it cannot determine what the ends of good practice should be or even, on its own, what are and are not appropriate means. These matters necessarily rely upon *judgements*, in which value assumptions play just as much of a role as factual ones. Furthermore, the effectiveness of any practical action usually depends not just on *what* is done but also on *how* it is done and *when*. Skill and timing can be crucial.

For these reasons, there are substantial limitations on what research can offer to policymaking and practice. This is not to argue that it can offer nothing, but rather to caution against excessive claims about its contribution.

THE NATURE OF PROFESSIONAL PRACTICE

Equally important is that a misleading conception of the nature of professional practice is built into some advocacy of evidence-based practice. In effect, it is assumed that it should take the form of pursuing explicitly stated goals (or 'targets'), selecting strategies for achieving them on the basis of objective evidence about their effectiveness, with the outcomes then being measured in order to assess their degree of success (thereby providing the knowledge required for improving future performance).[5]

This rationalistic model is not wholly inaccurate or undesirable, but it is defective in important respects. Forms of practice will vary in the degree to which they can usefully be made to approximate it, and it probably does not fit any sort of professional activity very closely. There are several reasons for this. One is that most forms of practice involve multiple goals that have to be pursued more or less simultaneously; that these goals cannot be fully specified in a way that avoids reliance upon professional judgement; that the same action will often have multiple consequences, some desirable and others less so; that these will be differentially distributed across

---

[4]Cochrane often seems to come close to this view in his advocacy of evidence-based practice in medicine: see Cochrane 1972: 30. For a useful discussion of problems that have arisen even where randomised controlled trial methodology has been extensively applied, from a perspective that is sympathetic to the movement, see Hampton 1997.

[5]Some versions of action research, notably that of Lewin, have the same character. See Chapter 7.

clients; that there is frequently uncertainty surrounding the likely consequences of many strategies; and that the situations being faced by practical actors are always unique, and generally undergo recurrent change, requiring continual adaptation.

As a result of these features, there can often be reasonable disagreement about what would be an improvement, and about what sorts of improvement are to be preferred, as well as about how these can best be achieved. And these are not matters that research findings can resolve, at least not on their own. Moreover, sometimes it will simply not be sensible to engage in elaborate explication of goals, to consider *all* possible alternatives, to engage in an extensive search for information about the relative effectiveness of various strategies, as against relying upon judgements based on experience about this, or to try to *measure* outcomes. Given other demands, and the likely low success of attempting to do these things in many cases, it will often not be worthwhile. The rationalistic model underpinning the notion of evidence-based practice tends to underplay the extent to which in many circumstances the only reasonable option is trial and error, or even 'muddling through' (Lindblom 1979), a point that applies as much to forms of occupational practice as it does to policymaking.

In this context, we should note that the very phrase 'what works', which the evidence-based practice movement sees as the proper focus for much social research, implies a view of practice as technical: as open to 'objective' assessment in terms of what is and is not effective, or what is more and what less effective. I do not want to deny that effectiveness, and even efficiency, are relevant considerations in professional practice, but the information necessary to judge them in the 'objective' way proposed will rarely be available, given the difficulties and costs involved. And, as we have seen, any such assessment cannot be separated from value judgements about desirable ends and appropriate means – not without missing a great deal that is important.

It is also essential to recognise that there is a significant difference between medicine and other fields in terms of the nature of professional practice. For whatever reason, much medicine is closer to the technical end of the spectrum, in the sense that there is less diversity in the goals and other considerations treated as relevant, and thereby in evaluative criteria. In addition, there seems to be more scope for identifying *relatively* simple causal relationships between treatment and outcome in this field than elsewhere. Of course, it is possible to exaggerate these differences. Davies claims that 'medicine and health care ... face very similar, if not identical, problems of complexity, context-specificity, measurement, and causation' to the other fields where the notion of evidence-based practice has been promoted (Davies 1999: 112). It is certainly true that there are such problems in medicine; and that in some areas, for example mental health, they are very similar in scale and character to those faced in non-medical fields. However, there are significant differences in this respect between some areas of medicine and the fields in which most social science operates. While what we are dealing with here is only a general difference in degree, it is still a substantial difference.

In short, in my view research usually cannot supply what the notion of evidence-based practice demands of it – specific and highly reliable answers to questions about what 'works' and what does not – and professional practice cannot be *governed* by research findings – because it necessarily relies upon multiple values, tacit judgement, local knowledge, and skills. Moreover, this is especially true in fields outside of medicine. When pressed, advocates of evidence-based practice often concede one or other, or both, of these points. Yet these points undermine the claim that rigorous research, and a reformed version of professional practice that gives more attention to research findings, will lead to a sharp improvement in professional performance and outcomes; and this was the key rationale for evidence-based practice in the first place.

THE TRANSMISSION OF RESEARCH FINDINGS

It is a central assumption of the evidence-based practice movement that research findings need to be presented to lay audiences via reviews of all the relevant and reliable studies, rather than through the findings of each study being disseminated separately. This is sensible, and an important corrective to current pressures on researchers to maximize the impact of individual studies. However, there are questions to be raised about the particular form of literature review promoted by the evidence-based practice movement, namely 'systematic reviews'.

The concept of systematic review shares some common elements with the notion of evidence-based practice more generally. It portrays the task of reviewing the literature as reducible to explicit procedures that can be replicated; in the same way that advocates of evidence-based practice see professional work as properly governed by explicit rules based upon research evidence. For example, the task of assessing the validity of research findings is portrayed as if this could be done properly simply by applying explicit and standard criteria relating to research design. Yet, validity assessment cannot rely entirely upon information about research design. Much depends upon the nature of the knowledge claims made, and assessment of them always relies upon substantive knowledge as well as on specifically methodological considerations (see Chapter 6). The result of this mistaken approach to validity assessment is that systematic reviews are likely to exclude or downplay some kinds of study that may be illuminating, especially qualitative work, while giving weight to other studies whose findings are open to serious question (see Chapter 8).

An illustration of the attitude underlying the notion of systematic review, and the evidence-based practice movement generally, is Oakley's recent adoption of what can only be described as a form of *naïve* positivism.[6] This is perhaps surprising because in the past she has been a proponent of qualitative methods, largely on feminist grounds (Oakley 1999; Westmarland 2001; Letherby 2004). However, she is now a strong advocate of randomised controlled trials. She insists that she never promoted qualitative method exclusively, and that she does not advocate

---

[6]Oakley was the first director of the Evidence for Policy and Practice Information Co-ordinating Centre (EPPI-Centre), which has responsibility for developing systematic reviews in the UK in the field of education. See its website: http://eppi.ioe.ac.uk/.

quantitative method exclusively now. Nevertheless, in some parts of her book *Experiments in Knowing*, she evidences a dismissal of qualitative work that is the obverse of her over-enthusiastic support for experimental research design. For example, she claims that the debate over Freeman's critique of Mead's anthropological study of Samoa is best read as an example of the 'untrustworthiness' of 'uncontrolled findings' (Oakley 2000: 57). The implication of this is that all research that does not involve physical or statistical control of variables is untrustworthy; a view that does not derive from, and was certainly not the position of, Freeman himself. Later she comments:

> Recent attitudes to evaluation in some quarters have been marked by a retreat into more 'naturalistic' and theory-driven approaches to public policy evaluation, but these serve the interests of academic careers more than they promote the goals of either an emancipatory social science or an informed evidence base for social and policy interventions. (Oakley 2000: 323)

Here we have dismissal of the views of those who disagree with her via the attribution of ulterior motives, and – ironically – in the form of assertion rather than any appeal to evidence.[7]

A more general problem about how research can be used by practitioners concerns the funnelling process through which research findings need to be refined into summary statements that policymakers and practitioners will have time to read and digest. The provision of any summary involves the paring away of many qualifications and of much methodological information. While summaries may be a very useful aid for those who have already read the whole review, or the original studies, they can sometimes be obscure or misleading for those who have not. To take a highly contentious example, one of the key points of Gillborn and Gipps's narrative review of the educational achievements of ethnic minority children, that was included in summaries of it, was that '"colour-blind" policies have failed' – but it soon became apparent after publication of the review that some audiences misread this conclusion or found it difficult to interpret (Gillborn and Gipps 1996: 80).[8]

Not only may research findings be misinterpreted but their validity is sometimes dismissed at face value because they conflict with what is taken to be commonsense. For example, a study which suggests that there is no positive, linear correlation between amount of homework set and level of pupil achievement may be interpreted as saying that homework should be abolished or is not important, and on

---

[7]Elsewhere, she has also dismissed her critics as Luddites: see Oakley 2006. For a response, see Hammersley 2008b. She is not alone in this sort of response: others have dismissed criticism as 'ideology parading as intellectual inquiry' (Chalmers, 2003: 26, quoting Mosteller and Boruch, 2002: 2). See Hammersley 2005b.

[8]For a discussion of how this review was represented in the mass media in diverse ways, see Hammersley 2003a and 2006. For discussion of some of the issues around summaries in the form of 'brief reviews' of research literatures, see Abrami et al. 2010.

these grounds its validity may be rejected.[9] These problems stem, in part, from the fact that the interpretive framework within which policymakers and practitioners approach research findings is often very different from that of researchers; in particular these audiences are likely to be much more directly concerned with practical or political implications, and to view these from within a particular ideological position. It is also not uncommon for summary findings to be seen by policymakers or practitioners as trivial, in the sense of repeating what is already known, because the actual contribution to current knowledge is only clear against the background of what can currently be taken to be well-established for research purposes, this frequently being different from what policymakers and practitioners believe is already well established (see Gage 1991).

So there are problems as regards the communication of research findings and how these relate to what policymakers and practitioners think they already know. These audiences tend to accept research findings that are supportive of, or compatible with, existing assumptions, and to reject them where they are not. This is partly because there is a genuine problem about how to weigh contradictory evidence, especially when it has been produced in different ways. In his argument for evidence-based health practice, Davies comments that 'there is no question of evidence replacing clinical judgement or experience', instead what is required is to '[unite] these two dimensions of knowledge to provide a sound basis for action' (Davies 1999: 111). Yet conflicting evidence from different sources cannot simply be 'united'.[10] One reason for this is that evidence from professional experience cannot be assessed in the same way as research evidence, since the process by which it was produced is not documented. Thus, it might appear that all one can do, when faced with contradictory evidence from research and practical experience, is either to trust one's instincts, as many lay people do, or to assume that research evidence is always sounder than other sources, which is what advocates of evidence-based practice sometimes seem to demand. Neither approach is satisfactory. What *is* perhaps required is that each source of evidence is subjected to internal scrutiny in its own terms: reflection on the sources, relations, and functions of particular beliefs, in the

---

[9]I am referring here to the response of a previous UK Secretary of State for Education, David Blunkett, to the findings of a study of the relationship between homework and achievement, in which he accused the researchers of double standards, of being unwilling to extend to other children the benefits their own children have had. See S. Farrow 'Insulted by Blunkett', *The Guardian* Wednesday 21 July 1999. In his speech to the CBI around the same time, Blunkett also included the following comment: 'Some researchers are so obsessed with "critique", so out of touch with reality that they churn out findings which no one with the slightest common sense could take seriously' (Blunkett 1999, quoted in Pring 2000: 76). Mr Blunkett's response was similar to research that suggested eviction laws were being applied over-zealously by some local authorities. His comment was: 'If this is what our money is going on, it is time for a review of the funding of social research', BBC News web page for 20 November 2000. His criticism of these studies was repeated in his speech to the ESRC: Blunkett 2000.

[10]Sackett et al. (1996: 72) talk of 'integrating individual clinical expertise with the best available external evidence from systematic research'. But 'integrating' is no better than 'uniting': it is a fudge that covers up a serious problem.

case of professional experience; and methodological assessment in the case of research. However, this is a time-consuming process, and it by no means guarantees that the result will be a satisfactory resolution of any conflict between the two sources. Moreover, any resolution will itself necessarily rely upon judgements that cannot be fully explicated.

Up to now, I have looked in fairly specific terms at the role that the evidence-based practice movement believes research should play in relation to policymaking and practice. However, it is important to take account of the socio-political context within which this movement arose, and which played an important part in its widespread influence.

EVIDENCE-BASED PRACTICE AND 'TRANSPARENCY'

The evidence-based practice movement was closely related to influential demands for 'transparent' accountability that are characteristic of what has come to be called managerialism, or the 'new public management' (Pollitt 1990; Ferlie et al. 1996; Clarke and Newman 1997; Power 1997; Lane 2000; Levy 2010). As Davies et al. note: 'In contrast to the preceding culture of largely judgement-based professional practice, there has arisen the important notion of evidence-based practice as a means of ensuring that what is being done is worthwhile and that it is being done in the best possible way' (Davies et al. 2000: 2). Thus, it is assumed that research can 'ensure' that the best is being done; both by providing information about 'what works', and by documenting whether practitioners are actually following 'best practice' so defined. Moreover, research is believed to be capable of doing this because it is objective and explicit; what it provides is open to public scrutiny, in a way that professional experience and judgement are not.

The demand for 'transparent' accountability seems to have arisen from two sources. The first lies in the field of business, and concerns the emergence of 'generic management'.[11] This is an idea that is exemplified by Lord Campbell's talk to his management group at London Weekend Television in the 1970s, as recalled by Frank Muir:

> You unit heads may think that managing talented producers and performers raises special problems but I have been in sugar all my life and I can assure you that the management of people in television is precisely the same as the management of sugar workers. (Muir 1997: 324–5; quoted in Collins and Evans 2007: 5)

Where, in the first half of the twentieth century, in the UK at least, managers had often spent all of their careers in a single sector, frequently working their way up to managerial positions within an individual firm, in the second half of the century there was increasing mobility of managers not only between firms but across sectors, the emergence of graduate entry to management, and closely associated with this a growing tendency to define management in terms of generic rather than sector-specific

---

[11]For the background to this development, see Burnham 1941, and Chandler 1977, and 1990.

knowledge and skills.[12] Along with growth in the average size of firms (see Devine et al. 1985: 85–90), often as a result of mergers and take-overs, this led to the problem of how senior managers were to assess the performance of different parts of their organisations. The solution proposed was to find objective indicators of performance, ones whose interpretation did not demand detailed knowledge of the kind of work being done. Over the course of the 1960s, 1970s and 1980s this reliance upon performance indicators spread to the public sector (initially to the publicly owned utilities, for example in the energy field, later to health, education, criminal justice, and other fields), on the back of arguments that this sector was inefficient by comparison with private enterprise.[13]

An equally important stimulus to the 'new public management', however, was recognition even by the political Left of the force, and electoral appeal, of the argument that citizens had a right to know that their taxes were being well spent. Public accountability of this kind now came to be widely regarded as central to democracy. But, of course, most citizens were in exactly the same position as the generic manager, in that they did not have direct knowledge of what was involved in the work of public sector agencies. What they *did* have, however, was some, albeit highly differentiated, experience as clients of those organisations, as well as access to others' anecdotes about failures of service, which were elaborated by media campaigns against the 'inefficiency' of the public sector. Here, too, the solution proposed was objective performance indicators: indicators that would allow politicians and the general public to judge what was happening and how it could be improved. Indeed, the new public management portrayed government ministers as managers of the public sector, and therefore as responsible for monitoring performance and intervening to improve it. Furthermore, in the context of the New Labour government in the UK in the late 1990s, politicians began to suggest that their *own* performance should be judged by whether promised improvements in the work of the public sector took place, as measured by performance indicators; an extension of transparent accountability encouraged by the media, for whom repeated publication of the results of such indicators constituted a useful source of news, but which politicians usually came to regret.[14]

More generally, criticism of the public sector for failing to 'deliver' a satisfactory level of service, and portrayal of it as inferior to the private sector, arose out of

---

[12]This was closely associated with the rise of management education, and the influence of the accounting profession (see Power 1997, but also Maltby 2008). The whole process was, of course, simply a further stage in the development of what Marris (1971) calls 'managerial' capitalism initiated by the invention of the public, joint-stock, limited liability company in the late nineteenth century.

[13]These claims about the superiority of the private sector relied upon a particular version of economic *theory* and anecdotes about 'over-manning', 'bureaucracy' etc. in the public sector, rather than on much empirical evidence.

[14]Performance indicator results have many of the key characteristics of newsworthiness: they are about the government, they offer apparently clear-cut and authoritative findings, and they often suggest serious failings. For a rather different, but not incompatible, account of the developments I have sketched here, see Aucoin 1990. Aucoin stresses the role of public choice theory and managerialism, portraying them both as anti-bureaucratic, and argues that there are tensions between the two, especially in relation to centralisation/decentralisation and control/delegation.

widespread attacks, in the second half of the twentieth century, on professionalism and on the role of the state. These came from both sides of the political spectrum, and from social scientists as well.[15] The claim of professional occupations to be guided by a service ethic, which justified their having autonomy in performing their work, was challenged on the grounds that they had misused this autonomy to serve their own interests. There was some evidence for this, but the charge also reflected a change in the prevalent 'vocabulary of motives', whereby claims to anything other than self-interest were subjected not just to suspicion but to disbelief. From the political Right, in particular, it was insisted that people would only do what was in the general interest if circumstances were arranged in such a way that it was in their self-interest to do it. The market was regarded as the model in this respect, and this fuelled not just privatisation but also the application of 'market discipline' within the public sector.

The assumption was that markets provide consumers with all the knowledge they need in order to assess the relative value of the goods on offer. As a result, it was concluded, consumers' purchasing decisions reward efficiency and punish inefficiency. This came to be widely believed, despite the fact that to a large extent it is simply a myth. It does not even hold true where conditions of perfect competition are approximated, a situation that is in any case very rare. This is because consumers do not usually have easy access to *all* of the information they would need to judge effectively the value of what is on offer. Reliable and comparable information about the relative quality of different products, even those from the same supplier, often is not available or is manipulated by sellers.[16] Moreover, most consumers would probably not have the background knowledge or the time necessary to make use of that information were it available. In fact, the tendency is for consumers to rely heavily upon just one type of information, that which is most easily accessible and open to assessment, namely price. In turn, this tendency distorts the production process, since it often leads to priority being given to lowering costs rather than ensuring quality.[17] The dangers of this in the public sector are perhaps especially obvious.

Of course, the attempt to introduce transparent accountability into the public sector is not in any simple sense a process of marketisation. Instead, efforts were made directly to measure the quality of services; and not so much as a basis for consumer decision making (though this was sometimes the case, as with institutional league tables) but rather so as to allow the public to judge whether the public services were

---

[15]One aspect of this was criticism of state regulation of industry. For an account of this in the United States, and of the pendulum swings towards and then away from regulation over the course of the twentieth century, see Vietor 1994: 312 and *passim*. For social scientific critiques of professionalism, see Macdonald 1995.

[16]This was why the Consumers' Association in the UK began to publish *Which?* magazine: see Sargant 1995: 190-2. However, even that publication cannot provide everything one would need to know in order to make the best choice among the many products available. The sheer number and diversity of products is too large, and subject to too frequent change.

[17]Quality may not even be given emphasis where fashion, technical hype or snobbery will support relatively high prices.

meeting satisfactory standards of performance and providing 'value for money'. However, for the reasons explained in the previous section, these performance indicators do not usually measure effectively what is important; and, indeed, advocates of transparent accountability will often acknowledge this, while insisting that they provide the best evidence available. Ironically, the severe problems associated with such performance indicators were demonstrated long ago in the attempts of Eastern European governments to control centrally the production of goods and the provision of services. Here, even attempts to specify industrial production targets and measure performance for relatively simple goods failed (Nove 1980: ch. 4).[18]

Moreover, this parallel shows that efforts to render people accountable in terms of performance indicators distort the production process at least as much as does the emphasis on lowering cost and price which is characteristic of the private sector. This is because it encourages, indeed to a large extent forces, individual practitioners to adopt an instrumental orientation in which scoring highly on the indicators becomes more important than doing what they judge to be a good job. Indeed, they may even lose the confidence to exercise such judgement.

Where professional services are concerned, the problems faced by lay people in assessing quality of service are especially severe, because of the level of specialised expertise and knowledge on which these services rely. Furthermore, what they involve is not a determinate process. For example, even the best surgeons do not succeed in all cases; and, to the degree that they deal with more difficult cases than their colleagues, their failure rates may be comparatively high. Similarly, schools vary considerably in how amenable their students are to the sort of education they are offering, and this variation cannot be easily measured. In this context, it is not just a matter of judging a product or service in terms of whether it meets requirements, or meets the requirements better than others – which is hard enough – but judging whether the best that could have been done has been done in particular circumstances. In some areas, for example running schools and prisons, this task is further complicated by the fact that practitioners deal with clients in batches, not on a one-by-one basis. So, here, judgement has to be according to whether what was done was the best for all concerned, on average (perhaps weighted), and this will involve trading benefits for some against costs for others. Further complications arise when we recognise that there are other stakeholders involved, with other interests, beyond the clients themselves.

The application of 'transparent accountability' to medicine, education, criminal justice, and other areas has been premised on the assumption that explicit information can be provided about all the factors relevant to judging the quality of professional

---

[18]Nove writes that in the Soviet Union 'many of the functions of government ministers and senior party officials can be regarded as a form of senior management, in some respects analogous to those of the senior directors of a big Western corporation' (Nove 1980: 88). He continues: 'how can the centre issue instructions in a form which does not give rise to ambiguities and contradictions? How can it encourage initiative, new techniques, the flow of desired and undistorted information? By what standards and in what way can we evaluate performance? Around these issues one finds grouped many of the most serious weaknesses of Soviet micro-economics. This is where many things go wrong' (Nove 1980: 89). Indeed it is, and not just in the old Soviet Union.

performance in these fields. And research is seen as playing a key role in this: the belief is that it can show what works and what does not work, and thereby provide a standard against which the practice of professionals can be assessed. Moreover, it is assumed that research is itself transparent: that it simply documents how things are in an objective fashion. However, for reasons already explained, research is unable to play this role.

Furthermore, efforts to make it do so have undesirable consequences. As already noted, in relation to practice the appeal to research findings may undermine the value of practical experience and common sense, and thus erode practitioners' capacity for sound judgement. While it is sometimes claimed that evidence-based practice represents an enhanced professionalism, its devaluing of professional experience and expertise relative to accountability in terms of externally produced research findings leads to a weakening of professionalism, in most senses of that term. Equally important, the attempt to make research serve this function has the effect of privileging practical against academic or scientific research, and of eroding the distinction between research and the work of management consultancy, audit, and inspection agencies.[19]

There is no doubt that evaluations of professional practice can be valuable; nor that some professional practice, in all fields, is poorer than it could be. However, not only is the notion of transparent accountability a myth, but it relies upon a version of perfectionism which implies that all failures and risks can be avoided, or at least can be progressively reduced in number and seriousness.[20] In these terms, it is assumed that performance can and should *always* be further improved, and that measures can be taken to ensure that any failures that have occurred in the past do not recur in the future. In promising this, transparent accountability encourages a climate in which clients demand that their needs and wants be fully met, while practitioners are increasingly concerned simply with protecting themselves from likely criticism (not to mention possible legal or managerial action). And, given that the indicators do not measure performance effectively, especially not across the whole range of each profession's activities, this frequently worsens rather than improves the quality of performance.

Advocates of evidence-based practice often deny that there is any link between it and attempts to introduce 'transparent accountability' into the public sector. Yet, governments have seen each as serving the other, and have acted on that basis so as to bring about 'reform'; and they view social research as playing a major part in this. This was exemplified in government attempts, at the end of the twentieth century in the UK, to bring educational research under increased central control, coordinating and

---

[19]Thus, in *What Works?* Davies et al. (2000: 3) comment that: 'the majority of research evidence considered in this text is the output from more formal and systematic enquiries, generated by government departments, research institutes, universities, charitable foundations, consultancy organisations, and a variety of agencies and intermediaries such as the Audit Commission, or Office for Standards in Education (Ofsted)'. For a useful discussion of the relationship between research and Ofsted inspection, see Smith 2000.

[20]This is an example of what Oakeshott (1962: 5-6) referred to as 'the politics of perfection'.

concentrating funding on issues directly relevant to policy and practice (National Educational Research Forum 2000 and Hodkinson 2001; see Introduction).

CONCLUSION

In this chapter I have argued that while few would disagree that professional practice could be improved if practitioners had better access to the products of a large body of relevant, good-quality research, the evidence-based practice movement is not well directed to lead to a dramatic improvement in performance, and may even result in a reduction in the quality of service. The reasons for this lie in misconceptions about the nature of both research and practice built into what it proposes. Its advocates have too much confidence in the validity of research findings – especially those coming from RCTs or equivalent – both in abstract terms and in comparison with knowledge deriving from professional experience. And they assume that research can play a much more direct role in relation to practice than it usually can. They tend to treat practice as the *application* of research-based knowledge, neglecting the extent to which it necessarily involves uncertainty, local knowledge and value judgements. Moreover, there are some serious difficulties involved in the use of research evidence by practitioners. One relates to problems in interpreting this evidence without background knowledge about the studies from which it arose. Another concerns how the general knowledge it produces is to be related to individual cases. There is also the question of how contradictions between research evidence and professional experience should be resolved.

Finally, I pointed to the close association between the evidence-based practice movement and the 'new public management', with its efforts to make the public sector transparently accountable and thereby to improve its performance dramatically. I argued that this notion of accountability is built on a mythology of the market that does not accurately capture how markets work, and that is peculiarly inappropriate in the case of providing services that necessarily rely upon a good deal of specialised expertise. I suggested that the search for transparent accountability is a futile enterprise, and one that has negative consequences for both professional practice and for research. It offers a false hope of substantial improvement in quality, while at the same time undermining the conditions necessary for professionalism to flourish. The entanglement of the notion of research for evidence-based practice with these developments means that it should be treated with the greatest caution.

2

THE MYTH OF RESEARCH-BASED POLICYMAKING AND PRACTICE

As I noted in the Introduction, the arguments for 'evidence-based' policymaking and practice must be seen against the background of recurrent crises in the relationship between social research and these other activities. It has long been agreed, both by many researchers and by many policymakers and practitioners, that research exercises insufficient influence. Researchers do not usually need much encouragement in wanting to maximise the impact of their research on policy or practice. Indeed, they often have strong commitments to particular policy ideas, and believe that these can be justified by research findings. This applies both to many of those who support government policies and current forms of socio-political organisation and also to those who are critical of them. Similarly, policymakers and practitioners frequently desire the 'right' kind of research evidence: there is much that they wish to know but do not, and much evidence they would welcome, perhaps especially if it supports current policies and practices.

There is often agreement, then, about the importance of research, and also that it does not currently play the role that it should. Where researchers and policymakers/practitioners tend to disagree is about who is to blame for this failure of research to influence policy and practice in the manner desired.

EXPLANATIONS FOR FAILURE

Not surprisingly, policymakers and practitioners tend to identify the problem as lying with researchers, though there have been some in the research camp who have joined this side of the argument. The complaint is that research:

- is not closely enough focused on practical concerns, that much of it is trivial and irrelevant;
- fails to produce findings at the time they are needed;
- generates conflicting and therefore confusing evidence;
- provides evidence that is at odds with what is well known to policymakers and practitioners, so that its validity seems to be weak; and/or
- produces conclusions that are inaccessible to policymakers and practitioners (because too elaborate and qualified, jargon-ridden, and/or published in journals they do not read).

Sometimes the remedy for these problems has been identified as increased effort by researchers in *disseminating* their findings. Thus, a great deal of emphasis is now placed by funding bodies upon researchers having 'dissemination plans', and engaging with potential users of their research findings in order to maximise the 'impact' of their work.

However, it is sometimes argued that the problem lies deeper: in the very nature of the research that is done. As we have seen, this was central to arguments for evidence-based practice, the complaint being that insufficient social research is aimed at determining 'what works' and that much of it is defective in terms of validity when judged by the standard of randomised controlled trials (RCTs). Along the same lines, Hargreaves' (1996) influential diagnosis of the failure of educational research argued that what is required is a transformation of research to make it more relevant and rigorous. As part of this he proposed that potential users of research be directly involved in setting the research agenda, and perhaps even in directing or carrying out the research. Only in this way, he argued, will research findings be produced that are capable of being implemented through policy and practice.

By contrast, researchers have generally put the blame for the perceived lack of impact of social science on policymakers and practitioners, in other words on the 'users' of research. In this explanation, practitioners – and especially policymakers – are portrayed as:

- closed-minded or set in their ways, and therefore resistant to new perspectives coming from research;
- committed to the dominant ideology and unwilling even to consider any radical challenges to it that research findings might imply;
- untrained in the capacity to understand and make use of research; and/or
- lacking in the motivation required to seek out research evidence and to reflect on their decisions in light of it.

In this spirit, not only policymakers but also occupational practitioners of particular kinds may be blamed for being conservative, or sometimes even for being ill-motivated, for example sexist or racist, in resisting what are regarded as the practical implications of research findings.

These two types of explanation are not necessarily incompatible: implicitly if not explicitly, criticism of the failure of research to inform policy and practice has often attacked both sides simultaneously, even if the emphasis has usually fallen primarily on one or the other. Even more important to notice is that the two explanations share the idea that if researchers and/or policymakers or practitioners were both to behave in a *rational* fashion, then research would feed smoothly into policymaking and practice. And it is further assumed that these activities would thereby become much more effective. Standards would be 'driven up'.

This is what I will refer to as the model of research-based policymaking or practice. In crude form, it treats research as producing conclusions that can be implemented, or 'translated into', policies or practices, whether at the level of national or institutional policy or 'on the ground'. A second assumption is that, if they were research-based, policies or practices would be more likely to maximise desirable outcomes.

QUESTIONING THE NOTION OF RESEARCH-BASED POLICY AND PRACTICE

I want to argue, first of all, that this model assumes too grand a role for research. Of course, many people believe that high expectations are a good thing, but unreasonably high expectations are not. And that is what we have here (Hammersley 2002). Moreover, as I have hinted, these excessive expectations of research are held not just by funders and potential users but also by many researchers themselves.

As I argued in the previous chapter, policy or practice cannot be *based on* research, in any exclusive sense, and to try to make it research-based will distort the activities on one or other, or both, sides of this relationship. The most likely outcome, and the one that I am especially concerned with here, is a damaging effect on research. I should emphasise that I am not suggesting that research has no role to play in relation to policymaking and practice, simply that it cannot play the highly determinate role that the notion of research-based policymaking or practice assumes, and that seeking to make it do this has negative consequences. These include:

- an increase in the likelihood of bias;
- further reduction in the funds available for research that is not directly related to what are currently high priority policy issues;
- a growth in the amount of research attempting to answer questions that, while practically important, simply cannot be answered effectively at the present time;
- a further reduction in the turn-around times demanded of research projects, which will make sustaining the quality of research work even more difficult than it is already.

In the long run, the result of unreasonably high expectations will be disillusionment and recrimination, or simply the abuse of research so as to support preferred policies and practices, or to discredit disliked ones.

Instead, we must recognise that the relationship between research, on one side, and policymaking and practice, on the other, is necessarily a highly mediated one, and that it involves considerable potential for conflict. The relationship between the two sides will never be smooth and direct (Hammersley 2002). The essence here is that not only do researchers, policymakers and practitioners not operate in the way that the research-based practice model assumes, but also that there are good reasons why they should not do so. The points I will make are summarised in Figure 2.1.

Research findings	must provide a basis for	Practice	so as to lead to	Desirable outcomes
BUT			BUT	
Research cannot provide all that practitioners need; they must draw on other sources of information and employ wisdom and judgement.			Research findings are always fallible, so that policies and practices drawing on them will *not* always lead to what is expected, and there may be unanticipated or unintended consequences.	
There is a difference between what researchers and practitioners take to be well-founded knowledge: organised scepticism versus a pragmatic orientation. This means that research will not provide what practitioners feel they need when they need it.			True factual knowledge is not sufficient for the success of a policy or practice. Indeed, false ideas can sometimes be more effective, and may even have desirable consequences.	
Practitioners will take account of other considerations than purely 'technical' ones, including what is and is not politically viable.			The impact of a policy or practice is always highly mediated by factors that are not under the policymaker's or the practitioner's control.	
Research can provide too much or too detailed information, or the picture it provides may be too complex.			What is a desirable outcome is a matter of value judgement, and there will often be widespread disagreement about what is desirable, and especially about what is the highest priority.	
Research findings cannot in themselves tell us what is good or bad and what should be done.				

Figure 2.1   Some problems with the idea of research-based policymaking or practice

Research and the needs of policymakers and practitioners

Let me start with the relationship between what research can produce and what policymakers and practitioners need. There are several issues. First, knowledge is not all that practitioners require: they must also necessarily rely upon experience and judgement. So, in a literal sense, practice cannot be *based* upon research, at least not exclusively. Furthermore, research could not supply even all of the *information* that policymakers and practitioners might need. The range of this is too great: there are not enough resources available to researchers, nor are there ever likely to be.

But the problem is more fundamental than just a matter of scarce resources. And this is the next main point: there are likely to be significant differences between policymakers/practitioners and researchers concerning the standards they use in accepting or rejecting knowledge claims, and with good reason. On some cogent accounts, social research modelled on science involves the requirement that, in determining what is and is not valid, researchers operate in such a way as to err on the side of rejecting what is true *rather than* of accepting as true what is in fact false. In other words, the emphasis is on avoiding false positives rather than false negatives. This is what is sometimes referred to as organised scepticism (see Merton 1973: ch. 13). This approach is necessary in order to ensure that research findings reach the threshold of likely validity required if social science is to be regarded as a source of reliable knowledge (Hammersley 2011: ch. 5).

By contrast, policymakers and practitioners' assessments do not usually have this consistent emphasis: what we might call the 'acceptability threshold' by which they judge the validity of information typically varies according to practical circumstances. In particular, policymakers and practitioners are likely to be concerned with the relative costs of different types of error, and also with the extent to which specific errors are remediable. Where the cost of error threatens to be high, or where it is irremediable, the standards of assessment adopted will usually be such as to minimise this danger. However, where the likely cost of a particular kind of error is judged to be low, or any error remediable, standards of assessment will not usually be designed to minimise it, other possible errors will be given a higher priority; or it may even be that the danger of error is of little concern. Moreover, this differential treatment of knowledge claims in terms of the likely costs of error is perfectly reasonable in the context of most forms of practice. While organised scepticism is the best policy in judging research findings, it is not a policy by which any of us could actually live our lives: it would often leave us with no basis for making decisions that we are nevertheless forced to make because we cannot afford to delay them.

A related point is that the possible costs that are addressed by policymakers and practitioners will often not be solely to do with what would be the best *technical* or *theoretical* solution to a problem, but will also relate to what we might call the politics of the situations in which they operate. For instance, some policy options will be seen as much more politically viable than others – even though they are not the best solutions in technical or theoretical terms. The politics of policymaking and practice cannot be just wished away by imagining a world where such considerations would not operate.

So, I am suggesting that there is a fundamental contrast in orientation between researchers, on the one hand, and policymakers/practitioners, on the other; and that the result of this is that there will often be a mismatch between what the two groups treat as valid knowledge. Furthermore, *there are good reasons for this difference*. One implication of this is that researchers' criticisms of policymakers and practitioners for not 'acting on' research findings are often naïve or utopian. Equally, practitioners' criticisms of research frequently betray a failure to understand, or to respect, what is involved in coming to sound research conclusions. Another way of putting the point is that what it is rational for researchers and for policymakers/practitioners to take as sound knowledge will sometimes be sharply discrepant.

It is also worth drawing attention to the fact that if research is governed by organised scepticism it will produce knowledge at a comparatively slow rate (Pels 2003); and this is another reason why it often cannot supply practitioners with the knowledge that they require. This is one reason why, even when knowledge relevant to practice *is* produced, it may not be sufficiently up-to-date to meet the needs of policymakers and practitioners. In other words, it is in the very nature of research, or at least research of an academic or scientific kind, that it will often not be able to supply the knowledge that policymakers and practitioners feel they need *at the time they need it*.

Another key main point, only superficially contradictory to the preceding one, is that research may generate *too much* information about a particular topic, or information that is *too detailed*, for practical purposes. After all, researchers study particular issues in depth, whereas policymakers and practitioners usually have to deal with a *range* of issues simultaneously, and often quite quickly. While we might assume that 'the more information the better', if policymakers or practitioners were to try to take full account of all the relevant research findings available on all the issues relating to their work, the result could be information-overload, and this might well damage what they do. In other words, it needs to be remembered that assimilating the information produced by research always takes time, and policymakers/practitioners often work under great time pressure. In short, we must take account of the fact that there are costs involved in making use of research information, and these may sometimes be prohibitive.

Another, closely related, point is that research tends to complexify rather than to simplify; at the very least it complexifies *before* it simplifies. Thus, it often shows that the world is more complicated than practitioners think it is, that widely held stereotypes are false or only true in a very approximate way, that assumed causal relationships are more contingent than often supposed, and so on. Under some circumstances, showing policymakers and practitioners the complexity and uncertainty of the phenomena they are dealing with, or revealing defects in their knowledge, can be beneficial. But recognising complexity will not *always* be advantageous in practical terms. It may confuse and de-motivate practitioners, or dissuade them from taking any action at all.

The final point I want to make in this section is that research can only validate *factual* claims, it cannot in itself justify practical evaluations and recommendations. Another way of putting this is to say that research 'under-determines' such evaluations and recommendations; analogous to how data under-determine theoretical conclusions (see Chalmers 1999). While we are often inclined to forget it, there is always the possibility of deriving quite different practical conclusions from any set of factual findings. To take an example from education, there are diverse conclusions that could be reached on the basis of the fact that boys underachieve in English by comparison with girls in terms of their 16+ examination results. It might be concluded that:

- special remedial schemes must be introduced to improve boys' performance;
- the way in which English is taught, or the nature of the English that is taught, discriminates against boys and must be changed;
- little can be done unless media and peer group images of masculinity are transformed;

- nothing should be done because the differential performance of girls and boys in this area reflects an inherent tendency for girls to have greater facility with language, or arises from the greater effort they put into learning. And, on this basis, it might be argued that taking steps to remedy the differential would be unfair on girls;
- nothing needs to be done because, for most pupils, once the basics of reading and writing have been acquired, English is not an important subject. Basic, functional language-use is all that is necessary.

As this example indicates, what (if anything) should be done cannot be derived from any particular research finding *in itself*, but depends upon other factual assumptions, and upon value-commitments of various kinds.

It is often proposed by advocates of evidence-based practice that research can provide evidence about 'what works' or about whether some particular treatment, policy, or practice 'works'. But 'works' is what the Americans call a 'weasel' word. The question that is really being addressed is whether a policy or practice is good or bad, or is better or worse than others. And this clearly depends upon value assumptions, as well as factual information, and it is important to underline that science, and research more generally, cannot validate value conclusions. In practice, there may sometimes be sufficient value consensus that, if it is shown that some treatment tends to produce a particular kind of effect, we can immediately judge it good or bad. However, this is rare: there is generally less value consensus than is often assumed, even in a field such as medicine. Evidence for this is the debates over hospital versus home birth, and those surrounding care of the terminally ill. Of course, in most fields of social practice, the contentiousness of the value issues involved is often all too obvious.

Moreover, it is hard to answer questions about what are good and bad policies or practices *in the abstract*, separated from particular circumstances. In fact, we can guess that most social policies and practices are good for some of the people on the receiving end of them, bad for others, and indifferent in their effects on still others. The issue in evaluating policies or practices, often, is what proportions and types of people fall into these three categories, and what contextual features determine the distribution. Furthermore, there will usually be more than one set of beneficiaries to (or cost-bearers of) a policy, so that we have to 'weigh' its benefits/costs for one type of stakeholder *against* those for others. For example, in the case of policy initiatives on street prostitution, what weight do we give to the interests and concerns of people living in the local area, those living in other areas nearby, citizens in general, and tax payers, as well as the prostitutes, and their clients?

Since policymakers and practitioners are primarily concerned with what is good or bad, acceptable or unacceptable, etc., and with what ought to be done in particular situations, the fact that research can only produce general factual conclusions limits considerably the contribution that it can make to their work. Certainly, it cannot solve their practical problems on its own. In these terms, the notion of 'applying' research to (or even 'translating' it into) practice, is misconceived; and so too is the idea of *basing* policy or practice on it.

The impact of research on the outcomes of policy and practice

It seems to be widely assumed that maximising the impact of research on policymaking and practice is always beneficial, that it will *always* produce good outcomes. This notion is on a par with, and sometimes closely related to, the idea that change is always a good thing, and that those who resist any particular change do so simply because they are resistant to all change.[1]

However, there are various reasons why this may not be desirable. One reason is that all research findings are fallible. We are not usually faced with a contrast between well-established scientific knowledge, on the one hand, and mere irrational opinion, on the other; but rather with a dimension along which are ranged judgements having varying degrees of likely validity. Moreover, researchers have no guaranteed access to truth, and no monopoly on it. The fallibility of even natural scientific knowledge is now widely accepted. And how much more true is this of the knowledge produced by social research? There are a variety of reasons for this, one of which is the complexity of the phenomena social researchers study. I am not suggesting that the conclusions of social inquiry are completely unreliable, simply that their validity is never absolutely certain, and is often seriously questionable. And for this reason, if for no other, policy or practice relying upon research evidence may not 'work'. This may even be true when the evidence comes from a meta-analysis, systematic review, or qualitative synthesis of a whole body of work that has been thoroughly evaluated by the relevant research community. On top of this, it is important to underline that a sound evidential base is not *all* that is required for practical success. Indeed, it may not always be necessary at all: false assumptions can be effective, most obviously as propaganda or public relations, but in other ways as well.

Another important point about the relationship between policymaking/practice and outcomes is that it is highly mediated. In the case of national policy, implementation is by no means entirely under policymakers' control. As many writers in the policy field have pointed out, policies have a trajectory that is highly contingent, interpreted and modified by various agencies along the way, so that what a policy looks like on the ground may be very different from what policymakers originally envisaged (see, for instance, Ball 1990), and from what they now desire (which may be different again).

This relates to a more general issue: about the limits to what anyone can do to improve a situation. Even where improvements are possible, they are rarely if ever cost-free. And not every problem *can* be solved or situation improved. A 'can-do' attitude does not always lead to significant, let alone to *desirable*, change; it may even cause serious damage. There are severe limits to the effectiveness of all policies and practices – the world is too diverse and uncertain a place for success to be guaranteed. Actions always have diverse consequences, not all of which were intended, and many of which will not have been foreseen. And the more ambitious policies or practices are, the more likely they are to fail, or to have serious unintended consequences.

---

[1]Oakley 2006 has applied this kind of argument to the critics of the evidence-based practice movement. See Hammersley 2008b.

The final point in this section is that what is a desirable outcome is a matter of judgement, and there will often be no consensus about this. The research-based policymaking and practice model tends to assume that there is agreement about what would count as a good (and a bad) outcome, when there is not. Potential disagreement is covered over by talk of, for instance, 'effective social work', 'effective policing', or 'effective teaching'. After all, who could be in favour of ineffective forms of occupational practice? But this is to ignore the plurality of values to which people are committed, and the different priorities that can be adopted amongst these, in judging what are good and bad outcomes, what are good and bad forms of practice, and so on. Furthermore, as already noted, policies and practices always have *multiple* consequences, some of which may be judged beneficial, others not. For both these reasons, the issue of whether the results of a policy or practice are desirable, or amount to improvement, is much less easy to determine than the model implies.

CONCLUSION

Underlying many of the points I have made here is an emphasis on the fact that social scientific research and policymaking/practice are activities that are very different in character from one another. This may seem an obvious point, but it is one that tends to be overlooked by some of those on both sides of the divide. For example, policymakers tend to see research as analogous to the collation of information from different sources that civil servants engage in when responding to a minister's request for background information. It is by comparison with this image that they often judge academic research to be insufficiently issue-focused, overly complex, and far too slow. By contrast, researchers frequently look on policymaking and practice as if they were, or ought to be, similar in character to academic research. An example is the charge that policymakers are closed-minded, this implying a contrast with the *open*-mindedness that is supposed to be characteristic of researchers – though this is, of course, far from always displayed. It tends to be forgotten that a degree of closed-mindedness is essential to getting anything done (and, in fact, this includes research).

What I have done in this chapter is to raise a whole set of questions about what I called the research-based model of policymaking and practice. In effect, I have complexified the relationship between research and practice. And, on my own account here, this is what one would expect from a researcher. But I believe that it is very important to be realistic about the nature of this relationship if we are to come to sound judgements about whether, and how, it can be improved.

3

IS SCIENTIFIC RESEARCH EVIDENCE-BASED?

As I noted in the Introduction, in recent years the notion that practice should be evidence-*based* has been liberalised in response to criticism. This has affected both the nature of what should count as evidence *and* its relationship to practice. Where, initially, evidence was to be largely restricted to that produced by scientific modes of investigation, exemplified by the randomised controlled trial (RCT), there came to be a broadening of the criteria by which evidence is assessed, sometimes so as to include qualitative research findings. Similarly, whereas in early accounts the implication was that practical decisions should be completely determined by what research evidence shows to be the most effective strategy, there has been increasing emphasis on the fact that research evidence must always be interpreted and evaluated by practitioners, and that they must combine it with considerations of other kinds in making *judgements* about what is the best course of action in particular situations.

While the revised demand that practice be 'evidence-informed' is more reasonable in many ways, as I suggested in the Introduction the result is to lose the distinctive force of the original notion of evidence-based practice. What was novel about this was the idea that research evidence could provide definitive conclusions about 'what works' that are reliably superior to professional judgements. It was precisely the emphasis on a particular kind of evidence, and the strong role assigned to it in making practical decisions, that marked calls for evidence-based practice off from recurrent previous insistence that research should shape policymaking and practice. Even more important, liberalising the notion of evidence-based practice significantly downgrades, and probably undercuts, the original argument that occupational practices and/or social science research need to be transformed; it also makes any assessment of whether or not a particular form of practice uses evidence appropriately much more difficult. What exactly is required of practitioners for their work to be judged 'evidence-informed'?

The shift from evidence-based to evidence-informed practice has remained largely un-theorised, mainly because advocates have generally claimed that the new term captures what they had intended all along. Given this, there is a danger that 'evidence-informed practice' will be taken merely as a more palatable synonym for 'evidence-based practice' and that, despite liberalising claims, practitioners will still be judged, bureaucratically and perhaps even legally, according to whether they have 'followed the recommendations' of research as embodied in institutional rules and policies. In other words, there is the danger that because of continuing demands for transparent accountability the shift to 'evidence-informed' practice will serve simply as an ideological cover for insistence that professional practice be rendered accountable in these terms.

A second problem with the un-theorised nature of this shift is that it hides some important issues, ones that are also obscured by simple rejection of the whole notion of evidence-based practice and its implications for research (see, for instance, Denzin and Giardina 2006). My focus here is the image of research on which much advocacy of evidence-based policymaking and practice relies. To a large extent, this reflects its origin in medicine, where research methods were broadly modelled on those of physics and chemistry as these had developed since the nineteenth century. The resulting conception of science is important for two reasons. First, research evidence is treated as uniquely reliable, in other words as far more likely to be valid than information from other sources. Secondly, perhaps less obviously but equally important, the notion of evidence-based practice requires that policymakers and practitioners act in a manner analogous to how scientists are thought to operate.

It is worth remembering that the original, classic notion of evidence-based medicine demanded a *transformation* of clinical practice. What was involved was not simply that clinicians employ scientific evidence about the effectiveness of different treatments – rather than relying on their own experience, tradition, occupational folklore, etc. – but also that they *employ it in a scientific way*. In effect, the requirement was that clinical practice should become a science rather than an art, which was the way it had previously been viewed by many clinicians. Of course, the demand that science be *the* privileged source of evidence in clinical decisions derived from an assumption that this evidence had itself been produced through a rigorous, evidence-based process. The fundamental point was that clinical practice must take on this character too. Thus, clinicians were not just required to access relevant research evidence, and follow its recommendations, but also to do this *in the same manner that researchers would*.

What this indicates is that the injunction to rely upon scientific evidence in making clinical decisions flowed from the idea that clinicians must be rational, in precisely the way that scientists were assumed to be rational. The use of scientific as against other kinds of evidence stemmed simply from the belief that a rational actor would privilege this because it is the most reliable source of evidence. Furthermore, the implicit model here is that of calculation as against judgement: of being able to move explicitly to a conclusion about what is the right thing to do with demonstrable certainty. In short, science, interpreted in a particular way, was treated as *the* paradigm-case of an evidence-based practice, and therefore as a *model*, as well as a source of evidence, for clinical work.

There is another aspect of this too, one that is particularly important for the way in which the evidence-based practice movement was sponsored by politicians and other policymakers, and how it spread its influence to other areas. This is that the model of science adopted is one in which what is done, and why, is rendered *explicit* because (it is assumed) scientists follow well-defined formal procedures, whose effectiveness has been demonstrated, for example through replication.

The question I want to address here is how far scientific research, even in the natural sciences, actually matches this assumed model.

A POSITIVIST VIEW OF SCIENCE

What is involved here is, of course, a broadly positivist conception of how scientific work is done, or of how it *should be* done. And, in many ways, the whole notion of evidence-based practice draws on central themes in nineteenth- and twentieth-century positivist thought: that science is the only genuine form of knowledge; that the kind of rationality exemplified in scientific research should provide the model for the pursuit of all other activities; that such research involves the logical or calculable inference of conclusions from a solid foundation of empirical data; and that this is done by following the prescriptions of objective methods having demonstrable effectiveness. The distinctiveness of the call for practice to be evidence-based, as against earlier arguments for research to serve policymaking and practice, derives in large part from this positivist view of science.[1]

In its simplest form, positivism treats the distinctive method of science as logical inference from empirical givens. Observation and measurement are seen as crucial in providing the empirical base on which inference can operate. These processes are to be methodical and repeatable, so as to ensure that the evidence produced is objective: that it is not a reflection of the particular way it was produced or of the characteristics of the researcher(s). Equally important, the process of inference from the empirical data is assumed to be analogous to deduction, in the sense that it guarantees valid conclusions, or at least approximates closely to this ideal in calculable terms, thereby ensuring that the validity of the premises is transmitted to the conclusions. On these grounds, it is argued that scientific results reliably reflect the nature of the world, or at least our experience of it, in a way that knowledge claims from other sources cannot.

This logic or method of science was regarded by positivists as the engine that enabled it to cumulate knowledge, to a degree that had not been possible prior to the scientific revolution of the seventeenth century, and one that is not achievable in any other manner. And the use of experimental method was regarded as central to

---

[1] By no means all of those involved in the evidence-based medicine movement adopted the assumptions outlined here, in simple form, but these assumptions do capture the force of that movement in the public realm. For a useful account of positivism, which stresses the different meanings of the term, see Halfpenny 1982. On positivist ideas about how scientific knowledge can be derived from empirical evidence, and early critics of these, see Gillies 1993. Scharff 1995 provides an illuminating account of the tensions within nineteenth-century positivism, and of the continuing relevance of some of the ideas. He emphasises Comte's rejection of the idea of an 'organon of proof', so central to later versions of positivism.

this revolution. Even some of those who rejected key aspects of this positivist model of science nevertheless retained the idea that science's distinctive logic generates findings that have a very high level of certainty. An instructive, and very influential, example here is Karl Popper (1959, 1963). He shared the idea that at the heart of science is a process of logical inference that guarantees the validity of the conclusions reached, even if in his case definitive conclusions could only be negative: that a particular hypothesis or theory is false.

Early advocates of evidence-based practice tended to rely upon a view of research that is very similar in character to this general model. They took experimental methodology, in the form of the RCT, as central to scientific research, and as able to produce findings with a very high level of validity. Particular emphasis was often placed upon the role of the randomisation procedure in eliminating competing explanations, and this was treated as more or less guaranteeing the validity of findings, and therefore as an essential feature of science (see, for example, Chalmers 2003; Hammersley 2005b). Any errors were to be ironed out through replication, or through synthesising the findings from multiple studies via statistical meta-analysis. The key point was that these methods were viewed as a means for producing definitive knowledge about 'what works', by contrast with the defective nature of practitioners' judgements (Cochrane 1972).

CHALLENGES TO THIS CONCEPT OF SCIENCE

The idea that applying some explicit and determinate method, or set of procedures, is the engine of science has, of course, been subjected to sharp criticism within the philosophy, history, and sociology of science. But we can begin by noting that many of those who originally put forward this view of science distinguished between what they called 'the context of discovery' and 'the context of justification' (see Reichenbach 1951: 231). The logic of science applied to the latter but not to the former. In other words, even for some early positivists, while research reports should show how findings are logically derivable from given data, this could not accurately represent how the research had been carried out, how the conclusions had in fact been reached. A parallel here is the contrast between the process of mathematical discovery and the mathematical proofs that it produces (see Pólya 1957). The actual process of research was seen as inevitably shaped by, and even requiring, all manner of psychological and social factors. In other words, it was acknowledged that scientific inquiry would not follow a clearly marked path of logical inference, that there would be many false starts and wrong turns, speculative hypotheses and false assumptions.

All that was required by these sophisticated positivist accounts was that any scientific inquiry move progressively towards being able to show that its conclusions could be logically or inductively derived from evidence whose validity is beyond all possible doubt. In other words, it was expected that by the time the research report was written the scientist would have filtered out the extraneous, subjective elements to produce a logical argument deriving sound conclusions entirely from obviously reliable evidence. So, while the *pursuit* of research could not be objective in this logical sense, the scientist should eventually be able to show that the *findings* are objective.

Popper's account of the logic of scientific research also adopts the distinction between contexts of discovery and justification, but gives it a radical twist. He insists that there cannot be a logic of scientific *discovery*, that how theoretical ideas are generated is necessarily subjective and speculative, rather than being evidence-based in the way that theory-testing is. Furthermore, while he believed that there could be a logic of theory-testing his restriction of this to refutation seems to carry the implication that science can never produce a sound knowledge base: it can only tell us with any certainty which theories are false, and which have not yet been refuted despite systematic attempts to do so. This limitation obviously has significant implications both for scientific research as a source of knowledge and for its role as a model for policymaking and practice.

Of course, these sophisticated, positivist and post-positivist, views about the character of natural science method have subsequently been subjected to considerable criticism themselves. Critics have pointed out, first, that there can be no data whose validity is simply given, and that is therefore beyond all possible doubt; and, secondly, that the kinds of inference employed by natural scientists, even in their research reports, are not, and cannot be, restricted to deduction or modes of inference approximating to its character. As a result, quite different theoretical conclusions can always be drawn from the same body of data. This has been referred to as 'the under-determination of theory by data'.[2] So, natural scientists do not, and could not, operate in the manner proposed even by sophisticated positivists and Popperians.

Some writers on social science methodology appear to have concluded from these arguments that any claim to superior knowledge or to rationality on the part of science is false (Woolgar 1988a, 1988b). This is not the inference I am drawing here, nor has it been the predominant interpretation among recent philosophers of science. Nevertheless, revisionist accounts of the nature of science over the past fifty years are significantly at odds with the assumptions built into advocacy of evidence-based practice.

Generally speaking, the knowledge produced by science is now recognised to be fallible, though it must be underlined that this is different from saying that it is false or completely uncertain in validity. The point is simply that it can never be shown to be true, or for that matter false, with *absolute* certainty. This reduces and makes less secure the difference in likely validity between knowledge claims produced by science and those from other sources. Moreover, it is now recognised, much more strongly than it was previously, that science is necessarily an activity that is carried out by human beings within the social world, and one that shares features with other human activities, including failings of various kinds. Also given greater emphasis are differences among the sciences, so that many commentators reject the idea that there could ever be any single 'scientific method', acknowledging that how research findings are produced will vary across different fields (Haack 2003). And there is also widespread rejection of the notion that scientists can or should seek to implement fixed, and transparent, methods. While making information about how scientific conclusions were reached available for scrutiny by colleagues is recognised to be an important aspect of the process by which knowledge can be assessed, the limitations

---

[2]For a good summary of these arguments, see Chalmers 1999.

on this, for example arising from the tacit knowledge that is essential for work in any scientific field, are recognised (Polanyi 1958).

The distinction between the context of discovery and the context of justification, and subsequent criticism of the positivist account of science, make clear that even in making epistemic decisions in the course of their work – in other words, decisions about which knowledge claims are true and which false – scientists cannot logically derive these from observational givens. Rather, they must rely upon background knowledge, on past experience about the likely validity of various sorts of inference, and on personal, situated judgements (albeit ones that are open to future revision).

It is also important to point out that scientists make many practical decisions that are non-epistemic in character. This is most obviously the case with the selection of topics for investigation, but it is also true of decisions about what would be the most effective data collection and analytic strategies to employ. And conclusions about these matters are not, and cannot be, logically derived from given data. Nor do natural scientists usually make them on the basis of *previous methodological research showing which research strategies 'work' and do not 'work'*. Here, too, scientists rely upon personal and collective experience and judgement, refined by methodological and theoretical reflection, along with trial and error.

In short, science is a practical matter that is not reducible to technique or to method. This means that, to a large extent, scientists make decisions in much the same way as practitioners of many other activities, albeit shaped to their own particular goals. In other words, they operate in precisely the manner that was subjected to such sharp criticism by early advocates of evidence-based practice.

CONCLUSION

I have argued that key assumptions of nineteenth- and twentieth-century positivist thought underpin the idea of research-based policymaking and practice. These include: that science is the only genuine source of knowledge, that it relies upon rational demonstration based on empirical evidence, and that the kind of rationality exemplified in scientific research should provide the paradigm for the rational pursuit of other activities. Much of the distinctiveness of the call for policymaking and practice to be 'evidence-based' derives from this.

I emphasised that, in its original, classical version, the idea of evidence-based practice required, in effect, that practice be *modelled* on scientific research, not simply that it should *draw on* research evidence – in other words, it was demanded that practitioners employ evidence *in the same way* that scientists were assumed to do. And this involved a particular conception of the nature of science: as governed by objective evidence and by a 'transparent' method that enables conclusions from that evidence to be derived by calculation rather than judgement.

The key image here is, of course, that of the experiment, notably as exemplified in the randomised controlled trial: a hypothesis is subjected to test through its treatment and outcome variables being operationalised, subjects randomly allocated to groups receiving different treatments, the outcomes measured, and the likelihood of any differences being the result of random error in allocation to the groups being calculated via statistical analysis. The results of this analysis are generally taken to tell us whether or not the hypothesis is true – in other words, whether or not the treatment 'works'.

However, I showed that work in the philosophy of science had made clear that even the *epistemic* judgements scientists make cannot simply involve the excavation of empirical givens, treated as having absolute validity, and the subsequent logical derivation from these of conclusions whose own validity is thereby guaranteed. Moreover, scientists' non-epistemic decisions, such as those about data collection and analysis strategies, are almost never based on prior studies that have demonstrated which strategy 'works best', nor could they be. What all of this makes clear is that natural science itself does not live up to the ideal assumed by the notion of evidence-based practice.

I began by noting how the classical notion of evidence-based practice had been liberalised or diluted in much subsequent debate. While this makes what it proposes more cogent, it threatens to obscure the important problems regarding the nature of research and its relationship to policymaking and practice that the classical model had usefully highlighted. These problems include:

1 Questions about the types of evidence (in addition to that from research) on which policymakers and practitioners can, and should, draw.
2 How they ought to handle these different kinds of evidence and relate them to one another (especially where their implications conflict).
3 What exactly is the nature of the judgements that are necessarily involved in different forms of practice?
4 What sorts of reflection are productive of good judgement? Are there some that actually undermine or erode it?
5 Which social conditions facilitate, and obstruct, the development of good judgement on the part of policymakers and practitioners?
6 What accountability regime is appropriate to occupations which necessarily rely upon professional judgment that cannot be fully explicated so as to be 'transparent'?

These issues do not arise only in relation to policymaking and practice, as we have seen they also apply to research as well. We may all agree that research cannot depend simply upon logical inference from brute data. But there is considerable disagreement about what should count as evidence, and about how it should be used in reaching research conclusions. Nor are these simple matters to resolve. Does the fact that social research necessarily relies upon culturally situated judgement mean that we must simply tolerate, even celebrate, diverse forms of research, abandoning evaluation of the likely validity of their findings in epistemic terms in favour of a concern with their political implications, ethical status, or aesthetic appeal (see, for example, Hodkinson 2004; Smith and Hodkinson 2005; Hammersley 2005a, 2009a, b)? This is no more appropriate, I suggest, than refusing to judge policymaking and practice in terms of how far it achieves its goals, or realises the values intrinsic to it. It is certainly true that, in neither case, can we rely upon transparent methods, but the alternative is not undecidable judgement, mysticism, or the celebration of diversity for its own sake. We need a clearer sense of what is involved in the exercise of reasonable, expert judgement (see Collins and Evans 2007). However, the model of research built into the notion of evidence-based practice does not help much with this.

4

WHAT COUNTS AS EVIDENCE FOR EVIDENCE-BASED PRACTICE?

In this chapter I want to examine what counts as evidence in the context of arguments for evidence-based practice. An important starting point is to recognise the complex nature of evidence as a phenomenon. Evidence is always evidence *for* or *against* some answer to a question; or *for* or *against* some proposed solution to a problem. The idea that there can be a neutral, all-purpose evidence-base that can supply answers to all of our questions is misleading. Another way of putting this is to say that what counts as evidence is always a functional or relational matter. For this reason, whether or not some item of knowledge is evidence cannot be determined by its intrinsic character.

It is also important not to assume that evidence must appeal to something ultimate that is beyond all possible doubt. One version of the idea that evidence needs to be absolutely valid in this way comes from an old-fashioned empiricism, according to which the only true evidence is given immediately to the senses, and so is beyond all interpretation. However, there is nothing we can access directly that is simply impressed upon our senses; all sense data are a biological and socio-cultural product, and inferences from them depend upon assumptions. An alternative kind of foundationalism appeals to a privileged method or research design as determining validity, for example experimental methodology in the form of the randomised controlled trial (RCT). Yet no method is infallible. All methods have advantages and disadvantages – they involve trade-offs among various threats to validity. Thus, they do not constitute a single hierarchy. Furthermore, other kinds of knowledge, besides that from empirical research, can serve an evidential function.

So, what counts as evidence, and what counts as supportive or conclusive evidence, depends upon the question(s) we are trying to answer, or the problem we are trying to solve, and the means available for doing this, and must be judged in these terms.

For example, in the context of medicine, an RCT, or a systematic review of several trials, may be able to tell us about survival rates following some treatment, but frequently will not tell us about survival rates for particular categories of person, or about the distribution of side effects across these. Thus, even in that part of medicine where RCTs offer a great deal of reliable knowledge, they often will not, and sometimes cannot, answer *all* the relevant questions.

There is also an important distinction between something being evidence and its being *strong* evidence. Too often the evidence/not evidence contrast is conflated with that between strong/weak evidence. Equally important, to say that there is no evidence for some knowledge claim is quite different from saying that it is known to be false. Clarity is required in observing these distinctions.

Given the functional and non-foundational character of evidence, any item of data only counts as evidence, or as good evidence, because of its relationship to a range of background assumptions. There is a strong temptation to forget this, seeing some sorts of evidence as decisive. In an interesting discussion of RCTs, Nancy Cartwright (2007) distinguishes between what she calls clinchers and vouchers. Clinchers provide decisive, logical reasons to accept or reject some proposition. Vouchers simply give us more warrant to believe something than we had before. She identifies the RCT as a clincher, though she goes on to argue that precisely because of this fact its usefulness is narrowly restricted. Yet there is an important sense in which there can be *no* clinching evidence in an absolute or logical sense; in other words independent of specific evidential relations. No kind of evidence can tell us, *on its own*, what is true or what is false; or, for that matter, 'what works'.

It is true that in phenomenological terms evidence can sometimes appear to function like this: there are occasions when a particular item of knowledge will serve, and legitimately serve, as a clincher. But this results from the background assumptions that are being taken for granted in using the evidence. If we were to move to a different framework, or modify it in significant ways, the force of the evidence might be changed. Furthermore, if any of the assumptions built into the framework came to be regarded as open to reasonable doubt then the evidence would stop being clinching, and might even become weak, or no evidence at all. Many of the background assumptions will, of course, be uncontroversial, and I am certainly not suggesting that we need to question *all* of our assumptions. How could we do this anyway? The point is, though, that it is wise to remember that there *are* always background assumptions, and that sometimes we *will* need to check their reliability.[1]

Another important point is that the strength of the evidence for any proposition or proposal depends upon the evidence available for competing knowledge claims. So the issue is not just whether the evidence is convincing in its own terms but also whether it shows that the knowledge claim or practical proposal to which it relates is better than alternatives.

Much advocacy of evidence-based policymaking and practice obscures these complexities about the nature of evidence. Equally important, it makes questionable claims about what particular research methods can offer in the way of evidence.

---

[1]On this whole issue, see Williams (Michael) 2001: chs 13 and 14 and *passim*.

PROBLEMS WITH THE GOLD STANDARD

One of the criticisms made of the idea that research should serve evidence-based practice has been that it involves a positivistic conception of research (Loughlin 2003; see Chapter 3). Of course, the term 'positivism' has to be handled very carefully, since it is often used simply as a means of dismissing an approach with which the speaker disagrees. So let me try to be clear about what I mean here.[2] One aspect of it is that many of the arguments for evidence-based practice exaggerate the capabilities of particular kinds of quantitative method in social science; notably, RCTs and systematic reviews.[3]

If we take the case of RCTs, often treated as the gold standard, this method often has great strengths in allowing us to rule out rival explanatory factors. Furthermore, even by comparison with smaller experiments, the large scale of RCTs means that we are more likely to be able to detect causal effects above the level of random error. As a result, for some purposes and in some contexts, this method will work well in providing us with factual information about the effects of particular treatments.

However, there are a series of problems associated with RCTs that need to be taken into account; just as there are with any other method. None of these problems are news to most people who have been closely involved in running RCTs, but their significance (and recognition of them) does vary considerably across areas of work. I will mention a couple of problems.[4]

First, the treatment being examined needs to be clearly specifiable and standardisable across applications. Yet this is hard, indeed probably impossible, to achieve where the treatment is primarily a social process operating in diverse contexts, and where the people administering the treatment are often not in total control, and may have other more pressing concerns than carrying out the research. In social work and education, for example, any application of a particular 'treatment' is likely to be significantly different in character across cases, both within any trial and more widely when the treatment is 'rolled out'. For instance, the behaviour of schoolteachers cannot easily be standardised because a requirement for effectiveness in the job is adaptation to circumstances, notably to the distinctive and changing characteristics of particular cohorts of children. Furthermore, how children respond to the use of a specific pedagogical strategy depends to some extent upon how they interpret the teacher's behaviour, both whether they understand what is being required of them and what attitude they take towards this. In more specific terms, a teacher's actions always carry potential messages for pupils about her or his

---

[2]Elsewhere, I have examined positivist philosophical ideas in some detail, in an attempt to indicate what can be learned from them: Hammersley 1995: ch. 1.

[3]For a useful discussion of the 'myths' surrounding the capabilities of RCTs as compared with other methods, see Scriven 2009.

[4]There are also some issues concerned with the logic and rationale for randomisation: see Worrall 2002 and the references cited there.

expectations about them; and what expectations pupils ascribe to the teacher can influence their learning (Rogers 1982).

Another way of putting the same point is that, strictly speaking, there can be no such thing as physical control in experiments on human beings because people respond in terms of signs and interpretations rather than on the basis of physical reflexes (Rosnow 1981). There is also the problem that people's reactions to variation in a single factor in an experimental situation cannot tell us how they will behave in contexts where other relevant considerations are not controlled.[5] This introduces a very significant potential source of error, and it may not just be random error. Equally important, the outcomes that are of concern in social, as opposed to some medical, fields are almost always multiple and hard to measure with any accuracy. Randomisation to reduce the effect of background differences, the great strength of randomised controlled trials, is not much help in tackling any of these problems, nor are they easily resolvable in any other way. Furthermore, attempts to deal with them will often worsen external validity. This is, of course, the key formal weakness of RCTs – they do not usually operate with representative samples of the population to whom the treatments will subsequently be applied, and employing such samples may weaken their claims to internal validity by introducing many more potentially confounding factors. Moreover, even where an attempt is made to employ a representative sample, variation in patient and doctor consent is likely to erode representativeness.[6]

The use of double-blind procedures is also usually recognised as being important for the effectiveness of RCTs.[7] The expectations of trial participants, both subjects and those involved in administering the research, can have a significant effect on outcomes. However, it is often impossible to operationalise double-blind procedures in investigating the effects of social policies or programmes. While it is sometimes relatively easy to disguise from a patient whether he or she is receiving the drug being tested rather than a placebo, many social 'treatments' cannot be disguised. The result of this is that a major source of potential error remains uncontrolled.[8]

So, the first element of positivism I am ascribing to much discussion of research-for-evidence-based-practice is an exaggerated respect for quantitative research, resulting from an underestimate of the seriousness of the methodological problems

---

[5] This is an issue that was addressed by Egon Brunswik, who proposed the notion of representational design, see Hammond and Stewart 2001, especially pp. 4-5.

[6] The use of so-called pragmatic trials has sometimes been advocated. These are designed to measure external validity at the expense of internal validity – testing out the effect of treatments on more 'realistic' populations, see Hotopf 2002.

[7] Not all advocates of evidence-based practice hold to this; see Chalmers 2003.

[8] There are other well-recognised sources of error that arise in practice in many RCTs, notably those concerned with differential dropout of cases from treatment and control groups ('attrition') and the danger that what happens in relation to one of these groups will be affected by what goes on in the other ('cross-contamination').

surrounding it.[9] This is not to imply that such research is of no value, nor to suggest that other kinds of research are free from problems – far from it. The point is that the case for evidence-based practice, especially in its classic version, is premised upon the idea that scientific research, of particular kinds, can produce knowledge whose validity is very secure, by comparison with evidence from other sources. But this is a matter of degree, and generally speaking in the literature on evidence-based practice there has been an exaggerated estimate of the likely validity of findings from RCTs, given the weaknesses I have just discussed. Furthermore, it is important to remember that RCTs also vary in the rigour with which they are carried out on particular occasions, just as much as do other research methods, so that their results should never be taken at face value.[10] Indeed, this is true even when they have been replicated, or synthesised via systematic reviews, since the same types of error may operate across all or most of the studies concerned. One reason why this can happen is precisely because subsequent studies model themselves on previous ones.

RELIANCE UPON EXPLICIT PROCEDURES

There is another important respect in which much of the thinking about research by some advocates of evidence-based practice is positivistic. This is that what is demanded is that research should follow an explicit set of procedures so that it is 'transparent' and repeatable. This applies to the production of 'systematic' reviews of research literatures, as well as to primary research (see Chapter 8).

It is certainly the case that in order to evaluate any piece of research, or any review, we need information about how it was done. And many research reports, and so-called traditional reviews, do not provide all of the information that could be relevant. Furthermore, we need to encourage people to read research reviews and reports in a more critical fashion, taking account of the fact that how the work was done will have consequences for the likely validity of the conclusions reached. But, having said this, there is no way in which one can make the process of research or reviewing transparent, in the sense of being open to sound assessment by *anyone*, irrespective of their background experience and knowledge. To believe that this is possible is to forget the expertise involved in doing research and in doing reviews, and how this relies upon tacit knowledge, judgement and skill. Indeed, readers who do not already have expertise in the relevant area of research and in reviewing may even have difficulty in making good use of information about how an inquiry or a review was carried out (see Chapter 6).

Furthermore, what people are likely to do, when they do not have all the relevant knowledge and skills, is to latch on to particular features of a study (for example, whether or not there was a control group, whether there was random allocation

---

[9]For further discussion of these problems, see Cooper et al. 2012: ch. 1. See also Chapter 5.

[10]For a discussion of some of the practical problems in carrying out RCTs and their implications for validity, see Gueron 2002.

between treatment and control groups, or how big the sample was) and draw conclusions about the likely validity of the findings solely on this basis. Yet even though these features can be important, they by no means *determine* the value of the research findings. Their importance will vary depending upon the nature of the knowledge claims, the likely threats to validity, and so on. Even if there are weaknesses in the above areas, this does not mean that the findings should be dismissed, but at most only that they should be treated with great caution. There is no perfect research design, or perfect review – *and the significance of any defects in a study or a review will vary depending upon the purposes for which we use its findings.*

Moreover, some of these defects arise not just because of human failings but because in carrying out research and producing reviews we always have to trade off some positive features against others. For example, in deciding how many cases to study, or how exhaustive to try to be in searching for relevant literature in doing a review, we have to weigh up the advantage of large numbers and near exhaustiveness against that of examining a smaller number of cases, or a less than exhaustive body of literature, in greater depth. None of us has infinite amounts of time and other resources, and for this reason we have to make hard choices that pit the value of one feature of research design against that of another.

What this implies is that there is no single, fixed hierarchy of methods or designs, with one (whether the randomised controlled trial or the qualitative case study) at the top and others ranked below. There are advantages and disadvantages to different ways of doing research, and it is never possible to maximise all the benefits. Not even combining quantitative and qualitative methods will do this, even though this strategy can sometimes be of value. This is because, when trying to relate evidence from more than one (necessarily) imperfect method, we are faced with difficult decisions about how to make sense of discrepancies, and even about how much reliance can be placed upon agreement in results from different sources (Hammersley 2008d).

Up to this point, I have outlined limits to what research can offer in terms of evidence, and underlined that there are advantages and disadvantages associated with any research approach – so that there is no single royal road to producing sound research evidence, and no research evidence that can play the role ascribed to it by the notion of evidence-based practice. But there are also limits to the use that policymakers and practitioners can make of research evidence.

EVIDENCE FOR POLICY AND PRACTICE?

I have argued that much discussion of evidence-based practice assumes that policymakers and practitioners should make decisions by following a set of transparent procedures, and relying solely upon what the evidence or data 'shows' (see Chapter 3). It is argued that the basis for decisions must be explicit evidence whose force anyone, lay audiences included, could recognise. In recent times, there has, of course, been a great deal of pressure on professionals in the public sector to make their practice transparent in this way. Targets must be set, courses of action must be specified in written plans, and performance must be measured. The requirement that policy and practice be evidence-based has become influential at least partly because it fits neatly into this managerialist programme (see Chapter 1).

Of course, professionals should not be allowed to be unaccountable, nor should they get away with mystical references to specialised knowledge or esoteric intuition. However, practice cannot be made *completely* transparent even to a knowledgeable audience. This point relates to a major dispute about the nature of professional practice, in fact about the nature of human practices in general, that goes back at least to Aristotle. In his book *Back to the Rough Ground*, Joseph Dunne provides an excellent history of some of the arguments about the nature of practice, in particular about the extent to which it necessarily involves what the ancient Greeks called *phronesis* (Dunne 1997).[11] This refers to the capacity for good judgement, which is required in deciding, in particular situations, what would count as acting well or badly. Phronesis involves analysis of concrete particulars, grasped through experience, but also guided by knowledge of theories and general principles (Nussbaum 1990). Central to it is 'the ability to recognise, acknowledge, respond to, and pick out certain salient features of a complex situation' (Nussbaum 1986: 305). It also involves the interpretation of relevant values, this providing the basis for the weighing of alternatives in order to decide how to act. What this indicates is that judgement is unavoidable, but it is not necessarily arbitrary or biased – it can be exercised in better and worse ways.[12]

Of course, advocates of evidence-based practice often deny that they are claiming that research should determine what practitioners ought to do in particular cases, and they sometimes acknowledge the role of professional judgement. This was central to the switch from 'evidence-based' to 'evidence-informed' practice. However, as I have noted in earlier chapters, this leaves us with genuine difficulties regarding how to weigh evidence coming from different sources, notably that from research (perhaps of various different types), on the one hand, and that from practical experience, on the other (see Oswald and Bateman 2000; Byrne 2004). What is required here is what Turner (2005) refers to as expertise about expertise. Moreover, when promoting evidence-informed practice its advocates frequently lapse back into privileging evidence that purports to be explicit and conclusive as against 'subjective' judgement.

It is also necessary to recognise that good practice, in many fields, allows for, indeed demands, the use of trial and error. Often the decisions involved are not as consequential as many of those involved in medical practice; nor are they usually irreversible. Trying out strategies to discover which one seems to work in a particular case may often be possible without significant cost, and indeed may be the only sensible option. This is an important source of evidence that the rhetoric of evidence-based practice denies.

So my point in this section has been that advocates of evidence-based practice exaggerate the role that research evidence can play in relation to policymaking and practice, downplaying the need for judgement, tacit knowledge, and trial-and-error.

---

[11]For a parallel discussion of expertise that resists the idea that it can be explicated in terms of rules, see Dreyfus and Dreyfus 1986.

[12]Another important source of this idea is Donald Schön's work on reflective practice (Schön 1983, 1987), though he had a rather narrow view of the role of research in relation to professional work.

Furthermore, if these are not given their due weight then the decisions made will be worse than they could otherwise have been.

EVIDENCE-BASED PRACTICE AS POLICY

Let me turn, finally, to policymaking as a form of practice, and what I see as the political role of the evidence-based practice movement. What was said above about the nature of practice – in particular, the necessary reliance on judgement and tacit knowledge – applies as much to policymaking as it does to forms of professional practice. Researchers often forget this when they complain that policymakers have not based policy on research findings. As we saw, it is false to assume that good policy can be directly derived from research findings; or that policymaking can follow the same logic as that involved in doing research. Here, too, there is necessary reliance upon expertise that is neither propositional nor explicit in character, and what amounts to good practice depends upon the goals being pursued and the characteristics of the situation in which this is being done.

Furthermore, as I noted in Chapter 2, policymakers have to take into account some considerations that are not specifically about whether or not a policy is likely to 'work'. For example, they need to judge whether it is going to be possible to persuade key stakeholders of the value of the policy, whether the policy is going to have significant knock-on effects in relation to other things they are doing or, in the case of politicians, whether it is likely to damage their chances of being re-elected. We might like to believe that new policies could be adopted purely on the basis of judgements about whether or not they will work better than current ones, but – given the way the world is (and probably not just the way it is at the moment) – this is not the only consideration that policymakers need to take into account. It is necessary to be realistic about the politics of policymaking.

Of course, I am not denying that policymakers may currently give too much emphasis to political considerations. In fact, I believe that much recent policymaking, at least in the UK, reflects this: it has been a case of trying to do too much, exercising too little deliberation and thought, giving too little weight to the knowledge and experience of those who deal with the problems first hand, and not making proper use of pilot schemes. But we should not assume that policymakers are ever likely to be able to act on the basis of the sort of 'rational model' that is assumed in much advocacy of evidence-based policymaking.[13]

I am not suggesting that all advocates of the evidence-based practice model are ignorant about the realities of policymaking. But I *am* saying that what they frequently assume about how policymakers will use research evidence betrays a naïve conception of the conditions under which policymakers operate, and of their primary concerns. I know that, in part, advocates of evidence-based policymaking are trying to make policymakers conform more closely to what they see as rational. And

---

[13]There is a considerable literature questioning this rational model of policymaking. See, for example, Lindblom and Cohen 1979.

this may be desirable up to a point. But, as I have indicated, the role of *phronesis* – of experience, expertise and judgement – is as important in policymaking as it is in other forms of practice, and the move to insist that all policy decisions should be validated in research terms can have undesirable consequences in this context just as much as elsewhere. It is also necessary to remember that even if policymaking were reformed to make it more rational than at present, it would still need to be realistic – it is always 'the art of the possible', in the sense of operating within significant practical constraints.

CONCLUSION

I began by arguing that what counts as evidence, and as good evidence, is always a functional or contextual matter: it is relative to the questions or problems being addressed. It cannot be determined in the abstract. I went on to suggest that there is a tendency for the evidence-based practice movement greatly to overestimate the reliability of scientific evidence, specifically that coming from RCTs. In this respect, the limits to what research can supply tend to be overlooked. Equally important there is a defective view of what is involved in policymaking and practice, these both necessarily depending upon phronesis, and involving additional considerations beyond evidence about 'what works'. Neglecting all this, the potential usefulness of research evidence comes to be exaggerated.

Throughout my discussion in this chapter I have taken its title to refer to the question of what should count as evidence for policymakers and practitioners, arguing that while social science research has a role it is not the only source of evidence, and that there is little justification for treating RCTs and systematic reviews as the only legitimate source of research evidence. There is, however, a different reading one can give to the title of this chapter: as raising the question of on what evidence we should determine the value of proposals for 'evidence-based practice'.

In fact, of course, this is simply the same question at a different level. Here, we would be asking whether this could and should be decided via a series of RCTs plus systematic review of their results, or whether other kinds of evidence must also be employed, perhaps including the sorts of methodological and philosophical argument presented in this chapter. Strictly speaking, it would seem that advocates of evidence-based practice ought to provide the sort of evidence they privilege to 'demonstrate' that their proposals 'work'. And yet, even if this were possible, it would not resolve the issue since the disagreement over what should count as evidence would remain.

The conclusion I draw from this is that the matter cannot be resolved by any simple demonstration – that the kind of discussion that some advocates of evidence-based or evidence-informed practice dismiss as 'theoretical' (see, for example, Chalmers 2005) or as evidence of 'resistance to new technology' (Oakley 2006) cannot be avoided. Here, as elsewhere, we are not faced with a choice between relying on demonstrable evidence or resorting to theory, prejudice, fashion, etc. but rather with the need above all for careful reflection, in which arguments and evidence of various kinds must be given due attention. The decisions we have to make – whether as practitioners, policymakers, or researchers – are more complex than most of the arguments for evidence-based practice allow, and what can count as evidence is also much more diverse.

5

IS SOCIAL MEASUREMENT POSSIBLE, AND IS IT NECESSARY?

In arguments for evidence-based practice, much of the rationale for the capacity of research, in the form of randomised controlled trials (RCTs), to provide reliable knowledge about 'what works', has focused upon the role of random allocation in controlling confounding factors (see Chalmers 2003). There is some force in this argument, even though randomisation does not control *all* the factors involved in documenting the effects of an intervention, and even though there are questions about what RCTs can tell us about how causal relationships actually operate 'in the wild'.[1] Given less attention, generally speaking, are the problems of measurement involved, particularly in the case of social variables. The capacity of researchers to measure the outcomes about which knowledge is required varies considerably. For instance, while it is *relatively* straightforward to measure birth and death rates, it is much more difficult to measure quality of life, improved learning, successful case outcomes in social work, and so on. The problem of measurement in the social realm is the topic of this chapter.

THE PRIORITY OF MEASUREMENT

Measurement has often been taken to be an essential feature of science, and measurement of 'nature's capacities' is possible – indeed to a considerable degree has been successfully accomplished (Cartwright 1989; see also Duncan 1984: ch. 5). In light of this, many social scientists have pursued rigorous measurement because they

---

[1]For discussion of these issues see Worrall 2002 and Cartwright 2007.

see it as required in order to produce scientific knowledge.[2] They take to heart what Merton et al. (1984) refer to as 'the Kelvin dictum', which (at the instigation of William F. Ogburn) was inscribed on the new Social Science Research Building at the University of Chicago in 1929 (see Wirth 1940). This dictum runs: 'when you cannot measure it, when you cannot express it in numbers, your knowledge is of a meagre and unsatisfactory kind' (Sir William Thomson [later Lord Kelvin] 1889: 73–4; cited in Merton et al. 1984).[3]

While the problems surrounding measurement have often been acknowledged by quantitative researchers, they have usually been treated as technical in character; in other words as remediable through further refinements in measurement technique (see, for example, Bulmer 2001). By contrast, critics have often taken these problems to indicate the folly of the whole enterprise. Qualitative researchers, especially, usually deny the feasibility of, and the need for, measurement. Indeed, the defects of many forms of psychological and social measurement have long been one of the grounds used in challenging the claims and the value of quantitative work.[4]

The critics have supported this conclusion by philosophical and methodological arguments of various kinds. They have insisted, for example, that human actions, unlike the behaviour of physical objects or even of animals, are constituted by meanings or reasons, and that by their very nature these are not susceptible to measurement. Quantitative researchers' attempts to measure them have been criticised, for instance for assuming that people employ standard meanings (ones that are common across a population and stable over time) that can be understood independently of the local social contexts in which they developed. Qualitative researchers have also argued that measurement falsely assumes the operation of fixed patterns of causal relation; instead, they claim, social phenomena are by their very nature processual and contingent in character, and therefore are not measurable. In more recent formulations, the argument has been that social phenomena are discursively constructed, and that the only feasible analytic task is to describe the discourse practices involved, or perhaps even to expose and challenge these. So, the assumptions about the nature of social inquiry built into much qualitative research and much current social theory are at odds with any conception of social science that puts rigorous measurement at its core.[5]

---

[2]On the history of measurement see, for example, Woolf 1961 and Robinson 2007. For the history of *social* measurement see Duncan 1984, who rightly points out that there is a sense in which 'all measurement is social' (p. 35). See Michell 2007 for a critical history of psychological and social measurement theory. For an account of the 'theory and practice' of measurement across both the natural and the social sciences, see Hand 2004; while Viswanathan 2005 provides a recent discussion of measurement in the context of social science. For an earlier discussion focusing on non-random error, see Zeller and Carmines 1980. Kempf-Leonard 2004 is an encyclopaedia that includes entries on many aspects of social measurement.

[3]The paper by Merton et al. recounts their efforts to discover the original form of 'Kelvin's dictum'. In fact, this had already been identified by Kaplan (1964: 172).

[4]For early examples see Cicourel 1964 and Phillips 1971: ch. 2 and *passim*.

[5]A glance at the *Handbook of Qualitative Research* (Denzin and Lincoln 2011) will provide confirmation of this statement. By contrast, earlier in his career Denzin treated measurement as an essential part of social research: see Denzin 1970.

At the same time, however, some commentators on qualitative research have argued that it cannot escape the need to measure the phenomena with which it deals (see Naroll 1962, 1973; Moles 1977; Denzin 1978; Hammersley 1986). In this spirit, it is often pointed out that, despite their frequent rejection of causal analysis in favour of interpretivism or constructionism, qualitative researchers nevertheless often aim at explaining outcomes of one kind or another in terms of the operation of various factors; so that, in practice, they are engaged in much the same task as any other kind of social scientist (Hammersley 2008c, 2012a). Furthermore, while the sensitising concepts that qualitative inquiry usually employs are important in the development of new theoretical ideas, it may be impossible to subject competing knowledge claims to effective assessment without clarifying and developing key concepts into more definitive forms; and without relating these to instances in a rigorous fashion (see Hammersley 1989b). Moreover, many of the knowledge claims that qualitative researchers put forward are intrinsically quantitative in character: they refer (albeit usually in verbal terms) to frequency, duration, degree, or extent. In short, it has been concluded by some commentators that it is impossible to do qualitative research, or at least to do it well, without employing measurement processes of *some* kind.

In this chapter I will employ a broad interpretation of the nature of social measurement, and consider some major obstacles it faces, as these relate to both qualitative and quantitative work. It seems to me that these obstacles are too often glossed over on both sides of the debate about evidence-based practice, and beyond.[6] Furthermore, we need to move the debate over measurement out of the context of paradigm battles between competing social science approaches, in order to recognise and address problems that virtually all social scientists face, and which at the moment they cannot deal with very effectively.

In offering any answer to the questions posed in my title, much depends of course upon what we mean by the term 'measurement'; and, also, on what we take the functions of measurement to be. These will be my first topics.

THE MEANING OF 'MEASUREMENT'

There are at least two quite different, but influential, definitions of 'measurement' within the methodological literature. First, there is what is probably the most common approach, exemplified by specifying so-called *levels* of measurement (Stevens 1946).[7] This is founded on Stevens' definition of 'measurement' as 'the assignment of numerals to objects or events according to rules' (p. 677). On his influential account, the assignment of instances to labelled categories constitutes the 'nominal level of measurement'. This is distinguished from ranking, and from two forms of metric measurement (interval and

---

[6]For a recent discussion of measurement theory that, like many others, effectively takes most of the issues discussed in this chapter for granted, see Bovaird and Embretson 2008.

[7]Kaplan (1964: ch. 5) and others have put forward more elaborate outlines of measurement levels.

ratio scales).[8] The second, more restrictive, definition of the term 'measurement' denies this title to categorisation counts and even to rankings, insisting that measurement is always concerned with the *degree* to which phenomena possess some particular characteristic. From this point of view, at least an interval scale and preferably a ratio scale is required for scientific measurement to take place: 'if the sums do not add up, the science is wrong. If there are no sums to be added up, no one can tell whether the science is right or wrong. If there are no ratio-scale measurements, there can be no sums to add up' (Laming, 2002: 691; see also Johnson 1936 and Michell 1999: 14).

There is another issue about what counts as measurement that is relevant here. This concerns the degree to which measurement must involve the use of explicit, standardised techniques – rather than reliance upon human judgement, whether that of researchers or informants. A central aspect of the development of at least some natural sciences has been the attempt to replace human judgement with mechanical or electronic forms of measurement, alongside efforts to extend the sources of evidence beyond human perceptual capabilities. On this precedent, many commentators would insist that measurement in the social sciences requires the use of explicit, standardised procedures that at least *minimise* the role of human judgement in producing evidence – in order to maximise the chances of valid measurement (Wilks 1961: 5). As Wilks indicates, the model here is not just that of natural science but also of modern, mass production methods. What is involved is a notion of procedural objectivity (Eisner 1992), and sometimes this is taken to *ensure* validity. For example, Bovaird and Embretson (2008: 283) claim that:

> A measure is standardized if there are uniform procedures to ensure that the measure is administered and scored the same way each time it is used. If so, two individuals who receive the same score can be interpreted to possess the same amount of the attribute.

A more fundamental issue than how 'measurement' is to be defined concerns what the function is of the activities that are included under this heading, interpreted in the broadest sense to include categorisation. This is the next issue I will explore.[9]

THE FUNCTIONS OF CATEGORISATION AND MEASUREMENT

It is important to recognise that typologies and quantitative dimensions are implicit in much ordinary everyday talk. Categories are used to describe events or persons,

---

[8]Producing a scale for temperature with an absolute zero, in other words a ratio scale, was of course one of Lord Kelvin's great scientific achievements. For discussions of Stevens' work on scales see Newman 1974 and Matheson 2006. While his approach has been extremely influential, within psychology and beyond, it has been subjected to considerable criticism. See, for example, Duncan 1984: ch. 4; Velleman and Wilkinson 1993; Michell 1997, 1999, 2000, 2002.

[9]For a discussion of the functions of measurement in the physical sciences, see Kuhn 1961. See also Duncan 1984: ch. 5.

and sometimes to count them, and people may also be represented verbally in ways that place them on one or more dimensions, such as 'bigger/smaller', 'more/less well-known', 'more/less important', 'more/less intelligent', 'more/less dogmatic', and so on. So, it is not the case that category schemes and conceptual dimensions are alien notions imposed upon social life by quantitative researchers; they are already built into it. What such researchers seek to do, often, is to render everyday schemes and dimensions, and their application, more systematic and rigorous *in particular ways*, in the belief that this is essential for scientific work. And this is usually regarded as especially necessary in applied research of the kind that is central to arguments for evidence-based practice. Here the outcome variables to be measured must more or less capture the meaning of the corresponding concepts used by policymakers and practitioners.

One of the tasks that the work of classification and measurement addresses, and the one I will focus on here, is what we might call the evidential grounding of concepts; in other words, the need to link them to evidence that will serve as grounds for allocating objects to categories, or to particular points on a scale, according to their possession of the relevant conceptual property. The implication of the term 'grounding' is not that concepts are generated out of pure thought, and therefore need to be linked to 'the empirical realm'. Generally speaking, the concepts that we employ in any research project will have come out of ordinary experience of the world and/or from the literature produced by previous research, itself connected to such experience. We may also generate concepts, or identify which ones are relevant to the phenomena being investigated, through a process of abduction. The key point is, though, that in carrying out any investigation we will need to link the concepts we have selected and developed to evidence that will allow us to check the likely validity of the knowledge claims in which those concepts are embedded. In the case of classification, we will need to be able to identify relevant objects and place them in categories that map the property which the concept implies. With measurement, it is a matter of identifying relevant objects and then assigning them to an appropriate position on a scale that accurately represents the character of the property. So, 'grounding' is a functional category, it does not refer to an empirical as against a theoretical realm, but rather to providing means for determining the validity of knowledge claims.

Occasionally, concepts themselves will relate directly to what can be used as evidence for classification or measurement. For example, for all practical purposes the issuing of death certificates can be taken as a direct measure in calculating the survival rates of those suffering from a life-threatening illness who were subject to different treatment regimes in a randomised controlled trial. By contrast, if the focus is on whether a condition has been cured, or whether symptoms have been relieved, or whether quality of life has been improved, a much more complex, difficult, and contentious measurement task is involved.

In the discussion above I have avoided the usual phrasing, to the effect that concepts must be 'operationalised', because this term is potentially misleading. It could be taken to imply that concepts can (and should) be *defined* in terms of standard measurement operations. While few quantitative researchers today would accept operationism in its full form, for example treating intelligence as no more than 'what intelligence tests measure', there is a very strong tendency for them to assume that, alongside any conceptual definition, there must be an 'operational definition' in terms of a standard set of indicators, usually a measurement instrument of some kind.[10] However, we need to distinguish clearly between the property being measured and any dimension this implies, a scale that would represent it, and any particular instrument that could be employed to locate objects at points on this scale in terms of amounts of the property.

One problem with the notion of operationalisation is that it tends to obscure these distinctions. Indeed, it is perhaps a legacy of operationism that it is very common, in the social and psychological sciences, for scales and measurement instruments to be conflated with one another, and also for them to be treated as effectively defining the property they are intended to measure.[11] By contrast, in physical measurement the distinctions are usually retained. For instance, mercury thermometers can be used to measure both degrees Fahrenheit and degrees Celsius, and there are other kinds of thermometer that can be used to measure on each of these scales. Moreover, heat as a dimensional property is conceptualised independently of both scales and measurement instruments. The key point is that how we think about any property we are investigating, how we devise a categorical scheme or scale to represent it, and how we assign objects to their appropriate category or place on the scale, are three quite different undertakings, even though the judgements we make in relation to each will affect the others.

The conflation of these three aspects of the process of grounding concepts in evidence is closely associated with, and reinforces, the tendency to assume that classification or measurement must, in the name of rigour, be carried out through the use of standard operations – explicit procedures that everyone can follow in the same way. Thus, in much quantitative research, including RCTs, measurement procedures have often taken the form of closely specified, standard routines that those involved must adhere to, on the grounds that this will increase measurement reliability (in the sense of consistency across observers and occasions).[12] However, while using standardised techniques may sometimes be possible and desirable in social science, there are good reasons to believe that it may not always be. More importantly, to assume that it is essential is to mistake a means for the function it performs. There is no intrinsic requirement that the grounding of concepts in any particular study be achieved via standardised operations. While each object must be classified or measured in terms of the

---

[10]The term 'definition' can, of course, mean different things: see Robinson 1954. There is also some dispute about what the term 'operational definition' meant for early operationists: see Hardcastle 1995 and Feest 2005.

[11]See, for instance, the discussion in Mueller 2004.

[12]While now entrenched in usage, it seems to me that this definition of 'reliability' as 'consistency' is ideological, in the sense that it trades on the commonsense connotation of 'can be relied upon' while meaning something quite different. Furthermore, as Zeller and Carmines (1980: ch. 1) note, consistency is only desirable in the absence of systematic error.

same concept definition, the indications we use to assign objects are not part of the concept and can legitimately differ when dealing with different objects. Furthermore, there is no reason to assume that such variation in measurement practice would increase the likelihood of error, though it could increase the likelihood of inconsistency between observers.

So, the use of a standard set of indicators, or of a measurement instrument, is simply one strategy that can be employed to classify or measure; furthermore, standardisation is not necessarily very effective in improving the validity of any attempt to ground concepts. There are at least three reasons why quantitative researchers often believe that standard operations or measuring instruments are required, and these need to be distinguished. First, there is the idea that by adopting a standard procedure the grounding process will be made more objective, in the sense that it will eliminate the effects of subjective or idiosyncratic factors on the part of the researcher and others. A second argument is that standard operations are necessary where more than one person is going to collect the data, so as to try to ensure that the same data would be collected irrespective of which researcher is involved. This may be an important consideration in RCTs, as in many social surveys. The third argument is that a specification of standard operations or procedures is essential if it is to be possible for the research to be replicated, so as to check that the results were not a product of extraneous factors, including those emanating from the subjective characteristics of the researcher.

These arguments are not as compelling as they are often taken to be. The first, and most fundamental, focuses upon how the subjectivity of both researchers and respondents/informants can threaten validity. However, this overlooks the fact that the influence of subjective factors can never be entirely eliminated, and that distinctive capabilities on the part of researchers (and informants) may be essential for producing the knowledge required. In most of its forms, in the physical as well as the social sciences, measurement involves some observational judgement, even if this is only looking at a dial to read off the figures, or making a decision about into which category a respondent's answer falls.[13] Indeed, even where data are produced entirely electronically, researchers must draw inferences from them; and this is never just a matter of deductive logic or mathematical inference. While some older models of the research process drew a very sharp boundary between theory and data, most recent philosophical views recognise that this is at most a functional distinction, which implies that judgement and interpretation are always likely to infuse what are treated as data. So, avoiding human judgement is

---

[13]Often it is more than this. It is important to remember that even the use of physical measurement devices are always located within some form of social practice, without which measurement could not take place. For example, in taking a person's temperature a thermometer must be applied to the right part of the body (in the mouth, under the arm, etc.) and in a context where the person's temperature is not likely to be 'artificially' raised or lowered, not to mention the fact that the thermometer must be read correctly. In short, measuring instruments are tools, and all tool use is dependent upon social practices that involve common understandings and the negotiation of contingent situations. Furthermore, as the case of medicine indicates, evidence from standardised instruments often needs to be combined with that from non-standardised sources.

impossible and undesirable; the key issue is how to improve the validity of the particular sorts of judgement employed.[14]

There is a fundamental fallacy that lies beneath the idea that grounding concepts must involve the use of standard operations. This is the false contrast that is sometimes drawn between procedures and judgements, with the former being treated as objective (or, at least, as potentially objective) and the latter as inevitably subjective, in other words as necessarily leading to error. Part of the problem here is that the term 'subjective' can have different meanings, and that these carry discrepant implications for the task of grounding concepts. 'Subjective' is often taken to refer to what goes on inside people's heads, rather than what occurs 'on the outside' in their behaviour. So, judgements are often treated as, by their very nature, private rather than public, and therefore as not open to checking by others. And, from this, the leap is frequently made to the conclusion that judgements are idiosyncratic, in the sense of simply reflecting the characteristics of the person rather than accurately representing what is being judged.[15] But this line of thought is defective. Much twentieth-century analytic philosophy, following Wittgenstein, was concerned with disabusing us of the misconception that first-person statements about subjective matters are simply expressions of inner experience. It has been pointed out that when we talk about such things, even to ourselves, we are using publicly available language and cultural conventions to do so. From this point of view, judgements, like other subjective phenomena, are not inscrutable, private experiences that cannot be evaluated, and which therefore must be simply accepted or rejected. Nor are they necessarily idiosyncratic; and neither does idiosyncrasy automatically imply inaccuracy. Of course, it is true that they *can* be inaccurate, and that we may need to employ means to check or improve them. But this is no reason always to avoid or minimise them; nor is there any alternative that can *ensure* accuracy.[16]

Not only is relying entirely upon procedures impossible, since some element of judgement will almost always remain, but attempting to do this will often be counterproductive. This is because reliance upon procedures can prevent us from using our observational and interpretive skills, and our relevant background knowledge, in drawing inferences about the nature of the phenomena with which we are dealing. While guidelines may be useful, these frequently operate best as an

---

[14]See Campbell's argument (1988a, 1988c) that 'qualitative knowing' always underpins 'quantitative knowing'. He writes: 'Qualitative, commonsense knowing of wholes and patterns provides the enveloping context necessary for the interpretation of particulate quantitative data' (1988c: 365). Also relevant in this context is Daston and Garrison's (2007) discussion of different notions of objectivity in physical science, and of the 'somersault' history of the meaning of the term (pp. 29-35). See also Hammersley 2011.

[15]One source of this tendency is the argument of Bacon and others to the effect that science should rely upon the abilities of ordinary human beings, not on specialised knowledge and skills, in the way that was true of humanistic scholarship in the Renaissance. See Gaukroger 2001: 127 and *passim*. Gaukroger notes the parallel between Bacon's conception of the collective work of scientists and the demand on Jesuits that they carry out instructions 'as if they were but corpses' (p. 128). It is perhaps from this context that the notion of scientific 'rigour' gets its sense!

[16]Newell (1986) covers this, and much other relevant, philosophical ground.

aid to judgement, for example in reminding us of what may need to be taken into account, or what could indicate what. However, to try to turn such guidelines into standardised decision rules that substitute for judgement will often increase rather than reduce error. For example, in observing and recording what actions are taking place in some situation, or in trying to understand people's reports of their experiences, we must have the capacity to 'read' the behaviour involved, and the environment to which it is attuned. In part, this is a matter of understanding the language that people are using to communicate with one another. But this is not just a matter of knowing the vocabulary and grammar of that language, we also need to have pragmatic competence in it, in order to grasp what it is being used to do on any particular occasion. And this is closely involved with understanding people's intentions, their likely reasons for doing what they are doing, and the motives that might lead them to react in the way that they do to others' actions. Where we are observing a scene that is already familiar to us, we probably already have these capabilities; it is usually only when we are a stranger that the need for them becomes obvious. Here, in order to be able even to describe what is going on, at least in terms that will allow us to develop and assess social science explanations, we need to 'learn the culture' of the people involved.[17]

Attempts to avoid bias coming from the subjectivity of the people being studied face similar problems. It is claimed that standardisation increases the chances that responses from experimental subjects or survey respondents are comparable because each has been presented with more or less the same stimulus. However, this argument is based on some highly questionable (in effect, behaviourist) assumptions concerning human communication. We must ask: Can it be assumed that standardisation of physical stimuli, for example in the form of printed items on a questionnaire, ensures that people's responses are equivalent? The answer to this is almost certainly 'no'. It cannot be assumed that people respond to stimuli on the basis of an algorithmic and universal model: for example, whereby the verbal elements of the stimulus are translated via rules, plus use of a semantic dictionary and perhaps also a factual encyclopaedia, into a standard meaning. There is a great deal of work in linguistics, philosophy, and the social sciences which makes clear that human communication does not operate in this fashion, that it is a more complex and indeterminate process: it involves mutual adaptation and negotiation of meaning in order to coordinate actions.[18] Thus, in interpreting questions in an interview, or items on a questionnaire, respondents will attribute intentions and motives to the researcher, these attributions will shape their answers, and people may differ in how they do this.[19]

---

[17]This is, of course, the longstanding argument about the need for Verstehen in social research (Becker 1950: ch. 4; Truzzi 1974; O'Hear 1996).

[18]See, for example, Grice 1991 and Sperber and Wilson 1986. There has been increasing recognition of this problem, if not usually of its depth, in the literature on survey research (see, for example, Johnson et al. 1997), though much actual social research practice ignores it.

[19]All human answering relies upon such attributions, as Schegloff (1971) illustrated many years ago in a study of the apparently simple matter of giving strangers directions.

There is also the problem that, in practice, it is never possible entirely to standardise the circumstances in which people respond to tests, answer questions in interviews, and so on. For instance, they may complete postal or online questionnaires in a variety of contexts (in their lunch break at work, lying in bed on a Sunday morning, alone or with other people, etc.), and these could affect their responses, for example about whether medical symptoms have been relieved, whether their lives have been improved by some social work intervention, etc. Nor is it clear that there is a positive, linear relationship between degrees of standardisation and degrees of validity; and, in the absence of this, approximations to standardisation cannot be treated as facilitating increased validity even 'other things being equal'.

For all these reasons, it is doubtful that standardisation of data collection processes can be relied upon to minimise the effects of extraneous factors. More than this, such standardisation, as well as efforts to render consistent how observers or interviewers code responses, may lead to systematic error. In other words, consistency may be attained at the cost of accuracy. For instance, in using standardised interviews to elicit responses that are taken to indicate whether or not someone's life has been improved by an intervention, the display of a negative attitude may derive from the particular way in which the question was formulated, from prior expectations about the level of improvement to be expected, from a desire to secure further treatment, and other factors. It can never indicate level of improvement in an unmediated fashion.

In the construction of attitude-measuring instruments problems of this kind are sometimes recognised, and attempts made to control for the error involved by comparing response patterns across several items intended to measure the same property.[20] But there are two potential problems here. The first is how to separate out consistency across responses produced by systematic error from that generated by the property being measured. The second arises from the fact that relying upon a questionnaire represents a very narrow range of indicators for the property. There is a diversity of indications that could be used for assessing whether people's lives have been significantly improved. However, what is frequently found when multiple, very different kinds of indicator are used to measure the same property is that there is limited correspondence among the results.[21] What this usually tells us is that much work remains to be done in clarifying the property concept that is being grounded, and in developing effective means for applying it. And the key point is that achieving improved grounding depends upon conceptual and empirical work: we must *discover* how best to ground our concepts.

The other two arguments often used to support the idea that reliance upon standardised measurement procedures is essential can be dealt with much more briefly. The second, about the need for consistency in experimental and survey research, draws upon the same assumptions as the first argument. Furthermore, it relates to only one, albeit important, kind of research: that where multiple experimenters, interviewers, or observers are employed. In this sense it is a pragmatic matter, rather

---

[20]Though Heath and Martin 1997 suggest that, in fact, this is rarely done in social measurement.

[21]The classic example is LaPiere's study of prejudice and discrimination against minority ethnic groups (LaPiere 1934; see also Deutscher 1973).

than relating to the essential character of measurement. As regards the third argument, it should be noted that replication is simply one means by which to assess the likely validity of the findings of a study, and interpreted in narrow terms it can only be used where the research process can be repeated in more or less the same way. There is no reason to argue that because replication is a useful strategy all research should be designed so as to facilitate it. This would be to put the cart before the horse.

So, it must *not* be assumed that, in seeking to ground concepts in evidence, it is essential to employ some standardised procedure or instrument, or that doing this will necessarily increase the accuracy of the results produced. Indeed, for the reasons I have suggested, doing so may introduce systematic error. In the next section I want to examine a rather different issue, but one that also raises serious questions about the usual approaches taken to the task of measurement, and about some treatments of categorisation.

CLASSICAL AND FUZZY CATEGORIES

Categorisation or classification is a key analytic strategy in its own right (see Becker 1940; McKinney 1954, 1966, 1970; Tiryakian 1968; Lofland 1971: 13–58; Bailey 1994). It is also fundamental to all measurement, in that we are always measuring a property that belongs to members of some *type* of phenomenon. The key point I want to make here is that it is often assumed, explicitly or implicitly, that a fundamental requirement of scientific categorisation is that it takes a classical or Aristotelian form. This requires that the categories belong to an explicit system, with each being defined in terms of a set of essential features, preferably ones that can serve as criteria for identifying members of the category.

However, there are some good reasons to believe that the categories used in social science not only often do not correspond to this classical model, but also cannot do so. First, it is important to note that considerable empirical work is often required in order to develop a categorical scheme that can represent variation in the phenomena being studied. Initially, in abducting categories – for example in the manner recommended by Glaser and Strauss (1967; see also Strauss and Corbin 1998) as part of grounded theorising – the aim cannot and should not be to produce a set of categories that are mutually exclusive and exhaustive. This would obstruct the creative process involved. Any form of more systematic, classical categorisation must represent a further step beyond the initial more flexible, overlapping categories generated in the process of abduction. This is because we often need to *discover* what are fruitful categories. For this reason too, our concepts should not always be taken over automatically from commonsense classifications or from existing theories, even when our research is designed directly to inform policymaking or practice.

What this indicates is that an important part of the research process can be to find good questions to ask about the topic of interest, and perhaps even the best way to characterise the topic itself. There is a tendency in much discussion of categorisation and measurement to overlook the need for this process of development: to treat clearly formulated research questions and their associated categories as the *starting point*, rather than as an important *product* of the inquiry process. What is neglected here is that reformulation of the initial research question, and development and refinement of the categories being used, may sometimes need to continue throughout data collection and well into data analysis within particular studies.

Beyond this, though, there are also a couple of reasons why achieving category systems that have the classical form may actually be impossible in social science. The first relates closely to the discussion in the previous section. It stems from the fact that the categories involved in social scientific work include not simply those that are key concepts in the arguments developed by researchers but also those that are embedded in any evidence used to generate, and to assess the likely validity of, those arguments. There is a common view that portrays science as founded upon transparent procedures 'all the way down', an idea that is built into many discussions of research for evidence-based practice (see Chapter 3). But it has been pointed out that scientists rely upon 'knowledge how' not just on 'knowledge that'; in other words, they place tacit reliance upon capabilities that necessarily operate outside the immediate focus of attention, and in some cases beyond the realm of consciousness altogether. Moreover, these capabilities or skills cannot be fully explicated in propositional terms. They are matters of practical competence that humans have developed in their ordinary engagement with the world, and there may also be specialised capabilities that researchers have developed. It is certainly true that, as I noted earlier, there has been much effort on the part of natural scientists to make explicit the procedures they use, and even to develop various kinds of mechanical or electronic apparatus that replace some of the human practices previously involved. However, these can never be replaced completely, and in the context of social science there is probably even less scope for reducing the role of human judgement.

But the key point here is that the categories involved in these practical capabilities on which researchers rely do not seem to take the classic Aristotelian form. In other words, they do not usually operate via a set of necessary and sufficient conditions that govern their usage. Instead, cultural categories generally seem to operate on the basis of family resemblances, with people using prototypes or exemplars as a basis for determining what counts and does not count as an instance (Rosch 1999; see also Taylor 2001, 2003).[22] Furthermore, the meaning of any cultural category is usually context-sensitive: what it includes, and does not include, depends upon the context in which it is being used, including the purposes it is serving. Not only will people interpret the same category in somewhat different ways according to circumstances, but also what level of clarity is required may vary in the same manner.

So, a first problem facing attempts to produce classically rigorous classifications stems from the fact that, at some level, social research will always depend upon social

---

[22]An alternative terminology here, drawn from biology, is the distinction between monothetic/monotypic (corresponding to what I have called classic or Aristotelian) and polythetic/polytypic categories: see Beckner 1959: ch. 2. This idea was applied in anthropology by Needham (1975). Also bearing on this issue, there has been considerable discussion within the philosophical literature about the nature of vagueness; on which see, for example, Williamson 1994. Equally relevant is Kuhn's (1970, 1977) discussion of the role of exemplars in science and Elgin's (1996: ch. 6) discussion of 'exemplification' in cognition more generally.

scientists' ordinary cultural capabilities; that it may not be possible to explicate these fully in propositional terms; and that these practices depend upon flexible, context-sensitive categorisation.

The character of people's everyday categorisations has consequences for social science in a second way too. This arises to the extent that, in order to describe and explain their behaviour, we need to include in our accounts some representation of the categories that underlie people's discriminations among situations, types of people, strategies available for use, and so on. And this is surely unavoidable in much social research.[23] The crucial point is that, if everyday categories have a flexible, fuzzy, context-sensitive character, then we should not pretend that they can be incorporated into analytic categories that have an Aristotelian form: to do so would be to introduce distortion. This suggests that, for this reason too, we may have to work with analytic categories that are themselves based more on family resemblances, and perhaps also rely on the use of prototypes or exemplars (rather than criteria specifying necessary and sufficient conditions) to identify instances. In addition, we will need to find a way of taking into account the contextual sensitivity of the categories that the people we are studying use.

These two problems are of significance not only for quantitative researchers' attempts to measure social phenomena, but also for any effort by qualitative researchers to engage in the kind of rigorous classification recommended by writers like McKinney, Tiryakian, and Bailey (McKinney 1954, 1966, 1970; Tiryakian 1968; Bailey 1994). And they represent major obstacles. However, a caveat is in order here. Whilst it is unlikely that we can avoid reliance upon everyday competences – replacing these with formal, fully explicit, classical categorisation procedures – there may well be a need for researchers to exercise these practical competences in ways that are more careful, reflective, and explicit than is frequently the case in everyday life – specifically in order to try to achieve research goals. We should note that reflective deliberation about how categories should be defined and interpreted, and collective discussion designed to bring interpretations into closer agreement, occur in several other areas of human activity, notably those where much hinges on the decisions that result. Examples include legal definition of offences and medical diagnosis of illnesses. So, the fact that we must rely upon practical cultural capabilities that involve fuzzy categories does not mean that we should simply accept the practical categorisations built into everyday usage as they stand: these can be refined for particular purposes, even if we will never be able fully to explicate them, or to turn them into classically defined, 'transparent' forms. Indeed, not only is such refinement possible, it will often be essential. For example, many years ago Lofland rightly criticised what he labelled as a tendency towards 'analytic interruptus' among qualitative researchers: the use of categories that had not been properly specified through the systematic development of typologies (Lofland 1970, 1971: ch. 2; see also Bendix 1963; Hammersley and Atkinson 2007: ch. 8, especially pp. 172–5). And his criticism continues to apply to much qualitative work today.

---

[23]One interpretation of the implications of this for measurement, somewhat at odds with my argument in this chapter, is Cicourel 1964.

So, we need not treat the fuzzy nature of our categories as an insurmountable barrier to social science, nor perhaps even to social measurement. What is required is a level of precision that is pragmatically sufficient. At the same time, we must recognise the serious problems that such fuzziness causes for current classification and measurement strategies. Furthermore, considerable work may be necessary in order to clarify categories and develop ways of identifying instances of them in effective ways.

MEASUREMENT BY FIAT?

The problems surrounding categorisation I have just discussed parallel some that relate more specifically to the task of measurement, defined in the narrow sense as involving interval and ratio scales. A key problem here concerns whether the object-properties to be measured have the character that is demanded by metric measurement; in other words, whether they have a quantitative structure. This is a point that is obscured by Stevens' definition of 'measurement', in which reference to capturing the nature of some property is omitted. Michell has argued that in the field of psychology, where attempts at measurement of human behaviour have been most highly developed, there has been a failure to investigate this fundamental issue (Michell 1997, 1999, 2000, 2002). He claims that it has simply been *assumed* that the properties to be measured are at least ordinal in character, and that the methods used to gauge them effectively generate an interval scale. He describes this as a scandal (Michell 2002: 103). In effect, he is identifying what, many years ago in the field of sociology, Cicourel labelled 'measurement-by-fiat' (Cicourel 1964: 12); in other words, measurement that fails to ensure that the assumptions built into the measurement procedure correspond to the structure of the phenomena being measured.[24] As these writers have pointed out, an instrumentalist attitude, according to which all that matters is whether the use of a measurement procedure generates 'significant' findings, is inadequate (see Michell 1999: 21). In social science any outcome differences discovered are generally probabilistic and small, and there are many sources of error, within measurement procedures and elsewhere, that could generate spurious findings, including stable ones across several studies.

Any adequate classification or measurement depends upon a sound understanding of the phenomena being classified or measured, and of the processes involved in any indirect indicators that are being relied upon. Duncan sums up the point with an example from physical measurement:

I hope it is clear that most of the story of temperature measurement has to do with experimental determination of the quantitative laws of expansion of substances and with the deepening of the theoretical understanding of heat and

---

[24]Cicourel borrowed this term from Torgerson 1958: 21-2. Duncan (1984: 144 and *passim*) takes a rather similar view to Michel in his evaluation of much social measurement. His doubts about the idea of a 'correlational science of inexact constructs', and his denunciations of 'statisticism' (pp. 226-33), remain as pertinent today as they were 25 years ago.

thermodynamics, as well as learning how to construct reliable and sturdy instruments. There is not really much to be learned from the concomitant contentions about how to assign numbers to objects ..., except that the strictly numerical part is quite secondary. The Kelvin scale is a scientific achievement of the first order, not merely because it provides a scale with mathematically powerful properties, but because it incorporates a profound understanding of how a certain class of phenomena works. (Duncan 1984: 149)

So, the argument is that we need to develop our understanding of the concepts we are employing, and that this is part and parcel of improving our knowledge of the phenomena to which they refer. Thus, as social scientists we must develop our understanding of the social processes underlying the indicators we use.[25] It is hardly a secret that there are fundamental uncertainties about many of the concepts that are central to social science (see Sartori et al. 1975; Sartori 1984; Walker 1995; Williams 2001). Furthermore, there is no reason to suppose that all these analytic categories will be open to metric measurement – and even some of the categories that are amenable to this, in principle, will not be open to it in practice at any particular time, given the limited capabilities and resources available to us. This may, of course, indicate that the research problem being addressed is simply not tractable, at least at present. However, alternatively, it may mean that we must rely upon ranking or categorisation instead of measurement in the narrow sense. I am not suggesting that whatever strategy is available to us should be treated as sufficient; very often it will not be. Rather, I am arguing that no research strategy ought to be ruled out simply on the grounds that it does not conform to some preconceived model of science, or because it does not allow mathematical inference of kinds thought desirable.[26] The key issue is whether it can help us provide an adequate answer to the research question(s) we are addressing.

Furthermore, there will often be a great deal of conceptual work, and basic exploration of the phenomena being studied, that needs to be done before any process of analytic classification or measurement can be developed very far. Nor will the need for this necessarily stop once attempts at classification or measurement begin. In short, we need a much more thoughtful approach to the grounding of concepts than is currently common in much quantitative and qualitative research.

---

[25] Closely associated with this is a need to ensure that the meanings of those terms which are integral to the evaluation of classifications and measurements, such as validity and reliability, are soundly based and clear. I do not believe this currently to be the case: see Hammersley 1987, 1991.

[26] The range of available statistical techniques has, of course, increased considerably since Stevens first identified differences in the kind of statistical analysis each level of measurement allows. In particular, there has been considerable development in the analysis of categorical data. However, this generally requires categorisation on what I have called the 'classical' model. For attempts to address this through notions of fuzzy sets and family resemblance relations, see Ragin 2008 and Goertz 2006.

CONCLUSION

In this chapter I have examined the problems of measurement in social science since this is a crucial issue for arguments about the role of evidence from social research in shaping policymaking and practice. In my view, the difficulties involved here have been underestimated and given insufficient attention. Moreover, these problems face qualitative as well as quantitative research.

I began by trying to clarify the nature of the task that classification and measurement are designed to address. I suggested that we must assess any attempts to categorise or measure phenomena in the context of how far these enable us to answer worthwhile research questions, rather than in terms of prior views about the form that categorisation and measurement *ought to* take, for example as specified in terms of some presumed 'gold standard', such as interval or ratio measurement. I have also identified some serious problems that these tasks involve; problems that arise, in large part, from what seems to be the nature of social phenomena, and in particular from the character of human social action.

Are we to conclude that these problems make social measurement impossible? I think it would be foolish to draw this conclusion. Whether or not some body of evidence provides adequate support for the answer offered to a particular research question will depend upon the nature of the question, the sorts of evidence that are available, and what is taken to be the appropriate level of adequacy. It is as dangerous to generalise about what is impossible as it is automatically to assume that something *is* possible. Furthermore, it is necessary to adopt a pragmatic attitude towards social research, to recognise that what is possible cannot be determined on the basis of philosophical or statistical argument alone. To a large degree, we must *find out* what is and is not possible. And this, in turn, depends upon our current capabilities and resources, which may develop over time.

Equally, though, we must make robust evaluations of our attempts at classification and measurement. It is essential to recognise that adopting a pragmatic approach does not mean treating whatever we find we *can* do as *good enough*, as if what is possible determines what is necessary. Furthermore, in my view most current social science is weak in this respect. The problems discussed in this chapter represent major obstacles; and – as Cicourel, Michell, Duncan and others have pointed out – there has been a longstanding and common tendency to turn a blind eye to them, in the hope that they will go away. What is required instead is, first of all, sober recognition of the limits on what it is possible for social science currently to achieve, and an avoidance of excessive claims about the validity of the findings produced. In my view such excess is not uncommon in both quantitative and qualitative studies, and it is encouraged by the demand that is characteristic of the evidence-based practice movement that research make a direct contribution to policymaking and practice. A second requirement is to pay more careful attention to the methodological problems we face. We need to understand their nature more clearly, to recognise their implications for what we can and cannot do, and to find ways of dealing with them that enable us to produce better quality knowledge about the social world.

6

THE QUESTION OF QUALITY IN QUALITATIVE RESEARCH

In recent years, the quality of qualitative research has come to be questioned in some fields, in large part because of the influence of the evidence-based practice movement. The criticism has been that much of it is of a poor standard; or at least that there are no clearly defined quality criteria available for judging it, so that it is of *uncertain* quality. There are two assumptions underpinning these criticisms that need to be addressed. First, what is involved here is, at least implicitly, a *comparative* assessment: it is assumed that clearly defined criteria of quality are already available for quantitative research.[1] The other assumption is that explicit assessment criteria are needed. It is believed that unless researchers operate on the basis of such criteria their work will be of poor quality or at least unusable; that users of research require some reliable means of judging its quality, and a set of criteria would meet this need.

In this chapter I will examine some of the arguments about whether criteria are necessary, and then go on to consider whether a single set is possible given the present state of qualitative inquiry.

ARE CRITERIA NECESSARY?

Whether there are criteria by which qualitative research should be judged, and if so what character these should have, are issues about which there has been much debate but little agreement. There have been many attempts to identify criteria.[2] Some writers have tried to apply what they see as traditional quantitative criteria, such as validity and

---

[1] I have suggested elsewhere that this is open to dispute: Hammersley 2008a.

[2] These are lucidly reviewed and consolidated by Spencer et al. 2003. See also Altheide and Johnson 1994.

reliability, to qualitative work. Others have reformulated these epistemic criteria and, very often, added non-epistemic ones, whether in terms of 'giving voice' to the marginalised or bringing about practical or political effects of some kind.[3]

At the same time, there are some writers who appear to reject the very possibility of criteria, at least as conventionally understood. For example, many years ago John Smith argued that 'there can be no criteria to reconcile discourse (to sort out the trustworthy from the untrustworthy results)' (Smith 1984: 384; see also Smith 1989 and Schwandt 1996, 2002). Smith claimed that attempts to apply criteria to qualitative research would inevitably result in confusion and inconsistency, because criteria are incompatible with the basic philosophical assumptions of this type of inquiry. Subsequently, he insisted that 'criteria should not be thought of in abstraction, but as a list of features that we think, or more or less agree at any given time, and place, characterize good versus bad inquiry'. Also: 'This is a list that can be challenged, added to, subtracted from, modified, and so on, as it is applied in actual practice – in its actual application to actual inquiries' (Smith and Deemer 2000: 894). I suspect that, despite appearances, Smith's views did not change much over the period concerned; the difference between the two formulations hinges on what is meant by the term 'criterion'. And this is a crucial issue.

We can provide two contrasting definitions that illustrate the scope for disagreement about this. At one end of the spectrum, 'criterion' means an observable indicator that can tell us (in combination with other indicators) whether or not the findings of a study are valid, or are of value in more general terms. In other words, a set of criteria here amounts to a checklist that is sufficiently explicit and concrete in its reference for it to be filled in with little error; moreover, it is comprehensive enough to cover everything that needs to be taken into account in judging quality. Very often these criteria will relate to the procedures employed in carrying out the research, on the implicit assumption that these determine the validity of the findings. Towards the other end of the spectrum are the sort of criteria outlined by Smith and Deemer: a list of considerations, never fully explicit, that it is agreed in local circumstances should be taken into account in judging research, a list that can serve as no more than a reminder and that is always open to revision in the process of being used – indeed, which only gains meaning in particular contexts.[4] It seems to me that the second definition comes closer to what is possible and desirable than the first, but it is still not entirely satisfactory.

The best place to start in thinking about the nature and role of assessment criteria is with how researchers actually go about judging quality in doing their work. It is probably beyond dispute that they do not do this by simply applying a set of explicit and concrete rules of assessment. Instead, they make specific, and often largely implicit, judgements. Nevertheless, to some extent they can, and often will, explicate these

---

[3] For an example of a very broad set of criteria designed for the field of education, see Furlong and Oancea 2005. For a critical assessment of this approach, see Hammersley 2008e.

[4] There could be a position that is even beyond that of Smith and Deemer, where the whole point of criteria is to transgress them. Near this far end of the spectrum would be Feyerabend's (1975) rejection of method. Along these lines, Lather (1993) has proposed 'transgressive validities', see also Scheurich 1997.

judgments in terms of methodological principles. I suggest that reliance upon judgement is inevitable. This is as true of quantitative as of qualitative researchers, whatever other differences there are between them. The task of judging quality in the context of a relatively complex activity like research cannot be sensibly reduced to the application of explicit, concrete and exhaustive indicators. Instead, formulations of criteria, in terms of considerations that might need to be taken into account, *come out of* the process of judgement and are modified by it – to one degree or another. At the same time, they also feed back into it: they are used subsequently by researchers in judging quality in other situations; but they always have to be interpreted and may be *redefined* in this process. Furthermore, they will be applied selectively, depending upon the nature of the knowledge claims and research involved.

While rejecting the idea of a finite set of explicit and exhaustive criteria that can substitute for judgement, or render its role minimal, this discussion at the same time indicates that criteria, in the form of broad and flexible guidelines, can play an important role in the work of researchers. They may facilitate reflection on previous judgements that enables us to learn from our own experience, and from one another. Such learning may also involve exploring the implications of applying locally used criteria in new contexts, and considering the extent to which there are commonalities across fields. This is important because such reflection can lead us to conclude that locally used criteria need to be changed or developed, even as regards their original context. In other words, it seems to me that changes in criteria arise not just, as Smith and Deemer suggest, from the practical work of particular researchers in particular situations but also from attempts to universalise and systematise current criteria. The aim of these efforts should not be to produce a single, universal system of assessment rules that will eliminate judgement, it is rather that the process of thinking about how the criteria would apply in other contexts and how they relate to one another, is a productive force in the development of research practice.

In a much more mundane way, but no less importantly, criteria, in the form of guidelines, can remind researchers of what they ought to take into account in assessing their own and others' research. This is no small matter. When engaged in any complex activity, it is easy to forget or overlook what ought to be taken into consideration. Guidelines may also facilitate student researchers' learning how to assess research, though here especially care must be taken to avoid the implication that stated criteria can in some sense be a substitute for acquiring the practical capacity to make sound judgements.

However, as noted earlier, much of the pressure for qualitative criteria comes not so much from the context of *researchers* judging research, or even students learning to do this, but rather from that of lay 'users' of research (notably policymakers and practitioners) assessing its quality. On the basis of the above discussion, it might seem that the problem here is that, by contrast with researchers, lay people will not have the background knowledge, skill and experience necessary to judge quality: so that they will be overly reliant upon the guidelines. This is true in one sense, but false in another. And this ambiguity points to the problems arising at the interface between research and other sorts of specialised activity. It is true that lay users will not usually have equivalent knowledge of research findings and processes to that of researchers, or the experience of and capacity for making judgements about research that comes from practising it. Furthermore, as I have indicated, no set of criteria can substitute for this. On the other hand, lay users of research are not simply ignorant or lacking in all skill in assessing knowledge claims for relevance and validity. Indeed, this capacity is an essential element of many forms of activity, indeed of everyday life generally. The problem that faces lay users, then, is twofold. First, how to assess research findings in the terms in which these present themselves. Second, how to relate these findings to what they already know or take for granted. There seems to be a built-in tendency here for extreme reactions: for lay users either to adopt too reverent an attitude towards the products of research, or simply to dismiss them if they conflict with their existing knowledge. They may even be oscillation between the two attitudes.

Any set of criteria offered by researchers could only deal with the first of these tasks – how to assess findings in research terms: it cannot help much with the problem of relating them to practical, experiential knowledge, not least because the latter will be highly variegated. And, to repeat the point, no set of guidelines can remedy lay users' lack of practical experience of research. The implication of this is that, to a considerable extent, lay users need to trust researchers: they must assume, unless there is evidence to the contrary, that the latter have carried out their work effectively, that they have presented their findings honestly, and that the normal processes of criticism within the research community have reduced the danger of error. Whether research-ers *deserve* such trust depends upon how they operate, but there is no mechanism that can check this independently of the operation of research communities themselves.

The need for trust cannot be eradicated in this context, any more than it can be in other forms of contact between specialised practitioners and lay people. As already hinted, however, this does not have to be blind trust: it may be possible for lay users to make some judgement about the coherence and reasonableness of what research-ers say. At the same time, they must take care not to dismiss what does not fit their current frame of reference for that reason alone. There is clearly a dilemma here. On the one hand, the whole point of research is that it may produce un-commonsensical conclusions, and therefore its findings must not be dismissed simply because they are counter-intuitive. On the other hand, people's experience and background knowl-edge will often give them important resources with which to interrogate, modify, or reject research findings, especially in terms of how these relate to particular contexts of action with which they are familiar, and to what ought to be done there. So, good judgement is required by lay users, just as much as it is by researchers.

In short, I am arguing that it is not possible for researchers to make their judge-ments about quality transparent, in the sense of fully intelligible to *anyone*, irrespective of background knowledge and experience. Indeed, there are limits to the extent to which these judgements can be made intelligible even to fellow researchers, because of the situated nature of judgement. Certainly, such intelligibility is an *achievement*, it is not automatic: speakers need to be able to formulate the situation, the reasons for making the judgements that they did, etc., in ways that facilitate understanding; and, equally importantly, the audience must be able to draw the right inferences from what is said, on the basis of the background resources they have. The greater the experien-tial distance between speaker and hearer, the larger this problem of communication will be. And because the use of guidelines always depends upon background knowledge and judgement, they cannot solve this problem even if they may serve as a useful resource in dealing with it. Moreover, sometimes their use can exacerbate it.

To a large extent, then, qualitative researchers are right to resist demands for a fully explicit set of evaluation criteria: the nature of research (in general, not just of qualitative work) is such that these cannot operate in the way that is frequently assumed by those who demand them. And the same is true as regards lay use of research findings: here, too, good judgement is required and this cannot be reduced to explicit rules.

Even so, I believe that qualitative researchers need to give much more attention than is currently done to thinking about the considerations that must be taken into account in assessing the likely validity of knowledge claims, exploring the consistency of these with one another, and considering how they apply in other situations from those in which they were generated. This is not so much a matter of producing lists of criteria, in the sense of considerations that might need to be taken into account, though this is useful, but rather of collectively developing and talking about what is involved in assessing the likely validity of findings from particular studies. There is, though, a major obstacle to this process: the plurality of approaches to qualitative research that now exists. This issue is the topic of the remainder of this chapter.

IS A SINGLE SET OF QUALITATIVE CRITERIA POSSIBLE?

It is an obvious fact about qualitative research today that it is divided not just in terms of substantive focus, or even according to the use of particular methods, but by divergent theoretical, methodological, and value assumptions: about the nature of the phenomena being investigated and about how they can and should be researched.[5] In other words, there are different, and to some extent competing, 'paradigms'. The key questions that this raises are, of course, whether it is possible and desirable to overcome these differences, and if so how this can be done. This would be essential for a single set of qualitative criteria to be produced.

The term 'paradigm', in the sense being used here, derives, of course, from the work of the historian and philosopher of science Thomas Kuhn (1970). There has been much discussion of what Kuhn meant by 'paradigm', and it is clear that he used the word in a variety of ways.[6] However, his core argument was that natural scientists working within a mature field operate with a set of assumptions, about the relevant region of the world and how to understand it, that are embodied in their use of certain studies or theoretical models as exemplars; in other words, they take these for granted as the basis for further work. Of course, there are always things that do not

---

[5]I am not suggesting that quantitative research is entirely homogeneous: for example experimental and survey research have conflicting orientations in some key respects. However, the differences here do not lie at as deep a level as the current differences in orientation among qualitative researchers.

[6]For excellent recent discussions of Kuhn's work, see Hoyningen-Huene 1993, Bird 2000 and Sharrock and Read 2002.

seem to fit into their current understanding, and the task of what he called 'normal science' is to treat these as puzzles that can be solved *without modification to paradigmatic assumptions*. However, Kuhn famously argued that, over time, some puzzles turn out to be anomalies that cannot be resolved within these limits; and that, at some point, an alternative paradigm will arise that takes over the field, because it is able to explain all of what the previous paradigm covered and can resolve the anomalies that had arisen within it. This is what he referred to as a scientific revolution.

Now there have been many disputes about the accuracy of Kuhn's account of natural science, but the task of applying it to social science is even more complex and uncertain. Kuhn regarded the social sciences as pre-paradigmatic, at best, and therefore as not characterised by competing paradigms, in his sense of the word. Moreover, even were we to ignore this, there is very little social research that approximates to his notion of normal science; instead, much of it, at least over the past five decades, seems to have been in a state of continual 'revolution', albeit of a kind that is not recognisably scientific in Kuhn's terms.

At the same time, it probably *is* the case that social scientists operate on the basis of exemplar studies and models, and that this is part of the reason why they often adopt rather different approaches to the same topic, and why they sometimes disagree so sharply about the nature of research, and the validity of the findings of particular studies. Read correctly, Kuhn's work is an important counter to any tendency to adopt too cognitivist a conception of conflicting approaches amongst researchers. It is not that people first acquire epistemological and ontological assumptions and then decide how they are going to investigate the social world. Rather, they acquire particular research practices and various methodological and philosophical assumptions, consciously and unconsciously, more or less simultaneously, and each shapes the other. This means that the differences among qualitative researchers are embedded in diverse forms of situated practice that incorporate characteristic ways of thinking about the research process and the world. Furthermore, we are not faced with a set of clearly differentiated qualitative approaches but rather with a complex landscape of variable practice in which the inhabitants use a variety of labels for their own and others' positions ('ethnography', 'discourse analysis', 'life history work', 'narrative study', 'activity theory', 'interpretivism', 'feminist standpoint epistemology', 'postmodernism', and so on) and do so in variable and open-ended ways.

So what is involved in paradigm conflict is both a clash of ideas about what form social research ought to take and a divergence in *practices*. This can be conceptualised in terms of at least three areas of conflict: different assumptions about scientific method or rigour; the opposition between constructionism and realism; and detachment versus activism.

Scientific method and rigour

The natural sciences were the main methodological model for a great deal of social research for much of the twentieth century. This shaped what counted as rigorous investigation. However, it did not prevent considerable disagreement about how social research ought to be pursued. There were several, interrelated, reasons for this.

First, different natural sciences were taken as exemplifying scientific method: for example, some researchers treated physics as the premier science, others took nineteenth-century biology as a more appropriate guide.[7] The point is, of course, that different exemplars of science or rigour can lead to very different prescriptions and forms of assessment.

Secondly, there were differing philosophical interpretations of the 'method' attributed to whatever was taken to be the model for scientific investigations. For instance, broadly speaking, moving from the nineteenth into the twentieth century there was a shift from an inductivist conception of inquiry, in which scientific laws were logically derived from the observation of repeated patterns of occurrence, towards one that stressed the testing of hypotheses deduced from theories that were necessarily a product of speculative thought and that perhaps could never be proven, only falsified at best. Quite a lot of the conflict between social scientists promoting quantitative and those adopting qualitative methods in the first seventy years of the twentieth century stemmed from commitment to different views of scientific method along these lines, with qualitative researchers tending to adopt a more inductivist approach.

Finally, there was variation in views about the differences between physical and social phenomena, and about the implications of these for how far the methods of natural science needed to be modified. At one extreme, even taking physics as exemplifying scientific method, some believed that there were no distinctive features of social phenomena, or that if there were these did not stand in the way of rigorous measurement and control of variables. By contrast, others insisted that social phenomena had to be approached quite differently from physical phenomena. Indeed, it was sometimes argued that whereas the latter could only be studied from outside, social phenomena could and should be understood from 'within', so that a deeper form of knowledge was available. And it was claimed that this inner understanding required the researcher to draw upon his or her psychological and/or cultural resources to grasp the meanings that informed the actions of the people being studied, since these meanings are crucial for what it is that people set out to do, and why. In particular, it was insisted that these meanings cannot be inferred from external behaviour. To use Clifford Geertz's example: there are significant differences between a facial tic that forces the closure of one eye, a wink, someone pretending to wink, and someone practising winking. It is not possible to infer from the physical behaviour alone which of these is taking place (Geertz 1973: 6). Given this, some additional means of access must be secured to the cultural meanings that inform people's behaviour if we are to be able even to describe it accurately, let alone to explain it. All this did not necessarily lead to a rejection of science, but often rather to attempts to construct what purported to be a new form of science, one that was believed to be specially suited to studying the human social world.

Now qualitative researchers today vary in whether they see their work as scientific and, if they do, in what they take this to imply. And, aside from this, there are

---

[7]There were also one or two disciplines broadly within the social sciences that at various times were treated by others as exemplifying scientific method. Key examples here are behaviourist psychology, neoclassical economics, and structuralist linguistics.

significant differences concerning what is regarded as possible or legitimate in epis-temic terms. One illustration is what has been called the 'radical critique of inter-views' (Murphy et al. 1998: 120–3). This does not just raise questions about over-reliance on interview data – a common complaint, for example, on the part of ethnographers who, in the past at least, tended to stress the centrality of participant observation. What makes recent critics of interview research radical is that they challenge the use of this type of data, both as providing data about the beliefs and attitudes of informants, and as a means of gaining information about the social world in which they live (Dingwall 1997; Silverman 1997; Atkinson and Coffey 2002; Potter and Hepburn 2005). The critics deny both that interviews can tap stable attitudes or perspectives that govern people's behaviour beyond the interview situation, and that informants can be a reliable source of witness information about what happened, or what happens, in the world. Thus, they reject the two main uses to which social scientists, including most qualitative researchers, have put interview data (Hammersley and Gomm 2008).

In effect, the radical critique of interviews challenges a conception of rigour that is characteristic of some forms of ethnography – for example that exemplified by Geertz's interpretive anthropology – and replaces it with a view of rigour that is typical of many forms of discourse analysis. Discourse analysts, of some kinds, insist that the data must be presented to readers so that they can assess directly the validity of the inferences made, and also require that inference must not range beyond what is 'observable' in the data. By contrast, ethnographers often argue that it is not pos-sible to make all their data available to readers, that the validity of their inferences depends upon the success with which they have learned the culture of the people they are studying, and thereby become able to interpret accurately what meanings various phenomena have for them. Moreover, some would question whether dis-course analysts are actually presenting, or can present, 'the data' to readers; given that transcriptions involve theoretical assumptions about language use, and that how they are read will depend upon cultural background (see Hammersley 2003b, 2010b).

So, without even touching on post-structuralism and postmodernism, the usual bogeymen in this context, it is clear that there are divergent conceptions of the require-ments of inquiry to be found amongst qualitative researchers. And it is not difficult to see how these can lead to disagreement in judgements about what is good-quality work.

Realism versus constructionism

Constructionism is one of the sources from which the radical critique of interview analysis arose. The generic move of constructionism against realism is to insist that social phenomena do not exist independently of people's understandings of them, in other words that those understandings play a crucial generative role. Of course, many realists would accept, indeed insist, that social phenomena are the product of 'people acting together' rather than a result of social forces operating entirely beyond their control. What is distinctive about constructionism, as I am using that term here, is that it takes the argument that social phenomena are culturally constituted and draws from it the conclusion that these phenomena can only be understood by describing *the processes through which* they are culturally constituted as the things that they are or appear to be. In other words, a fundamental re-specification of the goal of inquiry is involved. The focus becomes not the phenomena themselves, and certainly not what might have caused them or what effects they have – or even what the actors involved intended, their background beliefs, etc. – but rather the processes by which phenomena are identified, and in effect created through identification or action, by culture members.

For example, instead of studying families as a particular type of social group with characteristic patterns of behaviour that are linked to various other social institutions, the focus becomes how people talk about or enact family relationships, both explicitly and, perhaps even more importantly, implicitly: how they use notions of family form, ideas about kin obligations, and so on, in the course of their interactions with one another. It is through these processes that they constitute, for example, what they 'find' to be functional or dysfunctional families. So, for constructionists, notions like 'family' are not descriptions of patterns of social relations that exist independently of these descriptions; the social significance of such concepts lies in their functional use rather than in any representational capacity they have (see Gubrium and Holstein 1990, 1993; Morgan 1996, 2011a, 2011b).

It is worth emphasising that it is not just the realist/constructionist divide that generates divergences here in how research is assessed. There are important differences in orientation *within* constructionism. One version is modelled on ethnomethodology (see Lynch 1993; Zimmerman and Pollner 1971). It suggests that there are means whereby the constitutive processes by which social phenomena are ongoingly produced can be uncovered or displayed in a manner that does not involve any cultural interpretation or inference on the part of the researcher. All that is involved, it is claimed, is a process of explication. Moreover, the terms of this explication are entirely those of the culture embodied in the actions being explicated. This position does not imply epistemological scepticism; in other words, it need not be denied that the actions and institutions people produce through their actions have a real existence as particulars. What *is* denied, though, is that these phenomena can be grouped into natural kinds in any other way than in terms of the processes that constituted them. Furthermore, we must remember that there is no one-to-one correspondence between some constitutive cultural notion, like family form, and the actions it is used to produce and how they interrelate with other actions. This is because such notions may be 'honoured in the breach', 'stretched' in various ways, or joked about.

A very different approach, characteristic of radical forms of constructionism, is to treat people (or some other agent, whether Discourse, Desire, or Power) as effectively creating the world in and through discursive and other practices. Moreover, this argument can be extended to researchers themselves, portraying them as necessarily engaged in constituting the social world, or particular social phenomena, through the writing process or whatever other means of representation they employ. On this view it is not possible simply to describe or display how people construct the social world through their actions, since the analyst engages in constitutive work her or himself. The result of this position is often a blurring of the boundary between social research and imaginative literature. In fact, the whole of conventional social science may come to be seen as, in effect, a form of fiction that is falsely conscious of its own character.

These two approaches, which by no means exhaust the kinds of work constructionism has generated, imply very different approaches to assessing research from one another, as well as from realism. For the first, the concern, presumably, is with whether the descriptions of the constitutive processes of social life are accurate, in other words whether what is displayed is indeed these processes. By contrast, for the second position, any idea of validity in terms of correspondence is rejected, and the accounts produced by researchers must be judged in non-epistemic terms, according to aesthetic, ethical, and/or political criteria. One way of thinking about the shift from realism to this latter kind of constructionism is in terms of the replacement of Kuhn by Rorty as the patron philosopher of many qualitative researchers. Whereas Kuhn still sees natural science as engaged in a process of inquiry, in which knowledge is accumulated, albeit in a discontinuous rather than a continuous way, Rorty abandons the residual realism to be found in Kuhn's account. In effect, he erases the distinction between inquiry, which is concerned with gaining knowledge, and conversation, conceived as guided by an interest in 'edification' or 'solidarity'. Indeed, he treats inquiry, understood in its conventional way, as labouring under a mistaken conception of itself, one that assumes that it is possible (and desirable) to claim superior knowledge of reality.[8]

There are many varieties of both constructionism and realism, but this discussion gives some sense of the implications that such a divergence in orientation can have for judgements about the quality of particular pieces of research. The point is that these amount to fundamental differences that it may not be possible to bridge.[9]

Activism: the relationship of research to politics, policymaking, and practice

What comes under the heading of 'activism', like that of 'constructionism', is quite diverse in character. But my point is that there are various qualitative approaches that explicitly reject the idea that the production of knowledge should be the only immediate goal of inquiry – they insist on the need for action.[10] Advocates of these

---

[8]The issues involved here are complex ones. See Putnam's (2002: 99-100) criticisms of Rorty's position.

[9]There are many different varieties of constructionism, and the representatives of some kinds of work that I have included here would reject that label. See, for example, Button and Sharrock 1993. However, my aim has been to give some sense of the implications that a broadly defined constructionist argument can have.

[10]The term 'activism' is not entirely satisfactory, not least because it might seem to imply an acceptance of the arguments of activists: that conventional kinds of research are inactive, being the pastime of those closed off from the world in their ivory towers. Needless to say, I do not accept that implication.

approaches often believe that research should form an integral part of some other kind of social or political practice, and argue that it is rendered useless, or at least debased in value, when separated out from this (see Chapter 7). Furthermore, there are those who claim that the institutionalisation of knowledge production, for example in universities, should be dismantled (see Greenwood and Levin 2005); and, indeed, some claim that this is already happening through the rise of new modes of knowledge production outside these institutions (Gibbons et al. 1994; Gibbons 2000). Other approaches insist on the *political* character of research, insisting that it must be explicitly directed towards bringing about change of one sort or another: challenging capitalism, patriarchy, racism, homophobia, or the social conditions that generate disability.

What is important here is that all these approaches introduce extra or alternative considerations in judging the quality of research, additional to the traditional epistemic ones concerned with the production of knowledge. The nature of these criteria varies, of course, depending upon the form of practice to which research is to be tied, or with which it is to be integrated. In broad terms, once again, they may be political, ethical, aesthetic, or even economic – for example, concerned with whether there is demand for the knowledge being produced, whether the research offers value for money etc. (see Furlong and Oancea 2005; Hammersley 2008e).

In their early forms, these activist conceptions of research treated the goal of producing knowledge as compatible with, or even as directly conducive to, the pursuit of practical goals. For example, in some versions, Marxism conflated epistemic with other considerations, on the basis of the Hegelian assumption that the development of knowledge and the realisation of other ideals are strongly interrelated in a historical dialectic. More recently, that assumption has been abandoned by most of those advocating activist forms of social research; and, as a result, practical or political goals have often been raised above, or have replaced, epistemic ones. This has usually been based on the argument, associated with some kinds of constructionism, that the pursuit of knowledge, in the conventional sense of that term, is futile. Equally, there are arguments for interventionism that dismiss traditional kinds of qualitative research on ethical grounds as a form of voyeurism (see Denzin 1992: 131). There are also arguments for intervention that are aesthetic rather than either scientific or ethical in character. Here research is to be a form of performance art, indeed it may be argued that it cannot but be this, and the requirement is that it be consciously shaped aesthetically, at most only hiding behind the masks of science or ethics in an ironic, knowing way.[11] It is not difficult to see that the criteria of assessment relevant here would be significantly different again.

CONCLUSION

In this chapter I have explored some of the issues surrounding whether assessment criteria for qualitative research are possible and desirable. I raised questions about

---

[11] I have not been able to find any clear presentation of this argument for intervention, but an example of the approach is Miller and Whalley 2005.

what the term 'criterion' refers to, but suggested that broad and flexible guidelines can be desirable, so long as they are not seen as a substitute for the practical capacity to assess research. In the second half of the chapter I argued that some fundamental differences in epistemological and political assumptions generate the methodological pluralism that is characteristic of qualitative research today.

There have been various responses to this pluralism, including the following:

1   The argument that the apparent differences are spurious, perhaps amounting simply to rhetoric: that when it comes to actually doing research there is much less variation than the methodological debates suggest.[12]
2   It might be argued that there are deep-seated incompatibilities, so that we must simply recognise that there are diverse forms of social research, each having its own distinctive conception of what is good-quality work, and its own ways of applying this, which must be respected.[13]
3   There are serious differences in perspective, but some means needs to be found to at least reduce them, so as to increase the level of agreement across social scientists' judgements about what is and is not good-quality work.[14] Developing guidelines may serve a useful function in this.

My position is, broadly speaking, the third. However, the sources of division I have identified in this chapter vary in character and in their implications for assessing quality. I suspect that those relating to different views of what counts as rigour are open to resolution in the longer term. A rather different strategy may be required as regards the realism–constructionism divide: this may be resolvable by treating it as, to a large extent, a disciplinary difference. In other words, there is no need for competition or conflict here, so long as neither side formulates its position in such a way as to render the alternative illegitimate, and that each side is suitably modest in the claims it makes for itself. After all, one would not expect the same assessment criteria to hold across disciplines. It must be said, however, that there is little sign that such a resolution is currently viable.

Even more difficult to deal with are the differences generated by what I have referred to as activism. This either requires research to supplement its goal of producing knowledge with other goals, or proposes the substitution of these for the pursuit of knowledge. The former position is likely to render research incoherent, as unable to pursue any goal effectively, least of all the production of knowledge; while the latter, in my view, amounts to the abandonment of research in favour of some other

---

[12]Bryman 2008 comes close to this position.

[13]Hodkinson 2004 illustrates this position, on which see Hammersley 2005a. It is worth noting that this does not have to be taken as implying that there are incommensurable paradigms, the exponents of which simply cannot understand one another. An alternative metaphor is different language communities, where while true translation may not be possible, learning the other language is. This is an analogy that Kuhn uses in his later work (Kuhn 2000), as against the perceptual analogy on which he relies in *The Structure of Scientific Revolutions*.

[14]Feuer et al. 2002 exemplify this position.

activity. However, proponents of activist forms of social research do not accept these arguments. Furthermore, aside from the problem of reconciling activist and non-activist conceptions of research, we should note that there is likely to be little agreement as regards assessment criteria even *among* activist researchers, given that they can be motivated by very different political or practical enterprises. Clearly, here we need to clarify exactly what can and cannot count as research.

My conclusion, then, is that guidelines for qualitative research – of the broad kind I suggested in the first part of this chapter – are desirable, and indeed I believe there is scope for common sets of guidelines across the qualitative–quantitative divide (Hammersley 2008a). But the barriers to our being able to produce any set of common criteria are formidable. We should not pretend that there are no serious problems here. At the same time, neither should we simply accept methodological pluralism at face value, reinforcing it by treating each qualitative paradigm as having its own unique set of quality criteria.

7

ACTION RESEARCH: A CONTRADICTION IN TERMS?

The idea that research should serve the goals of social and political practice was not invented by the evidence-based practice movement. There are many versions of this idea, and amongst the most influential have been those given the label 'action research'. Indeed, some commentators have proposed this as an alternative to the notion of research for evidence-based practice (Elliott 2001), while others have effectively conflated the two (Hargreaves 1999). In this chapter I will examine the history of action research, and the assumptions on which it is based, since it represents an important version of the idea of research-based practice.

There are diverse types of action research, varying across several dimensions: in whether carried out solely by practitioners or involving researchers as external agents; in how far it is pursued individually or collectively; in whether it is concerned with local and specific problems or aimed at bringing about wider social change; in terms of which methods of data collection or analysis it favours; in what methodological or theoretical stances it draws on, for instance positivism, pragmatism, interpretivism, critical theory, or postmodernism.[1] However, abstracting from this diversity, the core feature of action research is the idea that there should be an intimate relationship between research and some form of practical or political

---

[1]There are some interesting hybrids in terms of philosophy; see for example Argyris et al.'s (1985) 'action science', which brings together the approaches of Dewey, Lewin, and Critical Theory. There are also lines of thought that have much in common with some versions of action research without employing that phrase. Examples of the latter include Popper's 'technological approach to sociology' (Popper 1957), Campbell's notion of the 'experimenting society' (see Bickman 2000: pt 2), Rothman and Thomas' 'intervention science' (Rothman and Thomas 1994), and the notion of 'interactive social science' (see *Science and Public Policy* 27 (3), 2000). On action research and postmodernism, see Brown and Jones 2001 and MacLure 2002.

activity – such that the focus of inquiry arises out of, and its results feed directly back into, the activity concerned, in a spiral of improvement.[2]

While not all of its advocates promote action research as the only legitimate kind of social inquiry, it is often very closely associated with an instrumentalist view that to be of value, research *must* serve practical and/or political goals directly.[3] In this chapter I will argue that while the concept of action research points to some important differences in the form that social inquiry can take, it suffers from internal contradictions.

THE DIVERSITY OF ACTION RESEARCH

The history of the term 'action research' is usually traced back to the work of the social psychologist Kurt Lewin, writing in the United States in the 1940s (see Lewin 1946; Adelman 1993).[4] An important starting point seems to have been a request in 1939 for Lewin to help a new manufacturing plant solve the problem of low productivity on the part of its workers (see Marrow 1969: ch. 14); and his involvement in this kind of consultancy work continued through membership of a US Government task force in the Second World War and via links with community development organisations.[5]

Lewin portrayed action research as involving a spiral process in which a hypothetical solution to a problem is formulated and tried out, its level of success monitored, the proposed solution reformulated in light of this, the new strategy implemented and assessed, and so on. The key notion is that the spiral promises closer and closer approximation to an ideal solution to the problem, *based on genuine theoretical understanding of the processes involved*. Thus, Lewin viewed applied social science

[2]Some of the diversity in action research arises from what sort of activity the research is designed to serve. It is perhaps also worth noting that, while the service relationship is central, it is not necessarily framed in terms that privilege practitioners. Indeed, as I have pointed out elsewhere, some forms of action research seem to involve what we might call researcher imperialism, in that they are directed towards a transformation of practice which re-makes it in the image of research (Hammersley 1993).

[3]Some advocates certainly do see action research as replacing other kinds. Here, for example, is Sanford: 'Like other industries, social science has been polluting its environment. Not only has it been spoiling its research subjects by treating them as means rather than ends; not only has it been disseminating a rather monstrous image of researchable man; it has been creating an enormous amount of waste in the form of useless information' (Sanford 1970: 18). For a more recent, and less vitriolic, version of the same position, see Greenwood and Levin 1998 and 2005.

[4]There are other sources. Gunz 1996 and Altrichter and Gstettner 1997 point to the work of Moreno, others have cited Collier 1945. There is also the interesting question of the influence of Marxism, notably through Lewin's relationship with Korsch, who emphasised early on the connection between theory and practice: see van Elteren 1992.

[5]However, in many ways, this work built on his earlier experience working in applied psychology in Germany: see John et al. 1989. It is important to note that Lewin saw action research as a supplement to, not a substitute for, basic – that is, experimental – inquiry.

as the pursuit of practical improvement *combined with* the search for theoretical understanding; he famously declared that 'there is nothing so useful as a good theory' (Lewin 1951: 169). In this respect, he was operating within what Stokes (1997) refers to as Pasteur's quadrant, aiming simultaneously at contributing to theory development and at solving practical problems. At the same time, Lewin did not see action research as simply a matter of external agents intervening to bring about improvement and develop theoretical knowledge. There was a democratic element built into his conception of action research: the aim was to generate participation and 'self-management'. And his assumption that there were close links between science, social improvement, and democracy was consonant with the ideas of other, even more influential, writers of the early twentieth century – notably, John Dewey (on whom see Westbrook 1991 and Ryan 1995).[6]

The idea of action research can now be found across many different fields, including education, organisational sociology, and development studies. Moreover, it takes a variety of different forms and is shaped by divergent theoretical perspectives, many of which are at odds in significant respects with the orientation of Lewin, and even with that of Dewey.[7] However, in this chapter I want to focus on what I identified earlier as the central idea of action research: that there should be a very close relationship between inquiry and some practical or political activity. I will explore the different forms that this relationship can take, and their implications.

AN ANCIENT VIEW REJECTED

Let me begin with a classical form of argument to the effect that action research is internally contradictory. This involves taking the two components of the phrase as representing, respectively, *praxis* (action) and *theoria* (research) in their ancient Greek senses. An influential strand of Greek thinking treated *praxis* and *theoria* as different ways of life; and, moreover, as ways of life occupying different positions on a status hierarchy (Lobkowicz 1967, 1977). For Plato and his followers, and in some places for Aristotle too, *theoria* is the superior way of life: it is the closest that humans can approach to the divine. It involves detached contemplation of the world, divorced from human activity, in which the universe's essential, and therefore eternal, characteristics are comprehended. By contrast, *praxis*, and the forms of thinking associated with it, are concerned with human affairs, which (for Aristotle) are temporal and contingent in character, and therefore of little significance for the universe as a whole. So, *theoria* involves detachment from, and *praxis* immersion in, the flux of ephemeral events that makes up human social life; what would later be referred to in some quarters as History, in contrast with Reason.

---

[6]Graebner (1986) documents the development of this notion of 'democratic social engineering', and raises questions about its democratic character. See Lippitt 1986 and M. Lewin 1987 for defences of Lewin.

[7]For a fairly comprehensive account of developments in action research see Reason and Bradbury 2001.

While much of this position has been abandoned or modified down the centuries, the idea that there is a discrepancy in status between *theoria* and *praxis* has persisted. In the Middle Ages, inquiry was closely associated with religious calling, and especially with the monastic movement; and this sometimes reinforced the idea of its detached, even other-worldly, character. Furthermore, the idea of the superiority of *theoria* over *praxis* survived the process of secularisation. To take an extreme example, when in the early twentieth century Julien Benda writes about the treachery of the intellectuals, what they are betraying are universal ideals that he regards as standing above history, and which are intrinsically related to intellectuals' proper pursuit of philosophical and scientific knowledge or imaginative understanding through literature and art. He treats these rational, universal ideals – and the occupations associated with them – as sacred by comparison with the profane, temporal activity of politics (Benda 1927).

It is not difficult to see that, in these terms, to tie research to action in the world would be to conflate two quite different ways of life, as well as to betray the higher nature of *theoria*.[8] And, indeed, some attitudes towards action research display opposition on these grounds. For example, many years ago in an attack on criminology for not studying 'adult, unreformed, "serious" criminals in their natural environment', Polsky explains this in terms of a failure on the part of criminologists to free themselves from 'traditional social-work concerns'. He continues: 'in the years immediately ahead [the struggle to do this] may be even more difficult, because of a recent retrograde development: lately a number of sociologists themselves have joined forces with social workers to promote extra-scientific goals in the name of science and have saddled us with new euphemisms for these goals, such as "applied sociology" and "action research"' (Polsky 1971: 115). From the tone of Polsky's discussion – at one point he talks of 'fouling the waters of science with muck about "the dual role of practitioner-researcher"' (Polsky 1971: 142) – what we have here is dismissal of action research as equivalent to do-gooding, as mere practical work, compared with the higher ideals of science.

Now, despite the continuing influence of this status hierarchy, often transmuted into a privileging of 'pure' or theoretical over 'applied' research, much late-nineteenth-century and twentieth-century thought was directed *against* the classical distinction between *theoria* and *praxis*, or at least against treatment of *theoria* as a higher calling. Over that period, science came to be conceived very differently from the way the ancient Greeks had thought about it: it was now regarded by many as specialised inquiry that had abandoned not only religious but most extrinsic normative concerns. And this perception was shared both by many of those who supported as well as by those who denounced this development. Furthermore, over the past two centuries, natural science has become more and more closely involved in the development of technologies. Indeed, in some areas it has become

---

[8]Aristotle recognised the existence of practical sciences, but he seems to treat them as subordinate in status to theoretical ones, and as unable to produce knowledge in the true sense. Interestingly, an influential ancient Greek view of practical inquiry was that, unlike theoretical inquiry, it could only be justified in terms of its usefulness. For a rather different interpretation of Aristotle, see the work of Gadamer (Zuckert 2002).

subordinated to the task of producing technological innovations, in the form of what Ravetz has called 'industrialised science' (Ravetz 1971; Ziman 2000).

There were also some other intellectual changes preceding this shift in the nature of science which challenged the ancient hierarchical relationship between *theoria* and *praxis*. Renaissance humanism, the linking of heaven and earth under the same explanatory scheme by Newton and Leibniz, and Kant's 'Copernican revolution' in philosophy, all worked against viewing human beings and their practical affairs as separated off from the rest of the universe, and/or treating them as subordinate in importance. And this was reinforced in the nineteenth century by the development of various forms of positivism, historicism, and life philosophy – in particular by the work of Comte, Marx, Dilthey, Kierkegaard and Nietzsche – and into the twentieth century by Marxism, pragmatism, and existentialism.[9]

I will focus here on just one of these philosophical movements, the one that, as I noted earlier, has probably been the most influential for notions of action research: Dewey's pragmatism. For Dewey, as for other pragmatists, scientific inquiry is not an activity that is set apart from ordinary life, involving detached contemplation as if from some Olympian vantage point. He spent much of his intellectual life trying to counter this view, along with other 'dualisms'. For him, inquiry does not begin from a philosophical decision to engage in sceptical questioning, in the manner of Descartes, where thinkers must seek to detach themselves cognitively from their taken-for-granted world in order to find some solid foundation on which true knowledge can be built. Rather, inquiry – even scientific and philosophical inquiry – arises within the course of human social life, is shaped by its context, and should feed back into the flow of ongoing collective activity that makes up the wider society.

The paradigmatic model of how inquiry arises, for many pragmatists, was when a course of action is interrupted by the frustration of expectations. Its purpose is to resolve the problem and thereby enable continuation of the activity (see, for example, Dewey 1929). Indeed, they saw all cognition as stimulated by mismatches between expectations and outcomes. So, while Dewey did not deny the need for occupational specialisation in modern societies, he did not see scientific modes of thought as restricted to scientists. Rather, properly interpreted, science represented the highest form of rational thinking about problems, and needed to be diffused throughout society. Thereby, so it was assumed, any tendency for science to become a source of expertise that undermines democracy is negated. In Dewey's view, when it is properly understood scientific inquiry is central to democracy, which he conceived as a process of collective deliberation about what policies are best for all in dealing with the various problems that a society faces.[10]

---

[9]There is a danger here of a false contrast between ancient and modern views. In fact, there is diversity on each side. For example, the Sophists, and Socrates too, reacted against philosophy's previous preoccupation with the nature of the universe and with mathematics in favour of a focus on the ideals that should guide human beings in their lives: see Guthrie 1971. And in *The Republic* Plato argues that the guardians, who have gained access to theoretical knowledge, must govern if the best form of social life is to be achieved for all.

[10]There are some parallels, as well as some tensions, between his perspective and Campbell's (1988a) 'experimenting society', see Dunn 1998.

Here, then, as in the ancient model, science is still given high status, but it is not regarded as cut off from everyday activity; it is treated, instead, as the model for how we should live our lives; and through education it is to become the guiding orientation of the whole society. In short, scientists are not an other-worldly elite, they are ordinary people using a rational method that can be applied beyond the specialised areas in which they work; an extension that can transform individual lives and whole societies for the better. This is the core of Dewey's scientific and democratic humanism (on which see Rockefeller 1991).

It is not difficult to identify affinities between this and much of the thinking associated with action research, and these are no accident. As indicated earlier, Dewey's writings had a pervasive influence in the early part of the twentieth century, especially in the United States where the notion of action research first developed. Moreover, Dewey's arguments are surely correct in some important respects. The classical idea of an absolute distinction between action and inquiry, with the latter operating on a higher plane, must be rejected. Inquiry is a human activity, and as such shares some features in common with others. Furthermore, much inquiry does indeed arise in the context of the experience of a problem, and is concerned with resolving that problem. Alfred Schütz notes that the Greek root of the term 'problem' means 'that which is thrown before me' (Schütz 1970: 26). This amounts, in his terms, to an 'imposed relevance'. And there is little doubt that inquiry can be stimulated by imposed relevances.[11] However, this is not the only source of inquiry. Equally important is the puzzlement that Aristotle regarded as central to human beings' relationship with their world: deriving from an instinctive curiosity (Lear 1988). This can range from sheer wonder at the existence and character of the world through to more mundane puzzles about particular features of it that we do not understand. These are what Schütz refers to as intrinsic, rather than imposed, relevances.

So, there are times when we initiate inquiry, or find ourselves embarked upon it, without having been stimulated by a practical problem, an interruption in some course of action. Moreover, science and philosophy have become institutionalised; in other words, they are specialised occupational activities that are carried on outside the immediate context of other activities – and they therefore generate their own intellectual problems. Even where they are oriented towards providing knowledge relevant to some practical issue, they do not usually form an immediate part of courses of action directed towards dealing with that issue. Instead, they are carried out 'off-line' from those activities, and very often by people who are not members of the relevant practitioner group. Of course, we might argue that this represents an alienation of inquiry from practice, that the two ought to be more closely related. But this is an argument that cannot be justified by appeal to how things naturally are – in other words, by appeal to a single paradigm for the emergence of inquiry from practical problems – for the reason I have explained: recognising intrinsic relevance as a stimulus to inquiry points to the possibility of a much looser relationship between research and other kinds of activity. It suggests that knowledge can be of value in its own right, in resolving intellectual problems, and perhaps even in stimulating new ones, rather

---

[11]It is perhaps worth noting that imposed relevance does not require that the problem be accepted as given; it can be reformulated.

than simply in terms of helping to solve practical problems. In this way, something of the idea of research as a form of detached contemplation of the world resurfaces – but without any implication that this represents the only, or a superior, mode of life.[12]

So, what is to be accepted and what rejected from the ancient Greek model? While we must reject the status hierarchy between *theoria* and *praxis*, it should be recognised that inquiry can be distinct from other activities, and can be stimulated by intrinsic not just imposed relevances. And while not all inquiry is a way of life, some inquiry is a specialised occupation, for which we might retain the label 'research' (see Hammersley 2000c, 2002). To summarise, then, the classical argument to the effect that action research is self-contradictory fails, but the opposing pragmatist argument does not establish that research must always be an integral part of some other activity.

'RESEARCH' AND 'ACTION' AS POTENTIALLY CONTRADICTORY

It is often not obvious what the intended relationship is between the two components of the phrase 'action research', as generally used. Nor is it usually made clear – the other side of the coin – what the category system is to which 'action research' belongs. A fundamental question is: which of the component terms refers to species and which to genus? In other words, is action research a form of research, as the ordering of the words implies, and as I have assumed up to now, or is it a form of action? Furthermore, what contrasting types of research, or of action, are assumed by the implicit typology; and what is the nature of the contrast?

In some versions, of course, action research claims to transcend the distinction between research and action. Thus, while inquiry is to be re-formed to make it serve practice, so also is practice to be transformed through the influence of research. Yet what typically happens instead, I suggest, is an oscillation between emphasis on each of the two component terms – rather than transcendence of the difference between them. And the reason for this is that no overcoming of the distinction between inquiry and other types of activity is possible. While Dewey's main aim was to transcend dualisms, including that between theory and practice, he was not successful; and the same is true of advocates of action research.[13] In some key respects, pluralism necessarily prevails, a range of distinct human activities exist, and it is important to recognise the differences amongst them (as well as the similarities). Indeed, distinctions are essential precisely for seeing the relationships *among* things.

The difference in character between inquiry and other activities can be obscured by an overemphasis on what they share in common. In reaction against the influence of the ancient Greek view I discussed earlier, where an absolute difference in character is claimed, it is often noted that many other activities, besides research, involve the collection and analysis of information; indeed, that in some cases this is central

---

[12]For an argument that some knowledge can be treated as of value in itself, see Hammersley 1995: 140–2.

[13]Perhaps the most fundamental dualism Dewey failed to transcend is that between instrumental and intrinsic value: see Rockefeller 1991: 253.

to them. And the conclusion occasionally drawn from this is that all practitioners are or ought to be researchers. For example this is to be found in the field of education where Stenhouse (1975) proposed that schoolteachers should be researchers (see Hammersley 1993), but also in other areas.

Another overlap that may be used to suggest a false isomorphism is the fact that both research and other activities involve processes of trial-and-error. A stimulus for this is Popper's account of scientific inquiry. However, a crucial point here is that in each case trial-and-error is directed towards a different goal: in the case of science towards discovering whether a hypothesis is false, and in the case of other activities towards finding solutions to practical problems or improving existing strategies for dealing with them. And these goals pull in contrary directions.

It is certainly true that there is overlap between inquiry and other forms of activity. Thus, policymakers and other occupational practitioners often face problems, and one strategy (though not the only one) that they may engage in to resolve these is some form of investigation. For example, if a social worker discovers that a child has run away from home he or she will probably investigate where the child is and what prompted the event, and whether it signals more fundamental problems with the family and/or the child that require attention. Social workers may also engage in inquiry as part of ongoing evaluation of their own work, for instance judging whether or not some particular intervention strategy worked in a desirable way on some occasion and under what conditions it seems likely to be successful; or indeed they may engage in reflection on the very goals of their profession. However, such overlap between social work and research does not imply identity, any more than it does in the case of other occupational activities. By no means all aspects of social work take the form of inquiry. Nor are the *goals* of social work the same as those of inquiry. And the kind of inquiry that social workers engage in as part of their work is not the only sort of inquiry there is, and is significantly different from research as a specialised occupation.[14]

So, while inquiry may be closely related to other forms of activity, it is never isomorphic with those activities. And any lack of isomorphism opens up the probability of contradictory tensions. Given that, by their very nature, different activities have different operational goals, there will be occasions when they demand divergent courses of action, and sometimes those courses of action will be fundamentally incompatible. In other words, rational pursuit of inquiry may often lead the actor in a different direction from rational pursuit of some other activity; or even in a direction that would be judged detrimental in terms of the latter. For example, if with

---

[14]The distinction between inquiry that is part of some other activity and specialised inquiry must not be conflated with the separate question of *who* carries out the inquiry. Just as action research may be carried out by external agents as well as by practitioners, so specialist inquiry can be carried out by people who are occupational practitioners of various kinds. For example, Whorf, an influential linguistic anthropologist in the early twentieth century, was a fire prevention officer. Even aside from this, many people engaged in practical activities will sometimes experience puzzlements of various kinds that have no immediate practical implications, both during the course of action and in reflecting later on their experience. And they may go beyond thinking about the matter to actively engaging in some inquiry about it, whether seeking illumination from relevant literature, talking to colleagues, or even engaging in data collection and analysis.

Stenhouse we see teaching as involving the testing out of curricular hypotheses, this might require practitioners to engage in actions, such as teaching different material to different groups of pupils, that from an educational point of view would be difficult to defend or could even be judged unacceptable.[15]

Any attempt to combine inquiry with some other activity can generate contradictory pressures in a variety of ways:

- while the information that could be produced by an inquiry may be regarded as necessary or valuable, the costs in terms of resources needed for doing the investigation could be judged too high in practical terms, for example because they come from funds needed for intervention;
- while the value of an inquiry may be accepted in principle, uncertainty about reaching a clear conclusion – or the amount of time it would take to reach such a conclusion – might be judged excessive and thereby not warrant engaging in inquiry as against other activities;
- the intrinsic value of an inquiry could be recognised, but the opportunity costs regarded as too high. In other words, to engage in inquiry at the time concerned would mean not doing something else that is judged to be of greater value: here there is direct incompatibility, and a choice has to be made between one course of action and another. To use an example from medicine, seeking to run a randomised controlled trial may mean that a particular patient is assigned a placebo rather than the drug that would normally have been prescribed and which the patient's doctor takes to be the most appropriate treatment. Here, there is a direct conflict between what is needed in order to gain sound knowledge for future policy and what is judged most appropriate in a particular case in treating a patient;
- the value of an inquiry may be recognised, but what we might call the effect costs are judged too high. In other words, some of the consequences of the practitioner engaging in the inquiry are evaluated as too damaging. For example, pursuing inquiry may reveal uncertainty on the part of the actor, and thereby undermine his or her authority with an important constituency. Alternatively, it may involve giving away inside information that could be consequential – it is important to remember that inquirers always give out and give off information about themselves in the course of an investigation.

Any attempt to combine inquiry with some other activity, or to relate the two closely together, is likely to generate contradictory tendencies of these kinds (see Marris and Rein 1967: ch. 8 and Rapoport 1970: 505–7). These tensions have usually been managed contextually in one of two main ways: by subordinating inquiry to the other activity, or by setting up institutional barriers around inquiry to protect it from, or to mediate the demands of, other activities. Of course, it is precisely such institutional boundaries that many advocates of action research, and other proponents of the notion of research-based practice, wish to demolish.

---

[15]This reflects the fact that ethical judgements are properly determined, in part, by social role: see Emmet 1966, especially ch. VII.

TYPOLOGY, NOT HIERARCHY

I have argued that 'action research' cannot refer to a fusion of, or a transcendence of the distinction between, research and some other activity; that while there may be overlap there cannot be isomorphism; and that, as a result, there is the likelihood of contradictory tensions. The existence of these tensions is obscured by what we might think of as an Enlightenment myth, whereby pursuit of the true and the good are always in harmony – in the long if not in the short term. While this might have been a plausible idea in the eighteenth century, it certainly is not today; given, for example, the experience of twentieth-century natural science and its role in technological developments that have had many negative as well as positive consequences.

In the nineteenth century this Enlightenment myth had already been modified by Hegel and Marx. They saw contradictions as inevitable, but as the driving force behind historical change which would eventually result in the overcoming of all conflicts among human ideals; this being the 'end' of History in both senses of that term. However, it was precisely this kind of meta-narrative that some nineteenth- and many twentieth-century conservatives, liberals and radicals rejected; and that is denounced most vociferously today by postmodernists, with good reason (see Hammersley 1992: 106–9).[16]

As already noted, there are two main ways in which the tensions between inquiry and other activities can be, and have been, managed. It is important to recognise the sharp contrast between these, but also to acknowledge that they are *both* legitimate and can coexist within the same society. In other words, what we need is a typology, rather than some all-purpose hierarchy – of either the ancient Greek kind or the inversion of it promoted by some pragmatists and action researchers. From this point of view, there are two fundamental types of inquiry: one that is subordinated to some other activity, and a second that is pursued in its own right. In the first type, any conflicts are resolved in favour of the other activity, in the second they are resolved in favour of inquiry. What is critical here is *which* set of goals is taken as the operational priority.

In the case of inquiry-subordinated-to-another-activity, inquiry is a sub-activity: its pursuit is geared to other prevailing concerns. It will be started and terminated in accordance with those concerns, and how it is conducted will be properly shaped by them. Of course, even here, there remains an analytic distinction to be drawn between inquiry and the activity to which it is subordinated. It is not that the two sets of goals are fused, but rather that a *context-specific* hierarchy operates between them, in which the goal of inquiry is subordinated to others.

The second way of managing tensions between research and other activities is to separate them institutionally. At the most primitive level, this involves an actor clearly distinguishing between the role of researcher and other roles. Further along the road, it is exemplified by an organisation setting up a research department, or buying in research from outside. In its most highly developed form, it involves organisations and institutions that are funded to do research, rather even than being contracted to

---

[16]An important source for some postmodernists here is Nietzsche. In 1886 he summarised the point: 'There is no pre-established harmony between the furtherance of truth and the well-being of mankind' (quoted in Hollingdale 1977: 198).

carry out particular pieces of research. Universities are the key example of this full institutionalisation, though it could be argued that they are currently undergoing de-institutionalisation in this regard, with increasing pressure for them to serve the surrounding society more directly (Hammersley 2011: Introduction).

In the more developed of these forms of institutionalisation, what we have is research as specialised inquiry. Rather than a practitioner temporarily suspending some other activity in order to carry out an investigation, inquiry becomes the primary occupational practice. Even where research is stimulated by some practical problem, and contracted by an organisation that needs information relevant to this problem, inquiry is pursued in the terms originally set (these perhaps even being adapted for research purposes), not continually re-shaped by subsequent changes in the on-going activity that it is required to assist. What is involved here is not just a difference in what is treated as the prime concern but also a difference in the distance between inquiry and other activities. In inquiry-subordinated-to-other-activities the relationship is very close, whereas in institutionalised research the relationship is more distant. In the latter case, the contradictory tendencies between different activities are to a considerable extent externalised: they are minimised within the inquiry process, so that conflict tends to arise at the interfaces – where research and other forms of practice meet.[17] This is the reason why, as noted in the Introduction, there have been recurrent crises between research and policymaking/practice, and why these are unavoidable (Hammersley 2002; and see Chapter 2).

The advantages and disadvantages of these two solutions to the problem of contradictory tendencies are mirror images of one another. What inquiry-subordinated-to-another-activity offers is inquiry that maximises the chance that relevant and usable information will be produced. However, this is achieved at the risk of over-looking the falsity of key assumptions built into the activity, of missing errors in conclusions, and/or of failing to provide knowledge of underlying generative processes or about wider social forces. By contrast, specialised inquiry maximises the chances of avoiding errors, and of discovering the wider range of causal factors involved and how they operate. However, at the same time, it is in danger of producing information whose relevance for any particular practical activity is remote; in other words, considerable work may be necessary to make this knowledge into a usable resource. Even in the case of practical (rather than academic) research, where the framework of inquiry is set by practical considerations, there is a risk that by the time the results are produced the relevance of the information aimed at will be eroded, or transformed; or that what is produced will be too complex and qualified to be found useful (Hammersley 2002; and see Chapter 2).

How does this typology relate to action research? Much of what goes under that heading would be classified in my terms as inquiry-subordinated-to-another-activity. This is exemplified by Wallace's treatment of 'action research' as a 'generic term covering a wide range of strategies intended to bring about improvement in some practical situation'

---

[17]Elsewhere, I have formulated this in terms of research and other forms of activity becoming different 'worlds', in the phenomenological sense of that term: see Hammersley 2002: ch. 3. Maasen and Weingart 2005 approach this in terms of the relationship between different social systems.

(Wallace 1986: 98). This makes clear that the immediate goal governing much action research is to bring about improvement or change in the world rather than to produce knowledge about it; inquiry is subordinated to practical goals. Other definitions carry more or less the same message, albeit in different words. Here, for example, is Reason and Bradbury: 'the primary purpose of action research is not to produce academic theories based on action; nor is it to produce theories about action; nor is it to produce theoretical or empirical knowledge that can be applied in action; it is to liberate the human body, mind and spirit in the search for a better, freer world' (Reason and Bradbury 2001: 2). Along the same lines, in the field of education, for Carr and Kemmis the goal of critical action research is to restructure professional practice and thereby to transform the education system and society at large, not simply to produce knowledge that is relevant to educational issues (Carr and Kemmis 1986; Kemmis 1988). For all these writers, in effect, action research involves the subordination of inquiry to some other form of practice.

Of course, many action researchers would resist this categorisation of their work. One reason is that, as noted earlier, while they want research to serve action of some kind, they also usually want to transform the conventional ways in which such action has previously been carried out; often the role envisaged for research is not just to serve as a source of valuable knowledge but in addition to provide a model for this transformation.[18] In this respect, action researchers appeal, implicitly or explicitly, to what they regard as the liberating potential of research.

There are at least two aspects to this. First of all, it may be seen as offering a more open-minded perspective in which taken-for-granted assumptions are questioned and explored, stock descriptions and explanations abandoned, new possibilities for interpretation and action envisaged, and so on. Thus, writing about the Girls into Science and Technology (GIST) project, Kelly expresses the hope that 'teachers have come to question their taken for granted assumptions about the world (that is, to take a research stance on their experience), and will continue to examine and evaluate their own actions now that the formal Project is finished' (Kelly 1985: 134). A second feature of research often valorised by action researchers is its allegedly democratic character. Thus, Kemmis writes: 'action research was (and is) an expression of the essentially democratic spirit in social research' (Kemmis 1982: 14). Very often research communities are treated as models for discursive or deliberative democracy, of precisely the kind that many action researchers believe need to be institutionalised in society as a whole.[19]

---

[18]Sometimes the model here is empirical research, but it may also be philosophical inquiry. There is a direct parallel here with the notion of evidence-based practice, see Chapter 3.

[19]On these forms of democracy, see Dryzek 1990 and House and Howe 2000. It is perhaps worth noting that research cannot operate on a completely open-minded basis – as with other activities, some assumptions have to be made if anything is to get done. Moreover, the function of criticism, and therefore the limits that should operate on it, are different for different activities: see Hammersley 2011: ch. 3. And while there are areas within the organisation of research where something like deliberative or discursive democracy takes place, this is not directed towards the production of central policies. Research communities are to a large extent spontaneously generated forms of organisation, and must be (Polanyi 1962). Finally, even if research communities were discursive or deliberative democracies, this would not in itself make them a good model for the organisation of other forms of practice. Further argument would be required to justify this; and the problems with these types of democracy are well known.

So, rather than simply subordinating inquiry to another activity, action researchers want instead to maintain a more equal relationship between inquiry and the other form of activity which it is to serve. Yet any attempt to do this will run into the problems discussed earlier; and it remains quite clear that their overriding goal is a practical one, not the pursuit of practice-relevant knowledge alone. It is in this form that 'action research' becomes a contradiction in terms: it amounts to the attempt to combine activities with different operational goals, simultaneous pursuit of which generates incompatible orientations.

CONCLUSION

While recognising the diversity of ideas and practices associated with the term 'action research', this chapter has focused on what seems to be its core idea: that there should be an intimate, two-way relationship between research and some form of practical or political activity; such that the focus of inquiry arises out of, and its results feed back into, the activity concerned. In this way, action research has operationalised the idea that research should directly serve practice in a rather different manner from the notion of research for evidence-based practice. The question I have raised here is whether there is a contradiction between its two components. An ancient Greek view about *theoria* and *praxis* was examined as one affirmative answer to that question. This was contrasted with the pragmatist philosophy which has been influential on some versions of action research. I accepted the pragmatist idea that inquiry arises out of human activity, but not the rather instrumental conception of inquiry that is sometimes derived from it. I argued that inquiry does not begin only from imposed relevances arising from practical problems but also from intrinsic relevances deriving from intellectual puzzlement.

In the second part of the chapter I suggested that inquiry and other activities must be treated as operating on the same plane, and that any relationship between them creates the potential for contradictory tensions. I noted that these can be, and have been, managed in two main ways: by subordinating inquiry to the other activity or by treating it as primary and insulating it from other demands. I argued that neither solution should be turned into a universal, all-purpose hierarchy, whether that of the ancient Greeks or its inversion by some pragmatists and action researchers. What is required is a typology that acknowledges the value and legitimacy of both solutions, but also recognises the distinctiveness of the two kinds of inquiry that result: inquiry-subordinated-to-another-activity and research as a specialised occupation.

In these terms, most action research would amount to inquiry-subordinated-to-another-activity. However, I noted that many action researchers would not find this categorisation acceptable. This is because they wish to use research as a model for transforming the practical or political activity with which they are concerned, for example in order to make it more open-minded or democratic. As a result, they demand a more equal relationship between research and the action it is to serve. Yet this gives rise to contradictory requirements, and thereby makes action research inherently unstable: in these circumstances, it will always tend to oscillate in the emphasis given to its two components. In this sense it *is* a contradiction in terms, and as a result it involves a damaging conflict in goals.

8

ON 'SYSTEMATIC' REVIEWS OF RESEARCH LITERATURES

From the late 1990s onwards there were arguments that reviews of research literatures must become 'systematic' if social research is to facilitate evidence-based policymaking and practice (see Davies 2000a; Evans 2000; Evans and Benefield 2001; Petticrew and Roberts 2006). And institutional moves were made to increase the production of such reviews. Internationally, the Campbell Collaboration was founded, in parallel with the Cochrane Collaboration, which had already begun producing systematic reviews in the field of medicine. And in the UK the Evidence for Policy and Practice Information Co-ordinating Centre (EPPI-Centre) was established at the Institute for Education, University of London, and the ESRC UK Centre for Evidence Based Policy and Practice at Queen Mary and Westfield College, later at King's College, London.[1]

The idea of systematic review emerged, in large part, out of a debate about the advantages and disadvantages of statistical meta-analysis as an alternative to traditional or 'narrative' reviews of research literatures. Many of the arguments advanced by advocates of meta-analysis against narrative reviews were taken over by proponents of systematic review; though they do not always accept the particular solutions meta-analysis offers to the problem of how to synthesise evidence from multiple studies.[2] Cooper displayed the spirit behind the systematic review movement in the introduction to his book *Synthesizing Research*:

---

[1]The website for the EPPI-Centre is: http://eppi.ioe.ac.uk/. That for the UK Centre for Evidence Based Policy and Practice is http://www.kcl.ac.uk/sspp/departments/politicaleconomy/research/cep/contact.aspx. And that for the Campbell Collaboration is: http://www.campbellcollaboration.org/.

[2]An important precursor of systematic review is Slavin's 'best evidence synthesis', and he presents this as standing between narrative reviews and meta-analysis (Slavin 1986). Other key texts include Light and Pillemer 1984, Cooper and Hedges 1994 and Cooper 1998, 2010.

The approach to research synthesis presented in this book represents a significant departure from how reviews had been conducted just 20 years ago. Instead of a subjective, narrative approach, this book presents an objective systematic approach. Here, the reader will learn how to carry out an integration of research according to scientific principles and rules. The intended result is a research synthesis that can be replicated by others, can create consensus among scholars, and can focus debate in a constructive fashion. (Cooper 1998: xi)[3]

Systematic reviews have a number of distinctive features. One concerns how studies for inclusion in the review are to be selected: the contrast drawn is with 'haphazard study selection procedures' or even 'arbitrary study selection procedures' (Slavin 1986: 6, 10). Relevance criteria must be specified and the available literature searched exhaustively, wherever possible using computer databases, but also 'hand-searching'. Indeed, Slavin argues that 'Once criteria for inclusion of studies in a best-evidence synthesis have been established, it is incumbent upon the reviewer to locate *every* study ever conducted that meets these criteria' (Slavin 1986: 8, emphasis added).

Equally important is that the evaluation of studies selected as relevant must be based upon an explicit hierarchy of types of research design, categorised according to the likely validity of the results they produce. In short, the criteria for inclusion and exclusion of studies must be operationalisable. As the quotation from Cooper above makes clear, the aim is to make the reviewing process replicable. Similarly, Slavin argues that 'the literature search procedure should be described in enough detail that the reader could theoretically regenerate an identical set of articles' (Slavin 1986: 10). The implication of this is that there must be minimal reliance upon judgement or discretion by the reviewer. While Slavin recognises that 'no set of procedural or statistical canons can make the review process immune to the reviewer's biases' (Slavin 1986: 7), he believes that the use of explicit procedures will usually make the reliability of the conclusions high, and that explicitness allows the reviewing process to be assessed by readers.

A third feature of systematic reviews – as the link with meta-analysis, and frequent use of the term 'synthesis', indicate – is that they do not simply discuss the separate contributions of individual studies. Rather, they seek to *combine* the findings produced by the various studies reviewed. In this way, it is argued, more robust conclusions can be drawn, because there is support from more cases than were available to any of the individual studies included in the review.

A final point is that advocacy of systematic literature reviews has been closely related to the pressure for 'evidence-based' policymaking and practice. As a result, systematic reviews are frequently seen as concerned with providing research-based answers to specific questions about 'what works', or what works best, in relation to some practical problem. They are treated as a bridge between research, on the one hand, and policymaking or some other sort of practice, on the other. While narrative reviews are also sometimes designed to serve this bridging function, they frequently

---

[3]This sales pitch is repeated more or less word for word in the latest edition of this book: Cooper 2010: vi.

address relatively large and complex areas involving multiple issues – with one intention being to provide a map of research in the relevant field. They do not usually focus exclusively on specific hypotheses about the effects of particular policies or practical techniques.[4]

In this chapter I will examine some of the assumptions that are built into the concept of systematic review, and which underpin the status it is given by its advocates.

THE UNDERLYING ASSUMPTIONS OF SYSTEMATIC REVIEW

A first point to be made is that systematic review assumes the superiority of what, for shorthand purposes, can be referred to as the positivist model of research. This is true in two respects. First, the methodological criteria which it applies in evaluating the validity of studies are characteristic of this model: in that what are treated as of highest value are studies involving explicit and replicable procedures that provide for physical or statistical control and/or statistical generalisation. So, experiments, quasi-experiments, randomised controlled trials (RCTs), and statistical analyses of system inputs and outcomes are towards the top of what we might call its 'credibility hierarchy'.[5]

The second point is that systematic review also applies the positivist approach to the task of producing reviews. Not only is the reviewer to judge the quality of particular studies in terms of positivist criteria, but the reviewing process itself must match similar criteria. In particular, as already noted, it must employ *explicit procedures* in selecting and evaluating studies: relevance criteria must be identified, and all studies meeting those criteria are to be included in the review and evaluated in terms of whether their designs meet the specified validity threshold. Very often, too, statistical analysis is used to integrate the findings of the studies, where these are quantitative in character.

A central feature of the positivist model is commitment to procedural objectivity (Newell 1986; Eisner 1992): to the idea that subjectivity is a source of bias, and that it can and must be minimised. In other words, it is assumed that both doing research and producing research reviews can be pursued best by following a set of formal rules, on the assumption that this minimizes the effect of subjective biases. Here, methodology amounts to a repository of best practice, and the researcher or reviewer is expected to follow those rules which have been shown to be most effective.[6] As we have seen, not only is this assumed to maximise the chances of producing valid conclusions, but it is also valued on the grounds that it makes the

---

[4]For discussion of some examples of narrative reviews and the issues they raise, see Foster and Hammersley 1998.

[5]See, for example, Oakley's argument for the priority of experimentation: Oakley 2000. Oakley was the first director of the EPPI-Centre. See also Chalmers 2003 and 2005; and Hammersley 2005b.

[6]Though, as I pointed out in Chapter 3, in fact even in the natural sciences this expertise is rarely 'evidence-based', in the sense of depending upon research findings about what are the most effective techniques.

study replicable – so that its reliability (and thereby, so the assumption goes, its validity) can be assessed.

Another important feature of the positivist model is commitment to what Sohn refers to as 'the hypothesis-testing view' of research (Sohn 1996). This portrays science as concerned with testing hypotheses about relationships between treatments and outcomes, and as relying upon statistical tests, such as effect-size measures, in order to do this.

THE FAILINGS OF POSITIVISM

What is curious about this dual application of the positivist model to the task of reviewing is that it takes little or no account of the considerable amount of criticism that has been made of that model since at least the middle of the twentieth century. The positivist model involves a view of science that, critics suggest, may not capture accurately the practice of natural scientists; and which may not be a sensible ideal in studying human social life. One does not need to regard positivism as wholly misguided, or to be attracted by the most *avant garde* forms of postmodernism, to view many of the criticisms directed against it as raising serious problems.[7] Indeed, much criticism of positivism has come from those whose commitment to scientific understanding is no less strong than that of the positivists. Putting on one side a huge literature within the social sciences, let me cite just one influential critical appraisal of the positivist project: Michael Polanyi's argument that natural science necessarily relies on personal or tacit knowledge (Polanyi 1958, 1966). He specifically denies that science can, or should attempt to, operate on the basis of fully explicit procedures.[8]

There has been virtually no engagement with these criticisms of positivism on the part of advocates of 'systematic' review. Instead, they put forward their views as patently rational and sensible, trading to a large extent on the idea that being systematic is obviously a good thing and that what has 'worked' in medical research will work in other fields. Moreover, their responses to criticism have often been dismissive – for example, Oakley has portrayed the critics as Luddites resisting a new technology (Oakley 2006; see Hammersley 2008c).

It is legitimate, in my view, to contrast science as a source of potential knowledge with those approaches which rely upon immediate appeal to intuition or tradition (see Peirce 1965). Underlying this contrast is the idea that science does not just

---

[7]For reasons explained elsewhere, I do not regard positivism as wholly misguided: see Hammersley 1995: ch. 1. For some illustration of the implications for the task of reviewing of what can be loosely labelled postmodernist views of research, see Meacham 1998, Lather 1999 and Livingston 1999. For a discussion, see Chapter 9.

[8]Sohn's critique of the hypothesis-testing approach on which meta-analysis relies – for failing to establish reliable knowledge about relationships or to provide understanding of causal mechanisms – shares much in common with Polanyi's arguments, and also with those of Bhaskar (see Archer et al. 1997).

present conclusions but provides evidence for them, and does so in ways that are open to reasonable judgement by others (via thought-experiments, relating the findings of one study to those of others, carrying out parallel or related investigations, etc.). However, the operation of science in this manner does *not* require that the process of inquiry be reduced to following a set of rules, in the way that calculating the results of a statistical test can be. This is perhaps just as well. As statisticians frequently emphasise, decisions about *which* test to use cannot be governed by rules in this manner: what is required is judgement that takes into account the purposes of the inquiry, the nature of the data available, and the character of the psychological or social processes that are being studied. Much the same is true of most other aspects of doing research: judgement is involved, it cannot be eradicated. Moreover, attempting to eradicate it is unlikely to serve the task of research well. It is also important to recognise that we are not faced with a dichotomy between rational rule-following and irrational judgement. Rather, even the most simple rule-following involves some judgement; and rational decision-making will often take the form of the *interpretation* of principles rather than the 'application' of rules.

This raises two sets of issues about systematic reviews. First, there is the question of the way in which they favour some kinds of research against others. Most obviously, they favour quantitative over qualitative studies, and some kinds of quantitative study over others. Is this simply a matter of including those studies that are sufficiently relevant and cogent, and excluding those that are not; or is valuable evidence being overlooked here, and/or misleading evidence being privileged? Secondly, there is the issue of whether systematic review is the only or the best way of representing the literature, either for other researchers or for external 'users'. I will deal with each of these issues in turn.

QUESTIONING THE ASSUMPTIONS ABOUT RESEARCH BUILT INTO SYSTEMATIC REVIEW

One issue here is the relationship between quantitative and qualitative method.[9] Some treat this contrast as reflecting a fundamental difference in orientation, perhaps one that hinges on a commitment for or against social *science*. Such views are to be found on both sides of the divide. There are still those who are committed to a scientific approach and *define* it in terms of quantitative measurement, experimental or statistical procedure, etc. For them, qualitative method can be no more than a useful supplement to the real, quantitative, work of social science.[10] On the other side, there are qualitative researchers who reject any commitment to science, or seek to redefine it in such a way that the work of natural scientists in the nineteenth and twentieth

---

[9]For discussion of this, see Cooper et al. 2012.

[10]For a sophisticated exposition of this position, see Goldthorpe 2000: ch. 4.

centuries is no longer the prime exemplar.[11] There is, however, much scope for positions between these two extremes.

So, advocates of systematic review do not necessarily deny the value of qualitative research. They may well acknowledge that, in some areas, it represents the best evidence available (see Harden 2006). Slavin introduces the idea of 'best evidence' as follows:

> In law, there is a principle that the same evidence that would be essential in one case might be disregarded in another because in the second case there is better evidence available. For example, in a case of disputed authorship, a typed manuscript might be critical evidence if no handwritten copy is available, but if a handwritten copy exists, the typed copy would be inadmissable because it is no longer the best evidence (because the handwritten copy would be conclusive evidence of authorship).

> I would propose extending the principle of best evidence to the practice of research review. For example, if a literature contains several studies high in internal and external validity, then lower quality studies might be largely excluded from the review. ... However, if a set of studies high in internal and external validity does not exist, we might cautiously examine the less well designed studies to see if there is adequate unbiased information to come to any conclusion. (Slavin 1986: 6)

So, rather than including all studies that are relevant in a review irrespective of judgements about the validity of their findings (as in some kinds of meta-analysis), or adopting a fixed validity threshold that excludes all those regarded as too weak (as would some proponents of systematic review), Slavin suggests operating a variable threshold, according to the amount and type of evidence available in the field being reviewed. However, despite this, like other advocates of systematic review, Slavin treats the credibility hierarchy of research designs as absolute.[12] Thus, advocates of systematic review, whether in favour of fixed or variable thresholds, apparently believe that the likely validity of studies' findings can and must be judged abstractly, according to the research design employed. Was a RCT involved?, What form of analysis was used?, and so on. In other words, a scale is deployed that differentiates research designs in terms of the likely level of internal and external validity of the findings they produce. This very much follows the pattern of Campbell and Stanley's

---

[11]See, for instance, Denzin and Lincoln's (2000: ch, 41) call for a 'sacred science'. See also Denzin and Lincoln 2011.

[12]Or at least he comes close to this. He does recognise that there is variation across areas of research in terms of how likely it is that the independent variable will be highly correlated with biasing factors, and that this has implications for the relative value of experimental versus correlational studies (Slavin 1986: 7). Slavin describes the variable criteria to be employed in best evidence syntheses as '*a priori*', but it is not clear that he intends this in the strictly philosophical sense of 'undeterminable by empirical evidence'. It seems more likely that what he means is that the criteria are specified before the review is carried out.

ranking of research designs in terms of their susceptibility to specified validity threats (Campbell and Stanley 1966).[13]

Now it is certainly true that research designs have different general advantages and disadvantages in relation to threats to validity. However, it is not the case, even in abstract terms, that some designs have all the advantages and others have none. Advantage in one respect is often bought at the expense of disadvantage in another. For instance, laboratory experiments allow maximum control over variables, and thereby – other things being equal – facilitate the identification of causal relationships of particular kinds. However, this is bought at the expense of weakness in relation to threats concerning external validity, especially ecological validity. Moreover, while quasi-experiments and field experiments involve a trade-off designed to gain reasonable levels of both internal and external validity, these designs carry losses as well as gains. It is certainly not true that they always achieve 'the best of both worlds'. For some purposes, strict experimental designs will be better, and for others case studies or surveys (see Hammersley 1992: ch. 11). Indeed, in any field, it may be desirable to have studies employing a range of different research designs, since their products will often be complementary. Much the same is true in relation to quantitative measurement. This has obvious advantages, but also disadvantages. The disadvantages concern the meaning that is often lost when complex concepts are operationalised in terms of quantitative scales (see Chapter 5). Here, too, the most advantageous situation could be studies exhibiting a variety of approaches to the problem of how to operationalise the central concepts of a field.

Aside from this general point, it is also important to recognise that assessing the likely validity of the findings of a study never simply amounts to assessing its research design. One does not have to believe that validity is a matter of insight, intuition, or epistemic standpoint to doubt the value of the procedural approach to assessing it which underlies systematic review.[14] How much evidence is required, and of what kinds, varies according to the nature of the knowledge claim made, both in terms of its type (descriptive, explanatory, or theoretical) and its own degree of plausibility and credibility (see Hammersley 1998). Using fixed, standard criteria specifying a hierarchy of research designs ignores these sources of variation. It neglects the extent to which assessing the validity of studies' findings is a matter of contextually sensitive judgement. As a result, the validity of some studies will be overestimated, while others will be excluded from the review even though they could have told us a great deal of relevance to its focus.

---

[13]Often, there is slippage in the meaning of 'validity' here, with the term coming to be applied to research designs rather than to findings. For a discussion of this and other problems with the notions of internal and external validity, see Hammersley 1991. It is not surprising that Campbell's name has been adopted by an organisation designed to produce systematic reviews in education and other social fields, but it should be noted that he seems to have changed his mind about the credibility hierarchy of research designs, at least as far as the position of case studies is concerned: see Campbell 1988b and c, and also Rosenblatt 1981.

[14]For a critique of the procedural model, and of some of the alternatives, see Hammersley and Gomm 1997.

QUESTIONING THE ASSUMPTIONS ABOUT REVIEWING BUILT INTO SYSTEMATIC REVIEW

A second issue is whether it is desirable to apply what I have called the positivist model to the reviewing process itself. If there are serious problems with this model in relation to research, might these not also arise in applying it to the task of producing reviews? Where is the evidence that systematic reviews generate more valid conclusions than narrative reviews? How could this be assessed? It seems to be assumed that they *must* do because they are 'systematic', 'explicit', etc. But this prejudges what is to be proven, since those terms have been narrowly interpreted in ways that rule out the claims that narrative reviewers make about the systematic and rigorous character of *their* work. As already noted, the assumption is that studies can be assessed in purely procedural or design terms, rather than on the basis of judgements that necessarily rely upon broader, and often tacit, knowledge of a whole range of methodological and substantive matters. But this is no more than an assumption; and not one that is very plausible in light of the criticisms of the positivist model I discussed in the previous section. Moreover, it seems likely that, where a process cannot be proceduralised, attempting to reduce it to procedures will lead to distortion; while at the same time it may induce excessive estimations of the likely validity of the results on the part of readers. This is perhaps the most important danger involved in applying the positivist model to the production of reviews: it portrays research findings as necessarily superior to other sources of evidence; and by using quantitative indicators may give a false sense of security about the reliability of these findings.[15]

Aside from these problems with the way in which systematic reviews deal with research studies, it can be argued that the idea of systematic review draws too close an analogy between doing research and producing a review.[16] This stems from the tendency to see reviewing as *synthesising* the findings from multiple studies, on the model of meta-analysis. In effect, this approach assumes that there is just one possible relationship among different studies: an additive one. All the studies are treated as having addressed the same specific issue, and as having investigated it in a sufficiently similar way that their findings can be aggregated. Yet this is not the only form of cumulation that is possible. For example, studies could be additive in the quite different sense in

---

[15]Shahar has highlighted this danger in relation to the evidence-based medicine movement: see Shahar 1997. See Chapter 5.

[16]The same is true, it seems to me, of Eisenhart's approach to what she calls 'interpretive reviewing' (Eisenhart 1998; see Chapter 9). Another feature of systematic reviews is worth mentioning in this context, one that was inherited from meta-analysis. This is the inclusion of what Slavin refers to as 'fugitive literature', and what others refer to as 'grey' literature: 'from conference papers to unsubmitted or rejected papers' but also including dissertations and reports to funding agencies (Slavin 1995: 10). Indeed, Evans and Benefield even include 'opinion pieces from political parties' (2001: 535). Curiously, this seems to amount to abandonment of any commitment to the scientificity of research: if reviews are seen as presenting conclusions that have been validated by the relevant research community, then work that has not been submitted to public scrutiny should not be included (see Foster and Hammersley 1998 and Hammersley 2011).

which the pieces of a mosaic are additive (Becker 1970: ch. 4). Here, the studies focus on different parts of a single picture. For example, one might investigate the aggregate pattern of distribution of a particular type of crime across the areas of a city. Another study could investigate a small number of cases of crime of this sort, seeking to identify underlying causes and trigger factors. Another investigation might study the police response to this type of crime and whether it varies across areas. And so on.

Nor does addition, of whatever kind, exhaust the ways in which studies might be complementary. They may also relate to one another by reinforcing or challenging each other's assumptions or conclusions. Thus, Freese quotes Popper to the effect that 'it is not the accumulation of observations which I have in mind when I speak of the growth of scientific knowledge but the repeated overthrow of scientific theories and their replacement by better or more satisfactory ones' (Popper 1963: 215; Freese 1980: 40–1). Freese continues: 'The unconstrained addition of new facts and principles ... is often deleterious. The problem for the growth of sociological knowledge is not how to add more and integrate it but how to add proportionately less and make that less count for more'. Even more ominously for the kind of synthesis involved in systematic review, he adds: 'Cumulation cannot be imposed after the fact. If investigations do not proceed in a cumulative way, then they are not cumulative, cannot be made cumulative, and cannot have the results that issue from genuine cumulation' (Freese 1980: 41). He refers to the growth of knowledge in this sense as 'multiplicative cumulation', and clarifies that term as follows: 'The cumulative progression of a family of knowledge claims should behave like a mathematical series, with successive summation of a sequence or sequences' (Freese 1980: 41). In other words, what a series of studies should produce is a theory that is continually modified to increase its explanatory power. The findings of different studies are not just added together; each one that makes a genuine contribution changes the emerging theory.[17]

What all this means, I suggest, is that producing a review of the literature is a distinctive task in its own right. It is not a matter of 'synthesising data' in an additive sense; or, at least, there is no reason why we should assume that reviewing *must* take this form. Rather, it can involve judging the validity of the findings and conclusions of particular studies, and then thinking about how these relate to one another, and how their interrelations can be used to illuminate the field under investigation. This will require the reviewer to draw on her or his tacit knowledge, derived from experience, and to *think* about the substantive and methodological issues, not just to 'apply' replicable procedures.[18]

It is also important to recognise that, like any form of writing, reviews can be designed to serve different purposes and audiences, and that seeking to impose any single model is unwise. Furthermore, the fact that reviewing involves addressing an audience means that there must be judgements about audience members' background

---

[17]For discussion of a sequence of studies that seems to me to meet this requirement, see Hammersley 1985. See Chapter 9 for further exploration of types of synthesis. Pawson's (2006) realist synthesis approximates to the form of cumulation outlined by Popper and Freese.

[18]In this context, MacLure's (2005) emphasis on the importance of careful reading is of significance.

knowledge and level of interest in the various aspects of the research concerned. So, given that reviews are written for a purpose and for an audience, they involve evaluating studies and putting them together in ways that serve that purpose and will be illuminating for that audience. In this respect, too, I submit, reviewing cannot be a matter of following standardised procedures.[19]

CONCLUSION

I have argued that advocates of systematic review rely upon a positivist conception of research, and of the task of reviewing research literature, and that this is defective – in particular in assuming that applying explicit procedures necessarily enhances the likely validity of the results.

It is striking that while advocates of systematic review emphasise that qualitative studies have a role, it is not at all clear how these studies would fit into its framework, given the positivist assumptions this framework involves. As Dixon-Woods, Bonas et al. (2006: 27) report, having attempted to incorporate qualitative research within a systematic review:

> We show how every stage of the review process, from asking the review question through to searching for and sampling the evidence, appraising the evidence and producing a synthesis, provoked profound questions about whether a review that includes qualitative research can remain consistent with the frame offered by current systematic review.[20]

Furthermore, qualitative work is clearly seen by many advocates of systematic review as of rather restricted value. For example, Oakley comments that, in the context of evaluation, anything else but randomised, controlled trials 'is a "disservice to vulnerable people" ...' (Oakley 2000: 318; quoting Macdonald 1996: 21). Evans and Benefield (2001: 528) take a less extreme position, but they nevertheless contrast experimental evaluations focusing on 'what works' with qualitative evaluations, which they claim are concerned with 'how does it feel'. This is a misrepresentation of the focus of qualitative evaluations: these have typically been concerned not just with the perspectives of those involved (nor have those perspectives been treated simply as 'feelings'), but also with the processes involved in the implementation of policies – which are often not those assumed by policymakers – and with unintended and unforeseen consequences.[21]

---

[19]See Bassey's discussion of the distinction between academic and user reviews (Bassey 2000). For a discussion of audience and other aspects of the production of 'narrative' research reviews, see Foster and Hammersley 1998.

[20]See also Konnerup and Kongsted (2012) on the case of observational studies.

[21]For a useful discussion of qualitative evaluation, see Shaw 1999. Davies 2000b provides a relatively sympathetic account of the potential contribution of qualitative research to evidence-based policymaking and practice, but in large part it is still treated as an adjunct to quantitative work. For an attempt to identify 'standards for the systematic review of qualitative literature' which takes more account of the distinctiveness of a qualitative approach, see Popay et al. 1998.

Another problem is the very instrumental model of the relationship between research and practice that the systematic review movement assumes; at least where the function of research is taken to be identifying 'what works' or 'what works best'. As Hodgkinson (2000) has pointed out, the preoccupation with 'what works' also reflects the influence of positivism, this time of Comtean ideas about the role that research can play in governing society. Yet there are serious questions about whether research can do this effectively; and about the effects of trying to make it fulfil this function (see Chapter 1). Providing solutions to practical problems, or evaluating them, is not the only, or necessarily the most important, contribution that research can make. As Weiss has argued, social science much more commonly fulfils an 'enlightenment' function than the 'engineering' function assumed by the evidence-based practice movement (see Weiss 1977, 1979, 1980). Furthermore, the search for technical solutions to what may be political problems involves a potential threat to democracy. The evidence-based practice movement tends to assume that research can specify not only what *has* been done but also whether it was *good* or *bad* and what *should* be done; yet it is clear that this necessarily involves value judgements, which research cannot validate on its own (Hammersley 1995; Foster et al. 2000). Equally, this instrumental view of the role of social research may undermine effective practice because it privileges *research* evidence over evidence from other sources, including that arising from the experience of practitioners (see Chapter 4).

The label 'systematic review' shares not just a close association but also an important feature in common with 'evidence-based practice'. Both labels are so formulated as implicitly to disqualify alternatives. After all, what use would *unsystematic* reviews be? Who would be in favour of them? The label 'systematic review' tends to portray those who advocate other kinds of review as supporting what is patently indefensible.[22] Rhetorical sleight-of-hand is involved here: just as it turns out that the evidence-based practice movement privileges particular *kinds* of evidence, so too advocates of systematic review are in favour of a particular *sort* of systematic approach, one which is different from that employed by those who produce narrative reviews. By implicitly dismissing what they oppose, these labels operate as highly effective slogans; especially in a climate that favours the sound-bite. But in doing so they stifle productive discourse.

This rhetorical strategy reflects the wider political context. And we would be unwise to overlook the question of why systematic reviews suddenly came to be prioritised. There is a striking parallel here between the notion of explicitness that is central to systematic reviewing and the demands for transparent accountability that have become so influential within government circles and among the media. Indeed, the parallel is a functional one: the idea is that systematic reviews can allow lay people to judge for themselves which policies and practices work (see Chapter 1).

---

[22]Advocates of systematic review sometimes reject the narrative approach on the basis of what would simply be bad practice. For example, Davies describes narrative reviews as 'almost always *selective*, if not haphazard' and as often '*opportunistic*'. He also suggests that they may involve 'discarding studies that use methodologies in which the researcher has little or no interest' (Davies 2000a: 367). Similarly, Oakley (2007: 96) claims that 'most literature reviews in social science are selective, opinionated and discursive rampages through literature'.

Systematic reviews purport to make research findings 'transparent', so as to enable users to judge what works without any mediation by professionals, including researchers. In these terms, perhaps the most serious charge to be laid against the systematic review movement is that it extends the myth of the audit society (Power 1997) to research. In my view, for the reasons explained, the consequences are likely to be negative, both for social inquiry and for policymaking and practice.

9

SYSTEMATIC OR UNSYSTEMATIC, IS THAT THE QUESTION? SOME REFLECTIONS ON THE SCIENCE, ART AND POLITICS OF REVIEWING

Literature reviews can play a crucial role both within research communities and as a bridge between research and various forms of policymaking and practice. This reflects the fact that there is a need for practical use of research to take in the whole range of findings on a topic, not just the results from one or two studies. There has been an increasing tendency for the mass media to report evidence from single studies in controversial areas, particularly in the health field. This may not only be dangerous in its immediate consequences, but also – down the line – it could lead to further erosion in the public authority of scientific research.

The bridging role of reviews in facilitating the usage of research findings by policymakers and practitioners was given particular emphasis by the evidence-based practice movement. It argued not just that there have been insufficient reviews to make research findings as widely accessible as they ought to be, but also that many reviews have not been of the right kind. A contrast was drawn between *systematic* reviews and the older forms of 'traditional' or 'narrative' review (see Chapter 8). However, while the quality of reviews is certainly an important issue, as we saw there are some questions to be raised about the notion of 'systematic review' and about its claimed superiority. These start from matters of semantics but move rapidly into the substantive.

'Systematic' is a word that, in most contexts, has a positive ring to it. At face value, then, it might be interpreted as referring simply to doing the job of reviewing well, and it might be thought that everyone would be in favour of it. The only exception would be those who want to select and interpret research evidence so as to support their own pre-given views or interests, and thereby to claim scientific backing for these. It is worth pointing out, however, that a review conducted in this way would also be systematic, in an important sense: it would display what we refer to as *systematic error*. This highlights the need to give careful attention to what the word 'systematic' means, and also illustrates the fact that being systematic should not be treated as a virtue in itself – much depends upon the goal being pursued. If it is an undesirable goal then unsystematic pursuit of it might be preferable.

So we should not take the meaning, or the virtue, of being systematic in carrying out reviews at face value. Here I want to begin by exploring some of the meanings associated with reviews being 'systematic': that they involve synthesis; that they are issue-focused; and that they are 'transparent'.

'SYSTEMATIC' AS SYNTHESISING

It frequently seems to be assumed that for a review to be systematic it must involve the *synthesis* of the findings or data from the studies reviewed. This is one of the respects in which systematic reviews are believed to go beyond traditional reviews. But what is meant by 'synthesis' here?

There are several meanings of this term, as I suggested in the previous chapter, and they are not always clearly distinguished. One key metaphor is aggregation or pooling. Here, each study reviewed is to be treated as investigating a different sample of cases drawn from the same population, and what 'synthesis' implies is that these various samples can be combined to make a much bigger sample, thereby increasing the chances that the conclusions drawn are valid for the population as a whole.

This, of course, relies upon a way of thinking that is central to survey analysis in the social sciences. It is less central – though not entirely inappropriate in my view – to both experimental and qualitative research. However, applied to the task of reviewing, there are serious questions about whether data from cases studied by different researchers on different occasions – often for somewhat varying, and uncoordinated, purposes – can be pooled in the way proposed. After all, each of the studies does not simply describe the cases that it is concerned with, but also carries out some analysis designed to determine what caused what and why. As a result, there is likely to be variation between studies in what intervening and outcome variables are taken into account, how they are measured, the time period involved, the local context, and so on. So the cases do not necessarily belong to a single population. Nor is it always clear what the intended target population might be in the aggregation process. Moreover, we are not working with randomly selected samples from a population, in the way that quantitative methodology usually demands.

A second interpretation of 'synthesis', sometimes mixed up with the first, is that the various studies reviewed can be treated as replications of one another. The argument here is that, to the extent that further studies of the same problem come to the same conclusion as the first one, it can be concluded that the original findings were reliable. This is a logic that is derived from experimental research. And it is important to notice how it differs from the notion of pooling. With pooling, other things being equal and up to some point, the larger the number of studies the better, and the product is a mean effect size which, it is assumed, gives a statistical prediction of what is likely to be found on average across the population. This pooling metaphor encourages the inclusion of unpublished material or grey literature, not just peer-reviewed studies. By contrast, in principle at least, replication requires only quite a small number of studies, but these must be well conducted and they must all either support or reject the hypothesis if any definite conclusion is to be reached.

The application of this second conception of synthesis to research reviewing may be quite reasonable in principle. However, we should note that the criteria of selection here are *very* restrictive. Each study must be virtually identical in its focus and procedures, or must display systematic variation designed to test specific threats to validity. And this means that the studies must conform fairly closely to the experimental model. It might be thought that the randomised controlled trial is not so much the gold standard here as the lower limit of what can be included.

A third interpretation of 'synthesis' portrays it as the comparative analysis of existing studies with a view to the systematic development and testing of theories. The logic here is central to a great deal of research, both quantitative and qualitative. It is the very core of experimental method, but the notions of analytic induction, grounded theorising, and Qualitative Comparative Analysis also conform broadly to it (see Hammersley 1989a; Cooper et al. 2012). Moreover, in principle, there is no reason why this logic should not be applied to extant studies rather than to new data. Indeed, this is similar to the approach that Pawson advocates in proposing theory-driven systematic reviews or realist syntheses (Pawson 2001a, 2001b, 2006).

At the same time, while examining existing studies may facilitate the development of theoretical ideas, I doubt whether in most fields this will be enough to provide a rigorous test of those ideas. After all, the logic of theory development and testing is sequential: what is required to develop and test a theory changes over time as the research progresses, and often cannot be predicted in advance. As a result, the task of testing a theory rigorously will frequently require the collection of primary data, because the research that has already been done will not provide sufficient resources.[1]

A fourth interpretation of 'synthesis', one that is quite common among qualitative researchers, employs the metaphor of a mosaic or map. Here, putting together different studies means looking at how they can be combined to give us a bigger picture. In this version of synthesis, what each study contributes is distinctive. What is needed is *complementarity* not similarity. The studies that are reviewed will look at different aspects of the same phenomenon, for example they may look at different types of clinical contact between doctor and patient, at patients' experience of these kinds of clinical encounter, at the management structures within which such encounters take place, at the history of clinical practice and so on. This sort of complementarity is often central to traditional narrative reviews; and, while it is by no

---

[1]This is presumably why Freese (1980: 41) argued that 'cumulation cannot be imposed after the fact', as quoted in the previous chapter.

means unproblematic (see Hammersley et al. 1985: 48–56), I will not discuss it further here because it is marginal, at best, to most versions of systematic review.

A fifth possibility has been put forward by some qualitative researchers, who argue that synthesis can involve translation of the findings of some studies into the terms of another, thereby developing key metaphors that will facilitate future understanding of the phenomena concerned (see Noblit and Hare 1988). As far as I understand it, this 'meta-ethnography' is quite similar to what some traditional reviews have done, and it contrasts with what is usually meant by 'synthesis' in the context of systematic review. It amounts to developing a new framework that encompasses existing studies and shows these in a novel and illuminating light, or one that is more inclusive or abstract than that in which they were originally framed (see Chapter 11).

So here we have at least five different meanings that can be given to the term 'synthesis', the first two of which seem to apply to systematic review while the others do not.[2] Evidently, we need to be clear about which sort of synthesis is implied by the term 'systematic review', its justification, and why this one is to be regarded as more valuable than the others. Furthermore, it is worth noting that an important respect in which these different sorts of synthesis may vary is in terms of how far they follow a pre-determined path. Pooling and replication seem actually to *require* a fixed course. The questions to be answered must be clearly specified at the beginning of the reviewing process, and procedures are then set up to identify all the studies relevant to them. However, some other kinds of synthesis appear to involve a more inductive or developmental approach, in which the reviewer may reformulate the focus of the review in the course of doing it, perhaps quite dramatically. It seems likely that both approaches could be of value.

Over and above noting different types of synthesis, we might ask whether reviews *must always* involve synthesis, in any of these senses. Could reviewers perhaps simply make judgements about what we do and do not currently know on the basis of careful evaluation of particular studies and their findings, without employing any of the above forms of synthesis? Furthermore, reviewing can also be designed to provide methodological lessons about how we might improve the success of our inquiries in the future. This, too, does not seem to require synthesis.

To be even more provocative, we could ask whether some of these forms of synthesis actually constitute reviewing the literature at all. A few seem to be closer to actually *doing* research, rather than reviewing it.[3] For example, research synthesis as the pooling of results is close in character to analysis of secondary data, and so one might wonder why it does not go the full distance. And there is at least one form of synthesis which, as I indicated, probably cannot be done properly without relying upon supplementary collection of primary data, and whose logic is very much that of research designed to develop and test theory. So, has the distinction between primary research and reviewing the literature been obliterated here? And is this desirable?

---

[2]Incidentally, these different senses of the word 'synthesis' do not exhaust its meaning. Some years ago, Strike and Posner identified 15 kinds of synthesis, along with some forms of what they call 'quasi-synthesis' (Strike and Posner 1983).

[3]And advocates of systematic review often insist that it is a form of research.

'SYSTEMATIC' AS 'ISSUE-FOCUSED'

A second aspect of what it means for a review to be 'systematic' seems to be that it is focused on a specific issue – often, but not always, the question of whether an identified policy, practice, or technique works well, or whether it works better or worse than alternatives. This may be one useful task that reviews can pursue, but it is not the only focus they can legitimately have. Often, traditional reviews have been concerned with evaluating what is known about some whole field of inquiry. And this too is a perfectly reasonable enterprise.

To say that traditional reviews are unfocused because they do not concentrate on a specific question is like complaining that a map is of no value because it covers a wider area than the one in which we are currently interested. Here, it seems to me, instead of the systematic/unsystematic distinction, what is required is a non-evaluative typology dealing with the different kinds of focus that reviews can have, perhaps varying in something like the way that maps vary in scale; though the analogy is only partial.

At the very least, we need to distinguish between issue-focused and field-mapping reviews. The latter would start from the findings of research in a particular field, with a view to providing an adequate account of it, rather than from a set of questions (for example, about the effectiveness of a particular policy) to which an answer is required. Both kinds of review can be of value, and each can involve problems. Reviews concerned with representing the findings of a particular body of research will often be highly complex, and will nevertheless necessarily be rather selective in what is included and what is given emphasis. Moreover, for some audiences, such reviews may not address the questions that are of most concern. By contrast, reviews focusing on particular questions involve the risk that very little research will be found that is relevant, and/or there may be a tendency to engage in speculative inferences from what research is available in order to try to answer the question that is driving the review. There is also the danger that research whose relevance to the questions is not immediately apparent will be neglected.

SYSTEMATIC REVIEWS AS 'TRANSPARENT'

As I noted in Chapter 8, perhaps the most important, and distinctive, meaning of the term 'systematic' is the idea that reviewing should be done in a way that makes the procedures employed explicit. In short, the aim is for transparency. However, this too is not unproblematic. The word 'transparency' is even more obviously a hurrah word than is the term 'systematic', at least in recent times. Who could be against transparency, aside from those who have something to hide? However, questions can be raised about the idea of transparent reviews, and transparency generally. There are three points here.

First, explicitness is a matter of degree. If we look at examples of old-style narrative reviews, we find that many of them *do* tell us quite a bit about how they were carried out. It may be true that in many cases more such information was required for readers to be able to make a sound judgement about the conclusions of the review. But not all systematic reviews are likely to be perfect in this respect either.

The second issue is more fundamental. This is that there is a point beyond which it is impossible to make any activity, including reviewing, explicit. The metaphor involved in the word 'transparency' implies that *anyone* can see, or perhaps can see *through*, what is going on. In other words, it is assumed that there are no audience requirements for understanding and evaluating any activity other than possession of a pair of eyes. Yet this can never be true. Explicitness is always relative to a particular category of audience, who have some given level of background knowledge and some range of likely interests or relevances. Nothing can be *absolutely* explicit or transparent. And when we are dealing with audiences who do not share much of the background knowledge relevant to the activity concerned, as is often the case with reviews of research literature aimed at policymakers or practitioners, we often have to struggle quite hard to help them understand what is involved. Moreover, what we usually do in such circumstances is not so much make things explicit as use parallels and analogies to enable them to relate what they do not understand to what they *do* already know. In other words, the concept of transparency, and the metaphor of vision on which it relies, can be misleading.[4]

Furthermore, even when we are addressing an audience who *does* know a lot about the activity we are describing, we still may not be able to make explicit exactly *why* we did what we did, in other words to specify the rationale *in terms of rules*. This is a fundamental philosophical argument, one that was developed into what I think is an illuminating account of science by Michael Polanyi many years ago (Polanyi 1958, 1966). He argues that tacit knowledge necessarily plays a key role in scientific investigation. And if it plays a key role in science, we can be fairly sure that it would play a key role in reviewing scientific evidence as well.

This links to the final point about the notion of transparency. As we have seen, the concept of systematic review seems to imply that transparency can be achieved if the task of reviewing is formulated in terms of a set of *procedures* to be followed. But while seeking to specify the approach that will be, or has been, employed in a piece of work may be useful, it is not helpful to insist that people follow a set of procedures rigidly. This may rule out, or at least discourage, any reflection on issues that actually need attention, encouraging a rather instrumental and thoughtless orientation. And this is especially likely where very limited time is available for producing reviews, as is often the case.

In short, if one tries to reduce science to the following of explicit procedures, one runs the risk of obstructing its progress. And I suggest that, in the same way, producing reviews cannot be reduced to the following of explicit procedures: it always involves skilled judgement on the part of the reviewer, about what is and is not likely to be valid, what is and is not significant, and so on. As a result, trying to govern it by transparent rules could lead to a worsening in the quality of reviews, in some key respects, rather than to improvement. Research, like other

---

[4] See, for example, the arguments of Lakoff and Johnson 1980 about the essential role of metaphor in understanding.

forms of practice, relies upon what Aristotle referred to as phronesis (see Dunne 1997; see Chapter 4).

For example, as I have argued in earlier chapters, it is not possible to make sound judgements about the validity of particular studies wholly in abstract terms, such as according to what research design they employed. While judgements should be informed by guidelines about the strengths and weaknesses of different kinds of methodological approach, *these are only guidelines* (see Chapter 6). One reason for this is that in assessing the findings of any study we necessarily rely upon what we currently take to be sound knowledge. This is not to say that we immediately dismiss evidence that conflicts with what we currently believe, even less that we *should* do this. Indeed, the most interesting studies are, other things being equal, precisely those that challenge what we currently assume we know. My point is that if a study makes such a challenge then it needs support from strong evidence, and our judgement of that evidence will itself necessarily rely, in part, upon other things that we take to be sound knowledge. In short, there is no foundation of absolute empirical givens to which we can make ultimate appeal as evidence: we always have to rely upon background knowledge. And our judgements of the findings of a study will vary according to their relationship to what we take to be already known.[5]

WHAT 'SYSTEMATIC/UNSYSTEMATIC' OBSCURES

The final points I want to make concern aspects of the task of reviewing which the systematic/unsystematic distinction neglects; though I am not suggesting that those involved in systematic reviewing are unaware of them.

Above all, here it is necessary to remember that reviews of research addressed to audiences outside the research community, perhaps more than others, are a matter of art and politics as much as of science. As to art, I do not mean that we should explore presenting reviews in rhyming couplets, as dialogues, or as fictions. What I mean is that, as I indicated earlier, whenever we address a particular audience we have to take account of what we can assume they already know, what they would and would not be interested in, and perhaps also what they might misinterpret.

Of course, in much writing, including the writing of reviews, we do not know for certain who the specific audience will be. And often there is not a single target audience. Instead, the review is seen as a resource that could be used by many different audiences. This is a perfectly reasonable approach to writing a review.

---

[5]The view I have presented here is more or less that offered by Susan Haack in her book *Evidence and Inquiry*, in which she uses the crossword puzzle as an illuminating metaphor for the logic of scientific investigation. She points out that we have to judge potential answers in crosswords both in terms of how well they fit the clue (equivalent to empirical evidence in the case of science) *and* according to whether their letters match those of the other words we have already filled in (which corresponds, in the case of science, to what is taken to be already known) (Haack 2009). Another important source, this time taking a more contextualist line, is Williams (Michael) 2001.

However, there is an important distinction between this sort of review and reviews that are targeted at specific types of audience. It seems to me that the gap that has to be jumped between the world of researchers and that of particular groups of policymakers and practitioners is sometimes so great that considerable bridge-building is required. And I insist that building bridges is as much an art as a science: it depends upon skill, judgement, and sensitivity to what might be important in the particular situation. What I am saying here is that to think of a review simply in terms of whether or not it is systematic does not take any account of who the audience is and whether it is appropriate for that audience.[6]

Furthermore, some audiences may not find the standard systematic review very helpful. Or, if they do, they may judge it useful for the wrong reason. In trying to explicate what the term 'systematic review' means here I have concentrated on what *researchers* mean by it. By contrast, for some policymakers it might mean a review which provides a clear recommendation, in the right direction, backed up by impressive-looking scientific paraphernalia that is guaranteed to dissuade journalists from asking too many questions. If a review matches this specification, does that make it appropriate?

Having just talked about what audiences find most helpful, and suggested that some reviews ought to be designed for particular audiences, we should ask: what limits must be placed upon this? At the beginning of this chapter I drew an evaluative distinction between reviews that aim at presenting all the relevant evidence, and at making reliable judgements about its validity and implications, and those that select and interpret research evidence so as to support a pre-given view or interest, thereby giving the illusion that it has scientific backing. While I believe that this distinction is very important, I do not think we can simply condemn what might be called the politically motivated use of research evidence. We need to take account of the politics of how reviews are received and read by audiences. The reception of reviews is often driven by audiences' current preoccupations, and guided by relatively fixed preconceptions. This is almost inevitable because of the very nature and pressures of policymaking, and the same goes for many other kinds of occupational practice.

I should underline that I do not think that it is the proper task of the researcher to try to use research evidence to promote or defend some particular policy or practice. That would be to exceed the authority of research. However, I *do* think that it is the responsibility of the researcher who is preparing a review for a specific audience to anticipate the interpretations and evaluations which that audience might leap to, and to point out that what is involved *is* a leap, and is not necessarily justified. An example of this comes from a traditional review of evidence about the educational performance of ethnic minority pupils (Gillborn and Gipps 1996). The authors were aware that, if they used the term 'underachievement' to refer to those cases where the average level of performance of a particular ethnic minority is lower than that of ethnic majority pupils, readers might assume that this results from the distinctive character of that ethnic minority rather than, for example, from the way that these

---

[6]In a recent article, Gough (2007) provides a typology of reviews, but a tendentious one that centres on a single ideal of being 'explicitly systematic' (p. 216).

pupils are treated by schools. And they sought to guard against this danger, though their efforts met with only limited success (Gillborn 1998; Hammersley 2006; see also Foster and Hammersley 1998).

Up to now I have assumed that reviews of research evidence are produced by researchers. But this is not always the case. For one thing, researchers are not always *only* researchers: very often they are also practitioners of some other relevant occupational activity. And they may produce the review wearing the hat of practitioner rather than that of researcher. Or, more likely, they will wear both hats, without being clear about under which set of auspices they are speaking at any particular time.

For me, this distinction between a researcher's review of research evidence and that carried out by a policymaker or practitioner, or someone assisting them, is perhaps the most basic of all. One reason for this is that some reviews of the latter kind may well be designed to highlight particular evidence that the author believes has been overlooked, and which points in a particular policy direction that, on the basis of practical experience, he or she believes ought to be given more attention. Such reviewing is not necessarily illegitimate in practical terms; indeed, it is probably an inevitable part of how people in the public sphere routinely read and use research, even though it is not acceptable for research purposes. We must not pretend that policymakers and practitioners can or ought to operate in the manner that is expected of researchers.

So, it is important that researchers do not expect that their work, including their reviews of research evidence, will be employed by policymakers or practitioners in exactly the same manner that researchers would (or ought to) use them. Policymaking and professional practice are not the same as research, they do not call for the same cognitive or ethical orientation. This is because they are not solely or even primarily concerned with producing sound knowledge, but rather with bringing about desirable practical outcomes, and this requires practical wisdom not just valid evidence. It seems to me that *some* accounts of evidence-based practice assume that policymakers and practitioners could act in more or less the same way as researchers are supposed to do: carefully considering all the alternatives, weighing the evidence available and searching for further evidence where it is not, suspending judgement until sufficient evidence is available, and so on. The conditions in which most policymakers and practitioners work do not allow this, most of the time. Of course, I am not saying that policymakers and practitioners should not draw on research evidence, even less that they need not take care in interpreting and evaluating all sources of evidence. My point is that they cannot do this in exactly the same way, nor to the same extent, as can researchers. Indeed, were they to try to act in the same manner as researchers they would probably do their work less well (see Chapter 2).

CONCLUSION

I have argued that the contrast between systematic and unsystematic reviews is unhelpful in some respects. For one thing, the term 'systematic' seems to be used to mean different things, and not all of them are unquestionably good. I noted that systematic reviews synthesise data or findings, but that what is meant by 'synthesis' is open to diverse interpretation. I also observed that the notion of systematic review tends to privilege reviews that have a specific focus on some type of policy or program, rather than reviews that summarise what is known in a particular field of inquiry. Yet, both types are legitimate. In addition, I questioned the notion of transparency, which is perhaps the most central idea behind systematic reviews. I argued that full transparency is impossible and that, beyond a certain point, the attempt to make reviewing transparent, through reducing it to procedures, may often worsen the quality of the reviews generated. Finally, I pointed to some important aspects of reviewing that the distinction between systematic and unsystematic reviews obscures, concerned with the art and politics of the task.

If we are to improve our understanding of research reviews and the functions they can serve, we need to move away from simplistic evaluative contrasts. A better understanding of the different purposes and audiences to which reviews might be directed is required, and also a more sophisticated and defensible understanding of the difficult methodological issues involved, and the options available for dealing with them.

10

THE INTERPRETIVE ATTACK ON THE TRADITIONAL REVIEW

Criticism of 'traditional' reviews of research has not only come from advocates of systematic reviewing. For example, some qualitative researchers have argued for what they call 'interpretive' reviews, challenging the character and assumptions of more conventional approaches.[1] Where systematic reviewing is based on ideas that are intrinsic to much quantitative methodology, interpretive reviewing draws on methodological ideas that are common today among qualitative researchers, especially those travelling under banners such as interpretivism, constructionism, 'critical' inquiry, and post-structuralism (see Hammersley 2012b).

In a key article introducing the notion of interpretive review, Eisenhart (1998) treats its functions as similar to those she sees as characteristic of interpretive research generally. First of all, the aim should be to reveal 'something surprising, startling or new' in a way that 'disrupts conventional understanding, or, in the vocabulary of ethnography, that "makes the familiar strange" ...' (Eisenhart 1998: 392). In other words, the aim is to challenge 'cultural complacency' (p. 394).[2] As this makes clear, emphasis falls on the imagination and interpretive insight of the reviewer, rather than on any attempt to attain an objective perspective. Part of the motivation for this orientation is that traditional literature reviews are dull (p. 391). The key sensibility here appears to be aesthetic, and a rather modernist one at that, focused on 'the shock of the new' (Hughes 1991). As we shall see, the notion of research as progressively building knowledge is rejected, being replaced by this idea that qualitative inquiry requires researchers to generate novel perspectives.

---

[1] Interpretive reviews are not to be confused with 'critical interpretive syntheses'. On the latter, see Dixon-Woods, Kirk et al. 2005, Dixon-Woods, Cavers et al. 2006.

[2] For a somewhat similar view applied to formulating research questions, see Alvesson and Sandberg 2013.

Another requirement is that interpretive reviews expose the logics of different perspectives, or multiple ways of understanding the world (Eisenhart 1998: 393). Thus, Eisenhart argues that an essential requirement for producing such reviews is a willingness to suspend one's assumptions in the face of discrepant points of view. And she sees this as serving to improve communication and understanding across human groups. At the same time, she believes that interpretive reviews must be aimed at having an *impact* on audiences, rather than simply informing them, and that it should involve the promotion of particular political or moral values:

> The authors write with the intent to increase the chances that their stories will inspire empathy, interest, and understanding (rather than dislike, dismissal, or distrust) in readers. They also write with conspicuous morals or politics; they take positions on public affairs and hope to influence public thinking and action. (Eisenhart 1998: 395)

The aim of interpretive reviews, then, is to 'disrupt conventional assumptions and help us to reconfigure new, more inclusive and more promising perspectives on human views and actions' (p. 397). At one point, Eisenhart illustrates what she has in mind through a brief discussion of a novel in which there is a story about a boy from a rural black community who grows up to become a social scientist and comes back to carry out a study of that community.[3] In doing this he adopts a theoretical perspective and employs 'objective ethnographic methods'. The result is that he fails to understand his own home community; and, furthermore, in the process reinforces 'well-known stereotypes of rural blacks', so that 'his findings would add strength to theories of cultural deficiency …' (p. 396). This makes clear that the criteria of evaluation to be deployed in assessing interpretive research, and therefore interpretive reviews, are practical and political, as well as hermeneutic and aesthetic.[4] Where in the case of systematic reviews the aim is to have a beneficial effect on policymaking and practice, through supplying knowledge about 'what works', here there is also a concern with 'impact' but this time the aim is to challenge common stereotypes and prevailing inequalities.

AGAINST 'STACKING UP KNOWLEDGE'

Eisenhart contrasts what is required for interpretive reviews with the more conventional notion of research reviews as 'stories about stone walls' (p. 394), by which she means accounts that document how existing knowledge 'stacks up'. Instead, she calls for 'reviews that offer surprising and enriching perspectives on meanings and circumstances', reviews that 'would have to shake things up, break down barriers and cause things (or thinking) to expand' (p. 394). So, rather than settling

---

[3]The novel is Naylor's (1988) *Mama Day*, and Eisenhart appeals to Heshusius's (1994) interpretation of the implications of this story for the 'subjective' character of qualitative research.

[4]For similar views about the evaluative criteria appropriate to qualitative research, see Smith and Hodkinson 2005. See also Hammersley 2008e, 2009a, b and Smith and Hodkinson 2009.

matters, compacting knowledge down to eliminate the gaps, which seems to be implied by the image of the wall, interpretive reviews 'should be more like ground swells: they need to heave up "what we already learned" (the wall) ...; they would reveal previously hidden or unexpected possibilities (i.e., lay bare the wall's supports and components or transform its shape). They would create a new but temporary order (stasis) for those things which were disrupted' (p. 394). In summary, 'reviews-as-groundswells wouldn't give readers stories of walls; they would give us stories that startle us with what we have failed to notice about a wall and the possibilities for new thinking that arise from different ways of viewing or using it and its parts' (p. 395).

So, Eisenhart is challenging the idea that, through research, knowledge gradually accumulates into a body of established findings that has a wall-like structure, with the task of each new study being to add another brick; and she questions the assumption that the purpose of reviews is to survey the architecture of what has been built so far. What she is challenging here is, of course, very much the picture of knowledge accumulation assumed by meta-analysis and systematic reviews (see Cooper and Hedges 1994: 4), but also one that is shared more widely. Instead, she views the function of both interpretive studies and interpretive reviews as to undermine or unsettle existing knowledge; perhaps to do some new building but always with the recognition that what is produced can only be temporary, destined to be overturned in a future upheaval.

There are parallels here with Kuhn's influential challenge to older views about the cumulative nature of scientific knowledge.[5] He claims that the history of natural science is punctuated by revolutions in which the whole basis on which previous work was carried out is overturned. Furthermore, the task of bringing about a revolution, and finding an alternative paradigm, necessarily relies upon imagination, interpretation, and judgement.

However, there are also illuminating differences between the positions of Eisenhart and Kuhn, over and above the fact that the first is concerned with social inquiry and the second with natural science. Kuhn sees mature scientific research as operating most of the time within the framework of a single paradigm, tackling the puzzles that it throws up, and seeking to develop knowledge within that paradigm rather than aiming to challenge it. Given this, during these periods of 'normal science' the traditional form of review would seem to be entirely appropriate.

Equally important, Kuhn argues that when a new paradigm takes over from an old one it must be able to explain what the previous paradigm could explain and also resolve the anomalies it faced. So there is still a notion of progress in the development of knowledge built into Kuhn's position: later paradigms are viewed as superior to earlier ones. By contrast, the value of the new perspectives that Eisenhart sees qualitative research and interpretive reviews as producing seem to be entirely contingent and local in character. Moreover, their value is to be assessed more broadly than in the narrow cognitive terms outlined by Kuhn.

In some respects Eisenhart's view of the nature of inquiry is also close to that of Popper (1963). He was certainly opposed to the view that scientific inquiry builds up

---

[5]See Kuhn 1970. Useful discussions of Kuhn's position are to be found in: Hoyningen-Huene 1993; Bird 2000; Sharrock and Read 2002.

facts about the world. Indeed, there are questions about whether, for Popper, the body of scientific knowledge can be any more than a set of hypotheses that have not yet been falsified (Stove 1982). For him, the task of the scientist is to engage in continual criticism. However, while for him inquiry always begins with the generation of bold hypotheses, he also stresses the need to subject these to the most rigorous possible test.

By contrast, Eisenhart appears to regard the value of the new interpretations put forward by interpretive work mainly in terms of their 'challenging' character, and their capacity to broaden perspectives so as to recognise a wider range of possibilities. She writes:

> Isn't it conceivable that were we to take … two accounts … and consider each of them with respect to their logic, contexts of production and use, and potential for improving communication across social boundaries, that we might be pleasantly surprised to find that both have something important to contribute to a new understanding …? We might also be surprised to find that *together* they enable us to grasp many more possibilities – for thought, action, and change – than either one alone. (p. 397)

While there is an emphasis on the value of newness and breadth here, there is little suggestion of progressive knowledge *development*. We are also not told why 'grasping many more possibilities' is desirable, or even why doing this would improve 'communication and understanding across human groups', which, as we have seen, Eisenhart regards as a key aim of interpretive research (p. 392).

OTHER PERSPECTIVES ON INTERPRETIVE AND QUALITATIVE REVIEWS

Eisenhart's article was prompted by a call from the then editors of the *Review of Educational Research* who were keen to generate discussion about the forms that reviews of research can take (Graue and Grant 1998), and there were two responses to her piece (Meacham 1998; Schwandt 1998). The editors of this journal made a later, similar call for papers in 1999 (Graue and Grant 1999), and several were published, again mainly coming from the direction of qualitative researchers (Apple 1999; Baker 1999; Gordon 1999; Lather 1999; Livingston 1999; and Popkewitz 1999). While these generally made no explicit reference to Eisenhart's earlier article or the responses to it, the positions they took once again mounted a challenge against more traditional forms of reviewing.

The initial responses to Eisenhart were largely supportive, though Meacham (1998: 402) did accuse her of 'othering' the researched. Thus, Schwandt (1998: 410) concurs with the desire to find an 'antidote' to 'terminally boring reviews'. And all of the contributors reject the conventional view that the task of reviews is 'collecting and organizing the results of previous studies so as to produce a composite of what we have already learned about a particular topic' (Schwandt 1998: 409). As Schwandt points out, this view assumes that 'knowledge accumulates within a field', and he claims that it also presupposes that 'understanding can be built up piece-by-piece, brick-by-brick, eventually yielding something like a more complete, thorough, and therefore, trustworthy understanding which, in turn, can be more confidently applied to solving a problem of a particular kind' (p. 409). He sees this vision of knowledge accumulation as deriving from the biomedical model, and as exemplified in 'systematic review' and 'integrative research reviews and meta-analyses' (p. 409). Against this, Schwandt emphasises the role of interpretation in reviews of qualitative research literatures: 'Reviewing is an interpretive undertaking insofar as it is an effort to make sense of … studies and to establish their meaning'. In the context of this, he argues that research is only properly intelligible as a form of praxis, 'a kind of morally informed and morally committed action that is guided by ethical criteria immanent within the practice itself' (p. 410).

The later discussions were also aligned with Eisenhart's opposition to more conventional views about the proper nature and function of literature reviews, though they go beyond this. Thus, Livingston (1999: 10) starts from rejection of the idea of reviewing as 'stocktaking', suggesting instead that the aim should be to *recast* 'both the academic literature and the lived'. What she means by 'the lived' here is 'that location of social relations which mediates the visceral recognition, reckoning, and witness of our at once layered and discursive-material experiences of living' (p. 10). For Livingston what is required is an approach that recognises the 'critical' function of research in understanding and changing lived reality, this having implications both for the kind of knowledge produced and for the relationship of researcher with researched, and of reviewer to what is reviewed.

Where traditional understandings of the review process assume that research is a distinctive field of activity, differentiated from other aspects of life, Livingston wants reviews to recast this background, as well as the relationship between researcher/reviewer and the wider society. One aspect of this is to change assumptions about what sorts of knowledge are to be privileged, for example by valorising forms of understanding and experience that are currently downgraded or subjugated in society. At the same time, she believes that there must be acknowledgment of the limits to researchers' understanding of these. In other words, the authority claimed for research must be tempered. The purpose of reviews, from this point of view, is simultaneously to re-position or reconstitute the relationship between researchers and society, and more specifically between research knowledge and marginalised forms of understanding, while at the same time conceptualising the socio-political structures operating within and outside the academy. As she comments, reviews must be sensitive to 'the relationship between the conditions for living and the conditions for thinking, writing and producing a review' (p. 14).

In these ways, Livingston radicalises one of the central points that Eisenhart makes when she discusses how through documenting others' experience qualitative research can 'force [us] to recognize the cultural *arbitrariness* of [our] taken-for-granted view[s]' (p. 393 emphasis added). Here Eisenhart was drawing on Heshusius's (1994) challenge to the idea that using 'objective' methods can allow us to understand human social life. Also picking up on this idea, Lather (1999) emphasises that the apparently 'neutral' character of reviews is deceptive, that they 'in effect police, produce, and constitute a field'. She emphasises post-structuralism's concern with 'how we might invent ourselves into "the surprise of what is not yet possible in the histories of the spaces in which we find ourselves" (Rajchman, 1991, p. 163)' (p. 2). She suggests the adoption of a 'non-mastery approach', challenging the positioning of the reviewer as 'the one who knows' or 'the expert in the field' (p. 4). At the same time, like Livingston, she sees an important function for reviews as 'a critically useful interpretation and unpacking of a problematic that situates the work historically and methodologically' (p. 3). So she insists that the reviewer must explicitly locate her or himself 'as an invested knower in the work of reviewing, implicating oneself in the process, and taking responsibility in the critique and its cultural reception' (p. 3).

Meacham (1998) had earlier exposed some of these tensions within Eisenhart's account: between an older interpretivism, committed to documenting real phenomena in their own terms, thereby implying distance between observer and observed – and, Meacham suggests, hierarchy too – and a form of constructionism that rules out any such venture because all accounts *constitute* the phenomena they 'represent'. He too emphasises that reviews reflect the character, culture, and social location of the writer. Echoing the claims of Eisenhart and Heshusius in their appeal to Naylor's novel, he argues that, if those outside the mainstream, for example African Americans, adopt the perceptual habits of the research community they 'become blind to [their] own culture and history' (p. 403). So, there is an ethical and political issue of complicity: 'do I voluntarily render myself invisible to conform to traditions of inquiry?', 'to what extent do I accommodate the perceptual habits of the main-stream reader?' or 'do I confront the reader with a picture based on alternative spatial and conceptual arrangements which are contrary to the mainstream perspective? (pp. 403–4). Here, prevailing 'traditions of inquiry', including traditional forms of review-ing, are identified as expressions of the dominant Western culture, and the forms of socio-political organisation that underpin it.

All these authors are opposed to what they see as the objectivism of traditional views of research and reviewing, where knowledge is treated as independent of the knower, and of the wider society within which it has been produced. Instead they argue that knowledge must be viewed as partial, socio-historically constituted, and necessarily personal in character, rather than simply as more or less accurately representing phenomena that are independent of it. Thus, for some of these critics, traditional forms of reviewing entail complicity in an objectivist conception of social research that is implicated in Western capitalism and neo-imperialism.

From this distinctive point of view, reviewing the literature should not be seen as a form of under-labouring: a relatively well-defined task concerned with taking stock of the current state of primary research in a field, identifying any significant gaps there may be, exploring how current understandings might be reformulated, and what practical implications could be drawn from this knowledge, for instance in order to prepare the way for further research. Instead, it has a grander role, one that is either indistinguishable from that of primary research, as in the case of Eisenhart, or, as with many of the other commentators, one that involves a reflexive analysis of the research field in terms of its socio-cultural constitution, in the manner of ideol-ogy critique, archaeology/genealogy, or deconstruction. Here the concern is with how the field is related to struggles both within the academy (Apple 1999; Gordon 1999), and outside of it, over 'redistribution and recognition' (Livingston 1999: 14; Popkewitz 1999). In short, the task of reviews is to open up to question the whole functioning of a particular research field, and of the society it is assumed to serve and reproduce.

ASSESSING THE INTERPRETIVE CRITIQUE

In evaluating these arguments, we can accept, to start with, that it is desirable that reviews of research literature are interesting rather than dull, and that (generally speaking) they should develop a line of argument rather than simply reporting the conclusions of the various studies they cover. Similarly, reviewers must be prepared to put forward interpretations that challenge conventional views, both those of the wider public and those of other researchers. As a result, reviews may well undermine what was previously taken to be well-founded knowledge, rather than simply giving an account of it. It is also true that they must draw on judgement and creativity, and on background knowledge and skill. Finally, it is important to recognise the role of reviews in shaping ideas about the nature of the field reviewed, rather than thinking of them simply as mirrors; and so the critics are right that reviews can amount to 'surveillance' or 'policing', and may therefore carry dangers.

Despite these points of agreement, it seems to me that these critiques of traditional reviewing are nevertheless exaggerated and seriously misconceived in important respects. Thus, while reviews can, like primary studies, challenge conventional views, they must not be motivated by 'an intent' (Eisenhart 1998: 392) to do this. Any challenge should arise indirectly, as a consequence of the review process, rather than being its motivating force. Furthermore, by no means every review will produce such a challenge, nor are those that do this automatically superior to those that provide illuminating accounts of existing knowledge in a field. Straining to be 'critical' or 'challenging' will rarely be desirable.

Equally, while it is necessary for reviewers to employ creative judgement, they must also assess the validity and value of what they propose. In writing reviews, no less than in carrying out primary research, the aim is to develop *knowledge* not simply to present novel points of view. As with advocacy of systematic reviews, there are signs here that goals are being displaced. For instance, contrary to Eisenhart, 'making the familiar strange' is a *means for producing knowledge*, it is not itself the purpose of research. Moreover, there is an important sense in which the reviewer should be speaking on behalf of the relevant research community, and must take seriously the responsibility that this implies – making clear what is and is not generally accepted as valid within that community.

My arguments here will not, of course, convince the critics. The reason for this is that quite fundamental differences in view are involved: about the nature and purpose of, indeed about the justification for, social inquiry. In significant ways these critiques of traditional reviews draw on 'critical' and post-structuralist traditions of thought that have become very influential in some areas of social science over the past few decades, especially amongst qualitative researchers. These traditions challenge many of the basic assumptions of conventional social science.[6]

While these radical traditions are neither internally coherent nor mutually compatible,[7] both break with a conception of research as a differentiated form of activity with its own independent goal and function, properly devoted exclusively to the production of knowledge. Indeed, the possibility and legitimacy of expert knowledge is sometimes itself challenged, and the goal of research is viewed in political, and occasionally also in aesthetic, terms. Of course, the idea that research should engage with political and social practice is by no means restricted to these traditions – it is also characteristic of those supporting the notion of research for evidence-based practice, and of positivism more generally. However, there is a crucial difference: as I indicated, many of the critics reject the idea that current Western governance is enlightened and progressive, and therefore do not believe that its policies should be made more effective. Furthermore, they regard 'objectivism' in social science as serving Western capitalism and neo-imperialism. And, under the influence of post-structuralism, 'Enlightenment values' themselves often come to be questioned, including the possibility and worth of knowledge.[8]

While I have sympathy for some of the political commitments underpinning these traditions, I find the arguments that their supporters put forward about the character and role of social science unconvincing and ultimately incoherent – and for me coherent understanding *is* an essential goal. It is false to assume that science or research is simply an expression and ideological tool of Western society: the capacity for reasoning, insistence on the need for clarity and evidence in argument, the concern with objectivity (in the sense of avoiding error), and so on, are not distinctively Western, nor are they intrinsically functional for Western capitalism and neo-imperialism.[9] The fact that social science can, and has, served these social forces in some respects does not mean that it is uniquely tied to them, though I am not suggesting that it is intrinsically subversive of them either. Furthermore, it is worth reiterating that, if pushed very far, the views of the critics about the nature and possibility of knowledge become self-undermining, and therefore cannot but result either in political quietism (Habermas 1987) or in irrational support for extremism on the Left or the Right; Foucault's politics might be cited as an example here – not only his links with Maoism but also his attitude towards the Iranian revolution (Afary and Anderson 2005).

---

[6]For arguments against these approaches, see Hammersley 1992, 1995, 2000b, 2008c.

[7]The post-structuralist tradition shares the modes of critique characteristic of 'critical' research but extends this to the kinds of meta-narrative and comprehensive socio-political perspective that critical theorists have often claimed to supply. Baker's (1999) examination of the notion of 'voice' illustrates this.

[8]Perhaps the most central feature of much that goes under the heading of post-structuralism or postmodernism – terms which it is now barely worth distinguishing – is rejection of any commitment to seeking, or any expectation of finding, coherent understanding. Instead, the aim is to subvert, playfully and/or politically, that very commitment.

[9]Following Marx, it is even possible to raise questions about whether capitalism and Western imperialism should be viewed in entirely negative terms (see Avineri 1968).

In my view, then, an excessively broad view of the purpose of social inquiry, and of the task of reviewing, underpins these critiques: one that includes bringing about socio-political change of some sort, and/or challenging the fundamental assumptions of Western thought. I have argued elsewhere that while these projects may be desirable there is no reason why social science should be subordinated to them. Indeed, there are very good reasons why it should not be (Hammersley 1995, 2008c). One is that this involves a considerable overestimate of the likely political impact of social research. And it is no accident that the politics associated with these traditions frequently verges on the naïve (see Hammersley 2012c). Thus, we get woolly expressions of what is desirable, such as Eisenhart's appeals to inspiring 'empathy, interest, and understanding (rather than dislike, dismissal, or distrust)' (p. 395), 'more inclusive and more promising perspectives on human views and actions' or 'grasping many more possibilities' (p. 397) and Meacham's (1998: 404) declaration of commitment to 'progressive cultural change'. Another reason to reject what is proposed by these critics is that it diverts energy and commitment away from the distinctive obligation of researchers: to develop knowledge, a task that is very demanding in itself (see Rule 1997). Furthermore, the sort of activism and constructionism to which the critics are committed frequently leads to bias and abuse of the authority of research (Hammersley 2000b, 2004).

Another key theme in these critiques is the idea that knowledge is always partial and situated. This can be understood in a variety of ways, some of them legitimate, others not. It is true that all knowledge is fallible, and one potential source of error is the personal and social characteristics of the researcher/reviewer. But these characteristics are also a source of insight, and this can be recognised without lapsing into a reflexive scepticism or relativism that undermines the very possibility of research, and also of any effective politics; a position to which some of these critics come perilously close, if they do not actually embrace. Similarly, while all knowledge consists of answers to some particular set of questions, and while different questions will produce different knowledge, this does not imply the kind of pseudo-sceptical position that is involved in referring to cultural interpretations, including those of researchers, as 'arbitrary'.

The approach of these critics is fundamentally at odds not just with the assumptions underpinning proposals for 'systematic review' but also with the actual reviewing practices of most qualitative researchers. However, any attempt to address, let alone to resolve, the disagreements I have identified is fraught with difficulty. This is not just because of the depth of the differences in view but also because there are defences built into some of the traditions informing these critiques that serve to disqualify external challenges. In the case of 'critical' research, criticism is frequently dismissed as simply representing dominant interests, whether defined in terms of social class, gender, ethnicity/race, ability/disability, sexual orientation or whatever. Meanwhile, as already noted, post-structuralism tends towards an epistemological scepticism that treats any claims to knowledge (apart from its own) as not only false but also as amounting to a strategy of domination. Both these tendencies block attempts at dialogue.

CONCLUSION

Just as advocates of systematic reviewing have identified weaknesses in how 'traditional' reviews of research literatures are carried out – in terms of failure to cover all the relevant literature, or to adopt a sufficiently critical approach to methodology – so interpretive critics highlight weaknesses in current practice, albeit very different ones. They challenge what they see as the boring character of traditional reviews, and argue that the aim instead should be to surprise and challenge. They charge that too cumulative a picture of the development of knowledge is adopted, one that fails to give due weight to discontinuities and to the need to question prevailing views. They also argue that insufficient attention has been paid to how reviews relate to the preconceptions, attitudes and social locations of researchers and reviewers, and to the functioning of social research within society.

As with advocacy of systematic reviews, there is much to be learned from these critics but there are assumptions built into their arguments that are open to serious question. And, ultimately, what is proposed amounts to abandoning any distinctive rationale for social research, and any specific function for reviews of research literatures.

11

WHAT IS QUALITATIVE SYNTHESIS AND WHY DO IT?

Reviews of relevant research literature have long been a key feature of qualitative inquiry, both as components of research reports and as stand-alone articles or occasionally even whole books.[1] By contrast, the notion of qualitative synthesis is a more recent development (Noblit and Hare 1988; Dixon Woods et al 2004; Thorne et al. 2004; Pope et al. 2007; Sandelowski and Barroso 2007; Howell Major and Savin-Baden 2010; Hannes and Lockwood 2012).[2] In large part, this was stimulated by the growing influence of statistical meta-analysis and systematic reviews, and consequent pressure to find ways of integrating findings from qualitative research, and also of combining them with quantitative data, with a view to serving policymaking and practice. This pressure was especially strong in the health field, but has been felt in other areas as well. Indeed, one of the earliest and most influential versions of qualitative synthesis, meta-ethnography, was developed in the field of education, in the context of a multi-site project on the implementation and effects of desegregation in US schools (Noblit and Hare 1988).

Statistical meta-analysis, systematic reviews, and qualitative synthesis have all been promoted as major improvements on 'traditional' or 'narrative' reviews, the latter being dismissed as 'subjective', 'unsystematic', 'lacking rigour' etc. In the context of quantitative

---

[1]There have, however, been disputes about what form they should take, as we have seen in previous chapters.

[2]Schofield (1990: 221-6) identifies Yin and Heald's (1975) 'case survey method' as an early form of 'generalising through aggregating or comparing case studies'. She also sees Ragin's Qualitative Comparative Method as serving this purpose. Dixon-Woods et al. (2007: 415-16) report that: 'Although there is growing interest in how qualitative research can be synthesized for purposes of informing policy and practice, we have identified only a modest body of literature published between 1988 and 2004 that has used explicit methods for synthesis'. At the same time, they note that it is 'rapidly expanding', a trend that has continued since they wrote this.

research, it was argued that it is anomalous for the statistical rigour that is characteristic of primary research not to be applied to the task of reviewing previous studies and drawing conclusions on the basis of them. Thus, meta-analysis was developed as a means of analysing existing studies so as to identify the effect of some treatment, policy or practice (see Glass 1976; Rosenthal 1984). The aim, then, was to produce summary measures of findings from multiple studies, usually in the form of a weighted average effect size accompanied by a confidence interval (Smith and Glass 1977; Hedges and Olkin 1985; Hunter and Schmidt 2004). Thus, even though the question addressed by any meta-analysis is broadly the same as that of each primary study it includes, the task is to go beyond simply summarising the findings of separate studies one-by-one. It is, in Glass's (2005) terms, a 'statistical analysis of statistical analyses'.

It is also significant that the fields in which meta-analysis and systematic review developed often contained a large number of studies dealing with the same issue, so that finding some means of integrating their findings was felt to be a priority, given that any account reporting them all would be very lengthy. For example, Glass (1976: 4) writes: 'The armchair literature review in which one cites a couple of dozen studies from the obvious journals can't do justice to the voluminous literature of educational research that we now confront.' Indeed, a central emphasis in these new developments has concerned the need to engage in exhaustive searches for relevant material and to include all of this in the synthesis, with 'traditional' reviews being dismissed as selective, and therefore biased, and as lacking rigour because the selection process is left implicit. At the same time, there have also been disagreements about whether all relevant studies should be included, or only those judged to lie above some threshold of likely validity as regards research design. Whereas most systematic reviews adopt such a threshold, this is by no means universal in meta-analysis. Thus, Glass (1976: 4) writes:

> my experience over the past two years with a body of literature on which I will report in a few minutes leads me to wonder whether well-designed and poorly-designed experiments give very different findings. At any rate, I believe the difference to be so small that to integrate research results by eliminating the 'poorly done' studies is to discard a vast amount of important data.

There has also sometimes been an insistence that synthesis is a form of research in its own right, not just a means of reviewing the literature, the aim of this being to heighten its status in the academic world.

The promotion of systematic reviews followed on the development not just of meta-analysis, but also of other forms of more 'rigorous' reviewing procedures, such as 'integrative review' (Cooper 1984, 2012) and 'best evidence synthesis' (Slavin 1986). While systematic reviews often employ meta-analysis, they need not do so. Indeed, in recent years, there have been attempts to incorporate qualitative evidence into systematic reviews (Dixon-Woods et al. 2004; Dixon-Woods, Agarwal et al. 2005; Dixon-Woods, Bonas et al. 2006; Harden 2006).

It is important to recognise, however, that the assumptions about the nature of social research underpinning systematic reviews are those that are characteristic of quantitative rather than qualitative methodology (see Chapter 8). Furthermore, generally speaking, this type of reviewing was developed with a very specific type of research in mind: that which is aimed at producing information about whether particular treatments, policies, or practices are effective. This involves distinctive assumptions about the relationship between research findings and policymaking/practice, ones that are less common among qualitative than quantitative researchers (see Hammersley 2002: ch. 4). Synthesis of quantitative research also seems to be tied to a particular vision of the development of knowledge in a scientific field. Cooper et al. (2009: 4) outline this as follows:

> Like the artisans who construct a building from blueprints, bricks, and mortar, scientists contribute to a common edifice called knowledge. Theorists provide the blueprints and researchers collect the data that are the bricks. To extend the analogy further we might say that research synthesists are the bricklayers and hodcarriers of the science guild. It is their job to stack the bricks according to the plan and apply the mortar that holds the structure together.

This is not an account that fits easily with many views of the nature of qualitative research (see Chapter 9); but it is also at odds with some influential views of scientific method (Popper 1959; Kuhn 1970; Willer and Willer 1973; Freese 1980; Haack 2003).

While responding to the development of meta-analysis and systematic reviewing, most of those involved in developing modes of qualitative synthesis have also emphasised the need for it to be sensitive to the distinctive character of qualitative work, despite some disagreement about what this might mean. Where some suggest that 'it is increasingly being argued that … paradigmatic divisions are overstated, and that they can be ignored (Bryman 1988)' (Dixon-Woods et al. 2004: 2), others insist on the significance of these divisions (Noblit and Hare 1988; Thorne et al. 2004).

The idea that, previously, reviews have been inadequate because they have not involved the application of the rigorous methods employed in primary research has been adopted not just by advocates of meta-analysis but also by many of those advocating qualitative synthesis, along with the idea that synthesis is itself a kind of research. Here, though, it is of course qualitative methods that are to supply the rigour, not statistical analysis. Thus, proponents of qualitative synthesis have frequently employed one or another method from primary qualitative research methodology as a basis for carrying out syntheses, such as grounded theorising (Kearney 2001), meta-matrices (Miles and Huberman 1994; McNaughton 2000), componential analysis (Sandelowski and Barroso 2007: 119–201), or framework analysis (Dixon-Woods 2011). As with meta-analysis and systematic reviewing, the aim of qualitative synthesis is usually formulated as going beyond summarising the findings of individual studies to produce some integrative result, and sometimes there is also emphasis on carrying out exhaustive searches and employing 'transparent' procedures of synthesis.[3]

An important starting point in assessing proposals for qualitative synthesis is to consider what it is aimed at producing, and what this adds over and above the

---

[3]However, Dixon-Woods et al. 2007 argue that most reports fail to meet the criterion of explicitness or 'transparency'. Interestingly, Sandelowski and Barroso (2007: 59-60) even propose that effect sizes can be produced through qualitative synthesis.

contribution of primary research studies. The usual meaning of the word 'synthesis' is 'putting things together to make a coherent whole' (see Strike and Posner 1983). And the contrast here is with 'analysis', whose core meaning is: breaking phenomena down into their elements or components. While this meaning of 'synthesis' broadly captures what is involved in both statistical meta-analysis and qualitative synthesis it is rather vague, and there is also some semantic uncertainty. It is, for example, thoroughly confusing that the main means of quantitative synthesis should be labelled 'meta-*analysis*'. Furthermore, the 'analysis of data' in primary research itself involves synthesis. Thus, accounts of grounded theorising portray the initial task as segmenting and coding the data (analysis) with this then being followed by the identification of relationships amongst categories, properties, etc. and the development of these into a well-structured theory, this clearly amounting to synthesis.[4] In parallel with this, outlining what they call 'meta-study', which is often seen as one kind of qualitative synthesis, Paterson et al. (2001: 2) insist, sensibly, that studies must be *analysed* before their results can be synthesised, so that meta-study involves both analysis and synthesis.[5]

Given that primary analysis also involves synthesis, we might ask: why is *secondary* synthesis necessary? What could it achieve? In the context of statistical meta-analysis the answer likely to be given is: it increases the probable external and/or internal validity of the conclusions reached in any of the individual studies. However, to the extent that many qualitative researchers reject any concern with empirical generalisation and replication, they may have to answer this question differently, and indeed they generally do.

There are several issues that need to be addressed, then. In what respect does qualitative synthesis differ from 'traditional' reviews? What does it add to primary research? Is it true that the kinds of synthesis built into systematic reviews are alien to qualitative work? What form of synthesis does qualitative synthesis aim at? And, finally, how can it contribute to the development of knowledge in a field, or to the information available to policymakers and practitioners?

---

[4]There is further semantic confusion in that the word 'data' is plural, which suggests that what it refers to is already segmented.

[5]Pope et al. (2007) refer to the following synonyms for 'synthesis': 'bring together', 'juxtapose', 're-analyse', and 'combine the findings from'. The prefix 'meta' is sometimes employed, as in meta-synthesis (Thorne et al. 2004), meta-study (Paterson et al. 2001), and meta-ethnography (Noblit and Hare 1988). The meaning of this prefix is not standard: it can indicate a concern with the study of the activity referred to, notably with its underlying assumptions, as in metamathematics. In the case of meta-ethnography, though, this prefix seems to refer to integration of theoretical ideas from primary ethnographic studies. Meta-study seems to involve both of these meanings, whereas neither of them appears to be involved in 'meta-synthesis': this does not typically refer either to the study of synthesis or to the synthesis of syntheses. It is worth adding that the original meaning of 'meta' seems to have been much more mundane, namely 'after'. Glass (2005) points out that '*meta*physics' is a term that derives from the compiling of Aristotle's writings, where his writings on the topics we now refer to as metaphysics were so-called because they were the books appearing *after* those on physics. See also van Inwagen 2007.

'TRADITIONAL' REVIEWS AND SYNTHESIS

Not only does primary research involve synthesis, along with analysis, but perhaps even more obviously *reviews* of research literatures have also generally sought to synthesise previous work, in some senses of that term. Reviews that consist of a string of paragraphs, each of which summarises a separate study along with its strengths and weaknesses, are not generally regarded as satisfactory (Ridley 2008: 2–3; Hart 1998; Jesson et al. 2011: ch. 5). Instead, it is usually argued that reviews must bring studies together in one or more of the following senses: so as to identify a gap that requires filling; as complementing one another in dealing with different aspects of a phenomenon; as confirming the likely validity of one another's findings; or as challenging certain findings, either through direct contradiction or by throwing doubt upon an assumption upon which some studies rely. Sometimes reviews have even aimed at producing an overarching scheme that makes sense of the findings of the various studies by formulating or reformulating them in more abstract or comprehensive terms.[6]

Not all 'traditional' reviews involve all these forms of synthesis, of course, and they can take divergent forms, for example because they have been designed to serve different purposes and audiences. Where they are produced as part of a primary research project, and published as a component of a research report, typically the aim is to establish what can be taken to be known in the relevant field, and what is still uncertain or not known, and thereby to provide a rationale for the new investigation that is about to be reported. Often, the primary audience here will be other researchers, whether in the same field or beyond. However, it is not uncommon for research reports to be also addressed to audiences outside the research community; indeed, separate research reports are sometimes prepared for these audiences. Who the intended audience is will obviously shape the nature of research reports to some extent; for example, where lay audiences are addressed it is not unusual for the literature review (and some other sections) to be omitted or cut down, and this may affect the character of any synthesis provided.

In the case of stand-alone reviews, the aim will often be to cover the whole of some field, identifying key issues and studies, and what conclusions can, and cannot, be drawn from them. Here, too, the main target audience has often been other researchers, with the aim of giving them a better overall sense of the field in which they are working, or to bring them up to date with what has been done in related fields to their own. Sometimes, such reviews may put different literatures together, with the aim of showing connections and relations that might not hitherto have been recognised, perhaps ones that are interdisciplinary in character. This too, presumably, counts as synthesis.

---

[6]See Foster and Hammersley 1998 for discussion of some traditional reviews. The promotion of qualitative synthesis, as with systematic reviews, often involves caricaturing and dismissing 'traditional' reviews. Thus, Noblit and Hare (1988: 14-15) write that 'positivists and interpretivists alike find literature reviews as usually practiced to be of little value. The study-by-study presentation of questions, methods, limitations, findings, and conclusions lacks some way to make sense of what the collection of studies is saying. As a result, literature reviews in practice are more rituals than substantive accomplishments'.

Stand-alone reviews may also sometimes be aimed at lay audiences. The task here is to provide policymakers, practitioners, citizens, or consumers with a summary of what is currently known, on the basis of research, about some specific issue or set of issues relevant to them. Here, again, audience considerations may have implications for the character of what is produced. Generally speaking, it is assumed that lay audiences will want a relatively short account of what is currently known rather than a lengthy, detailed, and highly qualified discussion. At the very least there may be a need for an 'executive summary'. Some sorts of synthesis may fit with these requirements, but others will not.

As this discussion makes clear, synthesis of various kinds seems to be involved in 'traditional' forms of reviewing, so that the distinctiveness of what is offered by qualitative synthesis will need to be examined carefully; especially when we remember that each of the studies included in a synthesis will itself probably contain some sort of literature review. Furthermore, given that traditional reviews have been designed to serve a variety of purposes and audiences, we might wonder whether the same is not also true of qualitative syntheses as well – how will they vary in this respect? My next task, however, is to determine whether the types of synthesis built into statistical meta-analysis and systematic review are compatible with qualitative research, given that it is frequently suggested that they are not (see, for example, Noblit and Hare 1988).

ARE SOME FORMS OF SYNTHESIS INCOMPATIBLE WITH QUALITATIVE RESEARCH?

In Chapter 8 I identified two kinds of synthesis involved in systematic reviews, what we might refer to as aggregative and replicative synthesis. I will examine each of these in turn as regards that relation to qualitative research.

Aggregative synthesis

This involves combining the findings of multiple studies, with the idea that this will provide a more accurate assessment of the effects of some treatment, policy or practice than any of the individual studies alone could do. The rationale for this aggregation is either that by pooling multiple studies the number of cases about which data are available has been increased, or that these studies can themselves be treated as a sample from some larger population of studies that could have been carried out. Either way, synthesis of the findings is believed to provide a better basis for estimating the effect than any single study.

Both the sampling rationales I have just sketched are open to question in particular instances, as regards whether the cases studied do in fact belong to the same larger population, how inferences are to be made from sample to population, and whether this sort of inference enables us to reduce likely error. Generally speaking, within primary quantitative social science there is reliance on the idea that if a random sample is drawn this maximises the chances of its being representative, but random selection of studies is not involved in either of these rationales.

Nevertheless, there is some force in the idea that by examining more cases from a population, up to some point, we reduce the danger of drawing false conclusions about what are typical characteristics of members of that population. And, on the face of it, this could apply to qualitative as well as to quantitative studies. Indeed, given that qualitative investigations tend to focus on a small number of cases, it might be seen as especially appropriate for them. By putting the findings of studies dealing with cases from the same population together, we may be able to provide a sounder basis for generalisation to that population than is offered by any single study.

There are, however, influential ideas among qualitative researchers that dismiss empirical generalisation in the context of primary research, and that would also rule out such aggregative synthesis. One is what might be called the idiographic discourse. This insists that qualitative research should be aimed at studying unique phenomena in their own terms (see, for example, Stake 1978, 1995), and that any form of generalisation obliterates their distinctiveness, with the result that all value is lost. Thus, Lincoln and Guba (1985: 238) have declared that 'the only generalization is: there is no generalization'. They argue that generalisation is not possible because all cases are unique, they are 'neither time- nor context-free'; although at the same time they add that 'some transferability of [the 'working hypotheses' developed to make sense of an individual case] may be possible from situation to situation, depending on the degree of temporal and contextual similarity' – what they refer to as 'fittingness'. From this point of view, each case should be described in its own terms rather than according to a framework provided by some prior theoretical idea, whether this is the product of arm-chair theorising or even of previous research. And, because of the uniqueness of each case, any attempt to draw general conclusions on the basis of studying more than one is regarded as futile. It is assumed that standard forms of generalisation abandon the uniqueness of what is being generalised *from*. So, it is denied that researchers must aim at producing general conclusions. Rather, the goal should be to provide thick descriptions of unique cases that allow readers either to select case studies that are most appropriate for their purpose, or to engage in what Stake calls naturalistic generalisation for themselves.[7]

There is also a second line of argument to be found within the literature on qualitative methodology that rules out, or seems to rule out, aggregation. This is what I will call the expressivist discourse. According to this, any account of the world produced by qualitative researchers (or, for that matter, by anyone else) is a product of their personal, socio-cultural background and socio-historical location, so that different people will necessarily produce different, and perhaps even incompatible, accounts of the 'same scene'. Furthermore, there is no means of deciding amongst these, as regards their validity, because there is no external position from which first-order interpretations can be evaluated that is not itself shaped by the characteristics

---

[7]This version of interpretivism is clearly at odds with that underpinning Eisenhart's notion of interpretive review (see Chapter 10), as well as with qualitative synthesis.

and locale of the evaluator. In these terms, there can be no objective account of the world, no 'view from nowhere'. Indeed, it is often argued within this discourse that there are no objective phenomena – that there are simply multiple realities which reflect the perspectives of different people or cultures.[8]

In the context of this discourse, too, it is hard to see what the warrant for, or the point of, aggregative synthesis could be: what sense does it make to put together or integrate accounts that reflect the diverse and distinctive perspectives of different researchers? Any attempt at this would surely produce a meaningless jumble.

Neither of these discourses is entirely convincing, in my view, and they do not succeed in ruling out empirical generalisation or aggregative synthesis. The first recognises that in social research we are not faced with cases that take standard forms, but rather with ones that are variegated along multiple dimensions. And this is an important point. However, the idiographic discourse involves a defective understanding of what 'unique' means. Uniqueness is no barrier to generalisation or aggregation. A case is always a case *of* something. What this indicates is that we cannot identify the uniqueness of any particular phenomenon without relying upon background assumptions about what cases of a particular kind *could* share in common, as well as how they might differ. In other words, we always describe particular cases by means of general categories that can be applied to many cases, whether deriving from some theory or from common sense. Any notion of absolute uniqueness would be unintelligible and inexpressible. Indeed, the term 'uniqueness', when it does not refer to the simple point that any phenomenon existing at a particular place and time is unlike all other phenomena in at least some respects (at a minimum in existing at that time and in that place), amounts to the argument that the case concerned is an outlier in some statistical distribution, and this is clearly by no means incompatible with empirical generalisation, even if the case cannot on its own tell us what is typical.

The second line of argument, the expressivist discourse, also contains some truth, but again only up to a point. There is an important sense in which all knowledge is perspectival, in that it is designed to answer particular questions; and if we address different questions the knowledge produced will vary – though the answers, if true, cannot be contradictory. It is also the case that producing any account – any set of answers to a set of questions – necessarily relies upon the linguistic and cognitive resources available to us, and is in addition shaped by our preconceptions, preferences, feelings, etc. However, this does not mean that what is produced is simply a reflection or expression of who we are, that it can tell us nothing about the world; even less that there are no phenomena existing independently of our perceptions and interpretations. The process of knowledge production is not one of invention or even mere construction. Rather, it involves, or should involve, attempts to check interpretations against evidence. And evidence is not just fabricated: there is an important sense in which data are 'given' as well as constructed; they are mediated rather than simply 'made up' (Hammersley 2010a, 2010b).

---

[8]Of course, this statement about multiple realities itself implicitly purports to be a 'view from nowhere'.

Ironically, while the expressivist discourse rejects the positivist idea that objective accounts can be produced by following procedures that eliminate the subjectivity of the researcher, it shares with its opponent the assumption that if accounts are subjective they must be arbitrary, in the sense of not corresponding to real phenomena existing independently of them. Sometimes this argument is applied to all kinds of phenomena, including the physical world, on other occasions it is restricted to social phenomena (Smith 1989). In effect, the argument is that all accounts are subjectively biased, though the term 'bias' here is in danger of losing its original sense (Hammersley and Gomm 1997).

While it is true that subjective judgements – in other words, ones that rely upon assumptions, interpretations, etc. – cannot be avoided, it is not true that this prevents an account being objective, in the sense either of being pursued in ways that minimise the danger of error, or of producing true answers to questions about some case or set of cases (Hammersley 2011: ch. 4). The plausibility of expressivism arises from the cogent idea that what sense we can make of any object is dependent upon what our interest in it is and the resources we bring along, and that we all have preconceptions and preferences. But there is a slide from this to the false conclusion that all accounts simply invent the phenomena to which they refer as expressions of the person who produced them. The implication seems to be that we live in a world of mirrors, and ones of our own making.

Given that neither the idiographic nor the expressive discourses are entirely cogent, they do not amount to a bar on empirical generalisation and aggregative synthesis in qualitative research. Furthermore, if we look at what qualitative researchers do *in practice* we find that empirical generalisation is common (Hammersley 1992: ch. 5). In other words, there is often practical reliance upon the logic of inference from samples to populations. This can occur in two ways, though these are not always explicitly distinguished. First of all, qualitative researchers frequently engage in empirical generalisation *within* the case or cases they are studying. For example, they often treat the perspectives of the people they interview as representative of all members of some category of informant inhabiting the case investigated. Secondly, in drawing conclusions from their studies, qualitative researchers often treat the case or cases they have focused on as representative of some larger existing population. For example, these cases may be portrayed as typical in key respects, or as representing a critical or extreme case that establishes some negative conclusion about the population as a whole.[9]

Of course, it is rarely, if ever, possible for qualitative researchers to study a sample of cases drawn randomly from a population so as to be able to use statistical theory to assess the likely validity of their inferences. However, it is a fallacy to treat this strategy as the only basis for empirical generalisation (see Hammersley 1992). One alternative that qualitative researchers sometimes employ is to select people, places, etc. in such a way as to try to capture significant known relevant heterogeneity within the population of interest – a strategy that parallels the use of stratified sampling in survey research.

---

[9]Schofield (1990) has provided a sophisticated account of various kinds of generalisation within qualitative research (see also Hammersley and Gomm 1997).

Given all this, we can conclude that qualitative synthesis could in principle take the form of aggregation, in the sense of determining how far what has been found to be true of some type of phenomenon in one study is true of other cases investigated by other researchers, with a view to drawing conclusions about some specified larger population. At the same time, there are practical difficulties in doing this. One is that there may not be a sufficiently large number of qualitative studies dealing with cases from the same population. A second is that even studies of the same type of case will often have adopted different foci, so that they will not provide all of the information needed to draw general conclusions in this way. Primary qualitative research would probably have to be carried out rather differently from how it usually is for aggregative synthesis to be possible. Whether or not this would be desirable I leave as an open question here.

Replicative synthesis

The other kind of synthesis I identified as possibly involved in systematic review is replicative in character. What I mean by this, in broad terms, is that the findings of multiple studies of the same type of phenomenon, or designed to answer the same questions, are tested against one another. Once again, this sort of synthesis would probably be widely rejected by qualitative researchers, for much the same reasons as they dismiss the possibility of aggregative synthesis. Yet here too it is far from clear that there can be any principled objection. The *underlying idea* of replication – that we can check an observation by doing it again – is not at odds with the practice of qualitative method. In fact, I suggest that it is commonly used: when, as part of an ethnographic study, we go to observe the same setting, again at a different time, we are interested not just in assessing whether the phenomena being observed vary over time but also in making sure that our previous observations were correct. Similarly, in interviewing several people who are involved in a setting, or in a particular line of work etc., we are often interested in checking whether the evidence we gained from earlier interviews is reliable, in addition to exploring variation in response across informants. In both these cases an elemental form of replication is involved. Furthermore, we could treat triangulation of different data sources, a strategy often appealed to by qualitative researchers, as a version of replication – one in which there is systematic variation of key elements of the process of investigation in order to check the validity of interpretations.[10] It has also been argued that in one kind of qualitative research – conversation analysis – replication is a central part of the analytic process: the data are provided in publications so that readers can replicate the analysis and thereby check its validity (Peräkylä 1997/2003).

All these examples refer, of course, to checking observations and interpretations *within* particular studies, rather than replication *between* studies; furthermore, they do not generally involve the use of multiple observers or analysts in the manner that is common in quantitative studies designed to assess the reliability of particular measures.

---

[10]See Denzin 1970. Of course, many qualitative researchers now reject this kind of triangulation, in large part as a result of what I referred to as expressivism, see Hammersley 2008d.

However, my argument here is simply that there is no fundamental incompatibility between the basic principle of replication and qualitative research. Moreover, while it is rarely, if ever, possible to carry out a strict replication of an earlier qualitative study – not least because research done in natural settings cannot be controlled by the researcher to anything like the same extent as in experimental and survey research – qualitative researchers *have* carried out *re-studies*: new investigations of settings that were previously studied by the same or a different researcher.

This was quite common in the field of community studies in the past, beginning with the Lynds' return to 'Middletown', which was followed by a later re-study by others (see Caccamo 2000). There is also the famous case of Lewis re-studying the town that had earlier been investigated by Redfield, the conflict in findings leading to considerable debate (Paddock 1961). Somewhat more recent re-studies, this time in the UK, include that of Banbury (Stacey et al. 1975), and in the field of education Burgess's (1987) re-study of the school that had been the focus for his own earlier ethnography. There are also examples of studies that were not intended as re-studies but where the relationship between the new study and a previous investigation in the same community subsequently came to be given attention. Here, similarity of findings may be treated as confirmation, while discrepancies throw doubt upon the validity of earlier findings. The best known example of the latter is Freeman's critique of the work of Mead on Samoa (see Mead 1928; Freeman 1983, 1999; Bryman 1994).[11]

Given all this, it is not clear why, in principle, a synthesis could not examine qualitative studies of the same setting or type of setting, addressing the same questions, with a view to determining how far they agree in their findings or challenge one another's conclusions. Indeed, this has sometimes been done in traditional reviews, and it seems to conform to one of the three types of synthesis identified by Noblit and Hare, what they call refutational synthesis.

While discussions of qualitative synthesis sometimes use the term 'aggregation', and others examine the possibility of one study 'confirming' or 'refuting' another, generally speaking they do not propose either aggregative or replicative synthesis. Instead, appeal is made to a rather different notion of what synthesis involves, concerned with theory development. In the next section I will consider what this involves.

SYNTHESIS AS THEORETICAL DEVELOPMENT

As noted earlier, many approaches to qualitative synthesis have been proposed.[12] Pope et al. (2007: ch. 4) reduce these to just two main forms: those that use comparative

---

[11]This was used as an example by Noblit and Hare (1988) in their development of meta-ethnography. Needless to say, there are some difficult questions around the relationship between replication and re-study. As already noted, it is almost never possible to carry out a second ethnographic study by following exactly the same procedures as were employed in the first. However, this is not required by the fundamental idea of replication.

[12]Barnett-Page and Thomas 2009 identify ten types. For other outlines of different approaches, see Finfgeld 2003 and Dixon-Woods et al. 2004.

method, for example grounded theorising, and those that adopt a 'translational' approach, as represented by meta-ethnography (Noblit and Hare 1988). This distinction is not clear-cut, since Noblit and Hare include grounded theorising as one model for what they call lines-of-argument synthesis. Furthermore, the notion of translation that they borrow from Turner (1980) specifically treats this as a comparative process. However, there are significant differences between the interpretive paradigm, derived from Geertz (1973), on which Noblit and Hare rely, and the assumptions of grounded theorising. Indeed, it is arguable that these two approaches are incompatible (see Glaser 2003, 2004). Given this, I will use Pope et al.'s distinction to organise my discussion.

Grounded theoretical synthesis

A few qualitative syntheses have been presented explicitly as modelled on grounded theorising (Kearney 1988, 1998, 2001; Dixon 1996; Finfgeld 1999). This is, of course, an extremely influential approach in primary qualitative research. It proposes a research design in which there is an inductive and iterative relationship between data collection and analysis, the latter subsequently providing the basis for theoretical sampling in further data collection, this again feeding back into data analysis, and so on. The whole process is aimed at the systematic development of emerging theoretical ideas into a coherent and comprehensive theory (Glaser and Strauss 1967; Bryant and Charmaz 2007).

Grounded theorising is by no means universally regarded as a sound approach to primary research amongst qualitative researchers. Problems have been raised, for example, about the nature of its intended product and the extent to which checks on the validity of the emerging theory are built into it (Brown 1973; Hammersley 1989a, 2012a; Dey 1999). Putting these issues on one side, there are also questions about how grounded theorising can be applied to the task of qualitative synthesis.

Interestingly, Glaser and Strauss specifically included a chapter in *The Discovery of Grounded Theory* about carrying out grounded theorising in the library. While elsewhere in the book they had advised researchers not to read other studies relevant to the field of investigation until the data collection process was well under way (Dunne 2011), here they emphasise the value of documentary material of various kinds for generating and developing theory. However, what they have in mind is much broader than simply drawing on previous research studies. They mention: 'letters, autobiographies, memoirs, speeches, novels and a multitude of nonfiction forms' (Glaser and Strauss 1967: 161). They also refer to 'quotations from informants' in social scientific studies, giving the example of the statements of 'taxi-dancers' to be found in Cressey's *The Taxi-Dance Hall* (Cressey 1932). In later discussions, they do specifically propose using the findings and theoretical categories generated by previous primary research (see, for example, Glaser and Strauss 1971: 6–7). In part the aim here is to remedy the 'incompleteness' of existing analyses: to combine studies in order to generate a more 'dense' theory. However, Glaser and Strauss also see this material as useful in developing *formal* theory as opposed to the substantive theory with which most primary research is concerned; and they themselves have developed grounded formal theories concerned with awareness contexts, status passage, and negotiation (Glaser 1968; Glaser and Strauss 1971; Strauss 1978).

Strauss defines 'formal theory' as concerned with 'a formal, or conceptual, area of inquiry such as stigma, formal organization, or socialization', as opposed to substantive theories concerned with 'substantive, or empirical' areas of inquiry 'such as patient care, professional education, or industrial relations' (Strauss 1987: 242). While these definitions are not as clear as they might be, what seems to be involved is not so much a *dichotomy* between two types of theory as a *dimension* concerned with a certain sort of abstraction: from concepts that relate only to particular types of socio-historical context to those that can be applied to all human societies. We can assume, for example, that socialisation processes, of one sort or another, are ubiquitous in human social life, whereas professional education only occurs on any scale in certain types of society (those where there is clear differentiation of occupations in terms of status and power), while socialisation processes amongst radiographers would be an even more 'substantive' concept.

There are hints in Glaser and Strauss's writings, then, of the possibility of something like qualitative synthesis of previous studies. Indeed, Kearney (in Thorne et al. 2004: 1353) quotes Glaser and Strauss as encouraging the building of formal theory 'from the research bricks of a multitude of sociologists', and cites their comment that 'there are too few good synthesizers who wish to search out the bricks and thus put the wall together' (Glaser and Strauss 1967: 82).[13] However, it is clear that for them the material to be used is not restricted to the findings of previous research. Strauss (1976: 247) comments that 'everything is grist for the formal theorist's mill'. Furthermore, what is proposed here is not a second-order activity but a form of primary research. Glaser and Strauss are arguing that the data a researcher collects her or himself can be supplemented by data from these other sources. For example, at one point in discussing the development of formal theories they say that 'we have used anecdotal comparisons, as well as actual field data and the published and unpublished research of social scientists', and they comment that 'although every reader will not agree that every bit of data is "warranted evidence" (to use Dewey's felicitous term), we do hope readers will not suppose that only materials drawn from actual sociological studies are fully evidential' (Glaser and Strauss 1971: 11).

Among the clearest examples of qualitative synthesis modelled on grounded theorising are those produced by Kearney to do with women recovering from substance abuse and women with violent partners. She claims that her goal was to generate formal theories, but she seems to interpret this in a different way from Glaser and Strauss. She describes the task as 'to construct more generally applicable "ready-to-wear" theoretical models that may fit a variety of users and populations and, thus, attain greater impact on nursing practice' (Kearney 1998: 179). The focus in her two qualitative syntheses does not seem close to being formal in Glaser and Strauss's terms, but instead more substantive in character.

---

[13]It is striking that here we find use of the metaphor of wall-building that Eisenhart (1998) and other interpretive critics of traditional reviews reject. See Chapter 10.

However, to assume that qualitative synthesis must be directed at formal theories would involve a restriction on its focus whose legitimacy seems questionable: substantive theories are surely an equally valuable and useful product. Still, the move from substantive to formal theory, as conceived by Glaser and Strauss, is one kind of higher level theoretical integration of the concepts and themes to be found in multiple studies that might be entailed by qualitative synthesis. We should note that what is involved here is, in part, a process of theoretical generalisation: of producing a theory that applies across different substantive settings, taking account of variations in these that are significant. An example that Strauss (1987) uses is moving from a theory about physician–patient relationships to one about professional–client relationships. He emphasises that, rather than assuming that the former provide an adequate model for the latter, it is important to work with data about different types of professional–client relationship.[14]

While Glaser and Strauss's substantive-formal dimension may be useful in this way, it is not clear that such qualitative synthesis can be pursued by applying grounded theory *method*: the full iterative mode of inductive data collection and subsequent theoretical sampling is surely not viable when one is working with a fixed (and often small) number of available studies within a field. Even if, in principle, studies could be selected on the grounds that they provide comparative leverage on significant differences that are likely to reveal important variation that a grounded theory needs to conceptualise, there will be considerable restriction on the theoretical sampling that is possible: the synthesiser, unlike the primary researcher, is not able to continue generating further data until her or his categories are 'saturated'.

There is also a significant ambiguity in Kearney's analysis regarding what constitutes the data for qualitative synthesis. In her work on women's experience of domestic violence, she reports that the total number of women included in the studies that she examines was 282, and she provides a breakdown of their ages, ethnicity and other characteristics. This seems to imply that individual people are the cases to be brought together in the synthesis, almost implying that the aim is aggregative synthesis. However, when she describes the synthesis process, she identifies the categories of data 'extracted' from the studies as follows:

> the year, source, and disciplinary and theoretical orientations of the report; methodological components (presence and adequacy of theoretical sampling, constant comparative analysis, and theory development); size, origins, recruitment source, social context, and other characteristics of the sample; scope and components of the findings, including concepts, relationships, stages, and substantiation; author conclusions; and critique by the formal theory analyst. (Kearney 2001: 274)

From this it seems clear that it is the *studies* that are the components of the synthesis, not the cases investigated by those studies. Moreover, in practice, the central thrust of Kearney's syntheses is to compare, and develop an integrated account of, the main

---

[14]Here 'professional' seems to be used to refer to a formal rather than a substantive category, illustrating that this is a dimension not a dichotomy.

concepts and findings of the studies. She goes on to describe how 'concepts across studies were identified and clustered into new categories, such as types of study origins, contexts, and stages or influences within the findings ...' (p. 274). What is involved here seems closer to the sorts of synthetic work that I identified earlier as forming part of many traditional reviews than it is to grounded theorising.

In summary, then, while grounded theorising offers some guidance for qualitative synthesis, particularly in supplying the idea that it could be aimed at producing more formal theories, it is not clear that it can provide an adequate model: there are too many discrepancies between the resources available for synthesis and those used by primary research. Furthermore, as we have seen, there is some ambiguity about what is being synthesised and the nature of the categories involved.

The second approach to qualitative synthesis that Pope et al. identify relies upon the metaphor of translation. The main example of this is 'meta-ethnography'.

META-ETHNOGRAPHY

Meta-ethnography is put forward as a form of synthesis that respects the distinctive character of each study, rather than 'stripping away' context in order to identify generic conclusions, in the way that a positivist approach, such as meta-analysis, is held to do. Noblit and Hare (1988: 12) draw a very sharp contrast between what they see as the two paradigms operating in social science – positivism and interpretivism – and in adopting the latter their approach is quite strongly influenced by what I referred to earlier as the idiographic and expressivist discourses.[15] While Noblit and Hare appeal to interpretivism, what they propose is, at face value and as subsequently interpreted, very different from the notion of interpretive reviews put forward by Eisenhart (1998); though their discussion of the role of metaphors and allegory towards the end of their book, in which they appeal to the work of Clifford (1986), obscures this.

Drawing on the work of Geertz, Turner, and others, Noblit and Hare view the ethnographer as interpreting human social life through understanding the cultural meanings involved, and then 'inscribing' this understanding via an idiomatic translation that makes it meaningful to an audience. And they see qualitative *synthesis* as sharing the same character, except that what is involved this time is attempting to translate studies into one another's terms, and conveying what can be learned from this to an audience, this itself involving an additional process of translation.

In the examples of meta-ethnography that Noblit and Hare (1988) provide, the focus of investigation adopted is relatively broad: school processes associated with desegregation, the role of the school principal, variation in student orientations

---

[15]For evidence of the influence of the idiographic discourse, see Noblit and Hare 1988: 17 and 22. Expressivism is evident in the following 'in the interpretive paradigm, any interpretation, metaphor, or translation is only one possible reading of that studied. Other investigations will have other readings. In many ways, a meta-ethnographic synthesis reveals as much about the perspective of the synthesizer as it does about the substance of the synthesis' (Noblit and Hare 1988: 14).

towards secondary schooling, and Samoan cultural practices regarding adolescence.[16] Later usage of meta-ethnography by others has tended to adopt rather more specific foci. For example, Britten et al. (2002) studied lay experiences of diabetes and diabetes care, and were concerned with the question 'How do the perceived meanings of medicines affect patients' medicine-taking behaviours and communication with health professionals?' Noblit and Hare place little emphasis on exhaustive searching of the literature. Indeed, generally speaking, the number of studies involved in their syntheses is low. By contrast, some later meta-ethnographies have involved searches of the literature that were designed to be relatively exhaustive, with the number of studies included being quite large (see, for example, Pound et al. 2005). Furthermore, they generally apply assessment criteria to filter out studies judged to fall below some threshold of likely validity, which Noblit and Hare do not seem to have done – or at least this is not explicitly stated.

What are being brought into relationship in meta-ethnography are the 'themes, perspectives, organizers and/or concepts' (Noblit and Hare 1988: 14) that each study employs. Noblit and Hare recognise that it will not always be possible simply to translate the terms of each study into one another, what they refer to as 'reciprocal translation'. Instead, where there is a conflict in findings among the studies a 'refutational synthesis' may be required, or where the topics addressed are different, but related, a 'line-of-argument' synthesis might be necessary (p. 36).

Noblit and Hare employ Geertz's (1973) notion of thick description to provide the basis for a kind of synthesis that is distinctive to qualitative research. His interpretive anthropology is primarily concerned with understanding particular phenomena in context, though it is not entirely idiographic in character: he sees the value of thick descriptions as lying in their capacity to illuminate general issues about human social life. This is possible because any particular situation studied involves general types of social process that will have occurred in other situations, and will occur in the future (Hammersley 2008c: ch. 3). The kind of general meaning involved here seems similar in character to the notion of literary truth, where a story exemplifies something important about human nature, modern society, etc. Noblit and Hare (1988: 24) take this over: 'as Geertz (1973) argues, the goal of qualitative research is to enrich human discourse not to produce a formal body of knowledge'. They declare that 'a meta-ethnography is complete when we understand the meaning of the synthesis to our life and the lives of others' (p. 81).[17]

Geertz argues that primary analysis involves producing 'constructions of constructions'. He writes: 'what we call our data are really our own constructions of other people's constructions of what they and their compatriots are up to' (Geertz 1973: 9). In fact, given that the ethnographer is faced with 'a multiplicity of complex conceptual structures, many of them superimposed upon or knotted into one another' (p. 10), there may be two or three constructional levels involved. There seem, then,

---

[16]Noblit and Hare (1988: 54-61) use Freeman's (1983) critique of Mead's work as an example of 'refutational synthesis'.

[17]Noblit (in Thorne et al. 2004: 1348) describes this as a 'modest' goal, but this claim is open to dispute.

to be several 'constructional levels' operating even before we reach qualitative syn-thesis where, presumably, a further one is added (see Noblit and Hare 1988: 35). Perhaps even underestimating what is involved, Sandelowski and Barroso (2007: xvi) describe syntheses as 'findings thrice removed': 'reviewers' constructions of researchers' constructions of the data they obtained from research participants, which are themselves constructed within the research encounter'.

The other major resource that Noblit and Hare draw upon is Stephen Turner's (1980) book *Sociological Explanation as Translation*, from whom they take the metaphor of translation. He starts from Peter Winch's (1958) critique of the positivist model of sociological knowledge as consisting of causal laws of human behaviour. Turner accepts Winch's argument that human action involves following rules, not least in applying concepts. However, he challenges his view that what is required to understand human behaviour is to learn the relevant culture – in other words, the rules – 'from the inside'. Instead, Turner argues that we cannot but start from our existing knowledge of human practices, applying what he calls 'the same practice hypothesis': we initially assume that what people are doing may conform to a practice with which we are already familiar. We only feel the need to try to build an explanation for their behaviour if this hypothesis is disconfirmed. Furthermore, when a puzzle of this kind arises, our only option is to consider whether the new practice might be a *variation* on one that we already know.

An illustration that Turner uses is Leach's (1969) discussion of 'virgin birth'. This concerns anthropological claims that there is ignorance of the relationship between copulation and pregnancy in some societies, on the grounds that informants some-times provide non-biological accounts of what led to a woman becoming pregnant. Leach argues that we should not be too quick to assume ignorance on the part of people in other societies, and should instead remember that there are practices within our own society where non-biological explanations of conception are put forward, such as the Christian idea that Christ was born to a virgin. In other words, Leach suggests that rather than assuming that when asked about conception and pregnancy people are presenting their factual knowledge, we must recognise that they may be providing what would be appropriate answers in other terms, for exam-ple in a religious context. And he goes on to make another important point: that the dogma associated with various rituals in which people participate within a society, and which they may present in interviews, does not necessarily represent their actual beliefs and knowledge.[18]

In taking over the concept of translation from Turner, Noblit and Hare seem to reinterpret it in a way that is closer to Winch. For example, they define an 'interpretive' approach as seeking 'an explanation for social or cultural events based upon the perspectives and experiences of the people being studied' (Noblit and Hare 1988: 12). Furthermore, they add to Turner's 'same practice hypothesis' the notion of a 'different practices hypothesis' (p. 30), where we assume that other people belong

---

[18]Incidentally, there is a sense in which Leach is himself engaged in informal qualitative synthesis in this article, in that he considers various anthropological studies relevant to his theme. In Noblit and Hare's terms it might be said that he is engaged in refutational synthesis.

to a different culture and that their behaviour can only be understood in terms that are entirely different from our own. Such a hypothesis can play no role in Turner's account. For him, the point is that we always begin by exploring whether a new practice we come across conforms to one with which we are already familiar. If it does not, we do not *hypothesise* that it is different, but rather explore *how* it varies and what the reasons for this might be, drawing on our own existing knowledge of human practices to make sense of this information.

The difference here can be brought out by noting some of Leach's (1969: 97) comments, these echoing the views of Claude Lévi-Strauss, who was a major influence upon him: 'the data of ethnography are interesting to me because they so often seem directly relevant to my own allegedly civilized experiences. It is not only the differences between Europeans and Trobrianders which interest me, it is their similarities'. Leach's approach, like that of Turner, contrasts with a Winchian/ culturalist point of view, for which the statement that women become pregnant because 'she may dream of having the child put inside her' (Leach 1969: 87) must be treated as equivalent, in the context of some other culture, to the biological account prevalent in the West and as equally valid in terms of that culture.

The complex relationship between what Turner proposes and the orientation of Noblit and Hare is also indicated by the following comment from Leach (1969: 86):

> Professor Clifford Geertz (1966: 35) has recently denounced my attitude to religious matters as that of 'vulgar positivism'. This intended insult I take as a compliment. Positivism is the view that serious scientific inquiry should not search for ultimate causes deriving from some outside source but must confine itself to the study of relations existing between facts which are directly accessible to observation. In consequence of this limitation, positivists, whether vulgar or otherwise, usually show signs of knowing what they are talking about, whereas theologians, even when disguised as Professors of Anthropology, do not.

At the very least, we get a hint here that Noblit and Hare's claim that there are just two 'paradigms' operating in social science is a misconception, and there is certainly an indication that the issues being dealt with are more complex than such a dichotomy allows.

In effect, Noblit and Hare treat each of the studies to be synthesised as representing a distinct culture: each setting is viewed as unique in cultural terms, and the qualitative study dealing with it is seen as inscribing its cultural meanings. The task of meta–ethnography, then, is to translate each study into the terms of the others, or into terms that provide the basis for a refutational or lines-of-argument synthesis.

Even putting aside the general problems with culturalist explanation already outlined, there are questions about this. While there might be some plausibility in the assumption that anthropological studies of different communities represent distinct cultures, the idea that this is true, say, of the studies of schools in various parts of the United States that Noblit and Hare (1988) synthesise is much less so. What sense does it make to try to 'translate the practices and conditions of one school into the practices and conditions of the other schools' (Noblit and Hare 1988: 106)? The notion of organisational cultures is a widely used one, but whatever its value there are obvious dangers that a culturalist approach in this context will overlook the political and social structural processes that operate *across* schools within a society. Indeed, perhaps not surprisingly, it is these on which Noblit and Hare's synthesis of desegregation studies focuses. This raises questions about the relationship between the rationale for and practice of meta-ethnography in this respect. Furthermore, in what sense are ethnographic studies simply *representations* of organisational cultures, rather than constructed accounts aimed at answering particular research questions about them?

There are other problems with the rationale for meta-ethnography too. One of these concerns Noblit and Hare's suggestion that what are being synthesised are the 'metaphors' used by the component studies. In fact, most of the themes they list from studies in their sample meta-ethnographies do not seem to be metaphors: for instance, 'proletarianization', 'growth, industrialization, and movement', and 'positive knowledge' (Noblit and Hare 1988: 50; see also pp. 53, 55–7 and 66–7). What does 'metaphor' mean here?

There is also the question of how such 'metaphors' should be evaluated. Noblit and Hare argue that meta-ethnographies must be judged in terms of the 'adequacy' of the metaphors they employ, this involving the following criteria: 'economy', 'cogency', 'range', 'apparency', and 'credibility' (Noblit and Hare 1988: 34). However, there is ambiguity here since some of these criteria (cogency and credibility) apparently relate to validity while the others concern rhetorical effectiveness.[19] Whether the authors would want to make any distinction between these two types of consideration remains to be seen. In practice, their main emphasis seems to be on *intelligibility* rather than truth. For example, they refer to cases being 'rendered *understandable* through a meta-ethnographic synthesis' (p.47, emphasis added). At the same time, they cannot reject the concept of truth, not least because the very idea of a 'refutational synthesis' assumes it.

Noblit and Hare are certainly not unique here: there is a decided ambivalence towards the concept of truth or validity among qualitative researchers today. Thus, in one of the most recent accounts of qualitative synthesis, Howell Major and Savin-Baden (2010: 20 and 73) first deny that validity is 'something for which qualitative researchers generally strive' but later emphasise the requirement that articles should include 'transparent explanations of validity' to show that 'efforts to ensure validity have been followed'. The key point is that if syntheses are intended to produce true results, we need a clearer sense of what this means and of how their validity is to be assessed.

In relation to this, it is surprising that Noblit and Hare give no attention to the metaphorical character of 'translation'. What does it mean to say that translations can be true, or indeed refutational? I have already pointed out that their usage of 'translation' seems to be significantly different from that of Turner. Moreover, they insist that what ethnography and meta-ethnography employ are idiomatic not literal translations. In fact, at one point they appear to abandon the source meaning of 'translation' completely, writing that: 'A meta-ethnographic synthesis does not

---

[19]The assessment criteria that should be applied to qualitative research have, of course, been a major source of contention within the literature on systematic reviewing and synthesis. See Chapter 6.

involve creating a text in a new language. Rather, it entails discovering the relationships between two existing texts' (Noblit and Hare 1988: 76). When they later add that ethnographic interpretation is allegorical (pp. 78–9), we might reasonably ask what the prospects are for any kind of translation, as well as about what 'truth' or 'refutation' could mean in this context.

If we put aside Noblit and Hare's culturalist rationale, we find that what they actually do in carrying out meta-ethnographies is very similar to what Kearney does under the auspices of producing grounded formal theory, and what is done in most other kinds of qualitative synthesis. Much the same is true of later meta-ethnographies, for example those by Britten et al. (2002), Campbell et al. (2003), and Pound et al. (2005). In practice, the aim is to identify the central categories employed in each study and to examine what relationships there might be between the two (or more) sets of these: are they different formulations of, or explanations for, the same phenomenon; do they represent conflicting interpretations; or are they complementary, for example in representing different stages of a process, different subtypes of a situation, person, or adding elements that were missed out of other studies?

Issues around validity are certainly not absent here. Given that the aim, often, has been to use multiple studies to generate an account of the range of factors, and variation in these, that leads to some outcome, there are questions about how strong the evidence can be for theories produced in this way. Qualitative synthesis cannot involve the sort of developmental process characteristic of grounded theorising or analytic induction (Cooper et al. 2012: ch. 5), in which theoretical ideas are systematically developed and tested through the collection of further data. Nor is the kind of systematic comparison characteristic of Qualitative Comparative Analysis deployed (Ragin 1987, 2008). Yet claims are made about the causal force of particular factors – for example that of gender difference on compliance/non-compliance with medical regimens (Pound et al. 2005: 140). On what grounds can such claims be judged cogent? There is some uncertainty here.

CONCLUSION

In this chapter I have examined some recently influential proposals for qualitative synthesis. One of my concerns has been to determine in what significant respects qualitative synthesis differs from what have come to be referred to as 'traditional' or 'narrative' reviews; how it compares to 'systematic reviewing' as regards the form of synthesis involved; and what contribution it can make over and above that of primary qualitative research. I argued that primary research already involves processes of synthesis as well as analysis, and that traditional reviewing frequently displays various kinds of synthesis, from those that treat studies as confirming or challenging one another's findings to those where relations of complementarity, of one sort or another, are identified. I also examined how far the two kinds of synthesis that appear to underpin systematic reviews – aggregative and replicative synthesis – are incompatible with qualitative research. I concluded that, in principle at least, they are not. Finally, I assessed two influential rationales for qualitative synthesis: that appealing to the development of grounded formal theories, and the 'cultural translation' proposed by meta-ethnography.

In my view, the suggestion that qualitative synthesis represents a form of research in its own right directed at producing new theories is hyperbole; it is no more convincing in this case than it is in that of meta-analysis or systematic review. Generally speaking, the findings and reported data available in existing studies cannot provide the resources necessary for this task: the collection of primary data or the use of secondary data would usually be required. Furthermore, formulating the goal of synthesis in this way loses its only claim to distinctiveness as compared with primary and secondary analysis: that it is aimed at formulating what is the current state of knowledge in some field, or in relation to some specific issue, at some point in time; and doing this in a way that is appropriate for a particular audience. Of course, if we take this to be its proper aim then its function is the same as traditional or narrative reviewing. While advocates of qualitative synthesis have been keen to emphasise the difference in goal between the two (Noblit and Hare 1988: 9; Thorne et al. 2004: 1343), this is not convincing.

If qualitative synthesis is aimed at the same task as traditional or narrative review, we must ask how far it represents an advance over this. There is much to be said for adopting a more systematic approach in both searching for relevant studies and comparing them, and for being more explicit about what has been done. However, these are matters of degree, and it is important to avoid caricaturing older forms of review in the way that has become common. It is also necessary to recognise that a systematic approach can degenerate into thoughtless following of procedure, and that there is a trade-off, for example, between exhaustive searching and the intensive examination of particular studies. Sometimes there appears to be a reduction of the reading of primary research reports to the 'extraction' of information in line with some protocol. Thus, Paterson et al. (2001: 46) write: 'We learned that the most expedient appraisal tool requires as little longhand as possible. By developing a form that could easily be distributed, completed, coded, and stored in computer databases … we improved the effectiveness and efficiency of the review process and had an ongoing record of the findings for analysis.' Furthermore, it is important to emphasise that the process of review/synthesis cannot be rendered fully 'transparent'; what is required is *sufficient* explicitness to allow likely threats to the validity of the conclusions to be assessed.

Moreover, as with reviews, the task of qualitative synthesis is to communicate an understanding of the current state of research *to an audience*. There sometimes appears to be a tendency to treat all qualitative synthesis as following a single standard model. While Noblit and Hare (1988) recognise the significance of audience, their focus in this respect is almost entirely upon the intelligibility of metaphors. As I noted earlier, it has long been widely recognised that reviews need to be different according to the audience being addressed, in terms of the background knowledge assumed and the information provided (for example about methods). The same must be true for qualitative synthesis.

Another point I want to make is that any clarification of the nature and purpose of qualitative synthesis depends upon clear and cogent understandings of the types of inference involved in primary research: what they require to be successful, how we can know that the conclusions they produce are sound, what the nature of these conclusions is, and so on. Unfortunately, at the present time such clarity and cogency are largely absent. In part this results from the fact that, as we saw in Chapter 9, qualitative research is currently riven by fundamental methodological, theoretical, and political disagreements. In this situation, attempts to conceptualise qualitative synthesis are likely to founder on the unresolved and contentious methodological issues that now plague primary qualitative research.

Indeed, speaking more broadly, there is a danger that the lack of coherence and methodological understanding that characterises a great deal of social science is simply being glossed over and reinforced by forms of synthesis that, not surprisingly, are similarly methodologically incoherent, as well as lacking clarity about exactly what sorts of claim they are aiming to produce, what sorts of question they are aiming to answer, and what is required if these goals are to be achieved. Qualitative synthesis cannot be a substitute for the failure of primary studies to build on existing knowledge, any more than can meta-analysis.

In this chapter I have been quite critical of the notion of qualitative synthesis. Yet I believe that it has great value in emphasising the need for careful reading and analysis of previous work (see Hammersley 1998). It may serve to counter the prevailing empiricist idea that new knowledge can only come from carrying out new data collection – a notion that is especially salient in some discussions of grounded theorising (Dunne 2011). In my view, qualitative researchers have often not dealt well with extant literature. Pound et al. (2005) found this in the field of research on non-compliance with medical prescriptions. They comment:

> Our synthesis revealed that only a minority of the studies referenced each other, even when papers were about the same medicines ... This suggests that research in this field, at least, is not an evolving process whereby new studies build on earlier ones and where research is only conducted after the relevant literature has been reviewed and important questions identified. Rather, among the later studies, there appeared to be little regard for earlier relevant studies and, certainly within the HIV literature, a tendency for studies to [repeat] each other. (p. 151)[20]

Moreover, citation of previous studies in primary research often amounts to little more than appeals for support, or to exemplars designed to dismiss alternative approaches or interpretations. In short, there has been insufficient work on previous research, both theoretical and methodological, with a view to learning what we can from it. If the growth of qualitative synthesis can remedy this, it will perform a valuable service.

---

[20]Pound et al. actually use the term 'replicate' here not 'repeat', but they seem to mean that studies have been carried out on exactly the same issue without any reference to one another, not that they were specifically designed to replicate one another.

REFERENCES

Abrami, P., Borokhovski, E., Bernard, R., Wade, C. A., Tamim, R., Persson, T., Bethel, E., Hanz, K. and Surkes, M. (2010) 'Issues in conducting and disseminating brief reviews of evidence', *Evidence and Policy*, 6 (3): 371–89.

Adelman, C. (1993) 'Kurt Lewin and the origins of action research', *Educational Action Research*, 1: 7–24.

Afary, J. and Anderson, K. (2005) *Foucault and the Iranian Revolution*. Chicago, IL: University of Chicago Press.

Altheide, D. and Johnson, J. (1994) 'Criteria for assessing interpretive validity in qualitative research', in N. Denzin and Y. Lincoln (eds), *Handbook of Qualitative Research*. Thousand Oaks, CA: Sage.

Altrichter, H. and Gstettner, P. (1997) 'Action research: a closed chapter in the history of German social science?', in R. McTaggart (ed.), *Participatory Action Research*. Albany, NY: State University of New York Press.

Alvesson, M. and Sandberg, J. (2013) *Constructing Research Questions: Doing Interesting Research*. London: Sage.

Apple, M. (1999) 'What counts as legitimate knowledge? The social production and use of reviews', *Review of Educational Research*, 69 (4): 343–6.

Archer, M., Bhaskar, R., Collier, A., Lawson, T. and Norrie, A. (eds) (1997) *Critical Realism: Essential Readings*. London: Routledge.

Argyris, C., Putnam, R. and Smith, D.M. (1985) *Action Science*. San Francisco, CA: Jossey–Bass.

Atkinson, E. (2004) 'Thinking outside the box: an exercise in heresy', *Qualitative Inquiry*, 10 (1): 111–29.

Atkinson, P. and Coffey, A. (2002) 'Revisiting the relationship between participant observation and interviewing', in J.F. Gubrium and J.A. Holstein (eds), *Handbook of Interview Research*. Thousand Oaks, CA: Sage.

Aucoin, P. (1990) 'Administrative reform in public management: paradigms, principles, paradoxes and pendulums', *Governance*, 3 (2): 115–37.

Avineri, S. (1968) *Karl Marx on Colonialism and Development*. Garden City, NY: Doubleday.

Bailey, K.D. (1994) *Typologies and Taxonomies: An Introduction to Classification Techniques*. Thousand Oaks, CA: Sage.

Baker, B. (1999) 'What is voice? Issues of identity and representation in the framing of reviews', *Review of Educational Research*, 69 (4): 365–83.

Ball, S.J. (1990) *Politics and Policy Making in Education: Explorations in Policy Sociology*. London: Routledge.

Barnett-Page, E. and Thomas, J. (2009) 'Methods for the synthesis of qualitative research: a critical review', *BioMed Central Medical Research Methodology*, 9: 59. Available at www.biomedcentral.com/content/pdf/1471-2288-9-59.pdf (accessed 19 March 2012).

Bassey, M. (2000) 'Reviews of educational research', *Research Intelligence*, 71: 22–9.

Bauman, Z. (1987) *Legislators and Interpreters*. Cambridge: Polity Press.

Becker, H.P. (1940) 'Constructive typology in the social sciences', in H.E. Barnes, H. Becker and F.B. Becker (eds), *Contemporary Social Theory*. New York: Russell and Russell.

Becker, H.P. (1950) *Through Values to Social Interpretation*. Durham, NC: Duke University Press.

Becker, H.S. (1970) *Sociological Work*. Chicago, IL: Aldine.

Becker, H.S. (1998) *Tricks of the Trade*. Chicago, IL: University of Chicago Press.

Beckner, M. (1959) *The Biological Way of Thought*. New York: Columbia University Press.

Benda, J. (1927) *The Treason of the Intellectuals* (English translation, 1955). Boston, MA, Beacon Press.

Bendix, R. (1963) 'Concepts and generalizations in comparative sociological studies', *American Sociological Review*, 28 (4): 532–9.

Bennett, W. (1986) *What Works: Research about Teaching and Learning*. Washington, DC, US Department of Education.

Bickman, L. (ed.) (2000) *Validity and Social Experimentation*. Thousand Oaks, CA: Sage.

Biesta, G. (2007) 'Why "what works" won't work: evidence based practice and the democratic deficit in educational research', *Educational Theory*, 57: 1–22.

Bird, A. (2000) *Thomas Kuhn*. Princeton, NJ: Princeton University Press.

Blunkett, D. (1999) Secretary of State's address to the annual conference of the Confederation of British Industry (cited in R. Pring (2000) *Philosophy of Educational Research*. London: Continuum).

Blunkett, D. (2000) 'Influence or irrelevance: can social science improve government?', *Research Intelligence*, 71: 12–21.

Bovaird, J.A. and Embretson, S.E. (2008) 'Modern measurement in the social sciences', in P. Alasuutari, L. Bickman and J. Brannen (eds), *The Sage Handbook of Social Research Methods*. London: Sage.

Braverman, H. (1974) *Labour and Monopoly Capital*. London: Monthly Review Press.

Britten, N., Campbell, R., Pope, C., Donovan, J., Morgan, M. and Pill, R. (2002) 'Using meta-ethnography to synthesis qualitative research: a worked example', *Journal of Health Service Research*, 7: 209–15.

Brown, G. (1973) 'Some thoughts on grounded theory', *Sociology*, 7: 1–16.

Brown, T. and Jones, L. (2001) *Action Research and Postmodernism*. Buckingham: Open University Press.

Bryant, A. and Charmaz, K. (eds) (2007) *The Sage Handbook of Grounded Theory*. London: Sage.

Bryman, A. (1988) *Quantity and Quality in Social Research*. London: Hyman Unwin.

Bryman, A. (1994) 'The Freeman/Mead controversy: some implications for qualitative researchers', in R. Burgess (ed.), *Studies in Qualitative Methodology*, Volume 4. Greenwich, CT: JAI Press.

Bryman, A. (2008) 'The end of the paradigm wars?', in P. Alasuutari, L. Bickman, and J. Brannen (eds), *The Sage Handbook of Social Research Methods*. London: Sage.

Bulmer, M. (2001) 'Social measurement: what stands in its way?', *Social Research*, 68 (2): 455–80.

Burgess, R. (1987) 'Studying and re-studying Bishop McGregor School', in G. Walford (ed.), *Doing the Sociology of Education*. London: Falmer.

Burnham, J. (1941) *The Managerial Revolution*. Harmondsworth: Penguin.

Button, G. and Sharrock, W. (1993) 'A disagreement over agreement and consensus in constructionist sociology', *Journal for the Theory of Social Behaviour*, 23 (1): 1–25.

Byrne, D. (2004) 'Evidence based? What constitutes valid evidence?', in A. Gray and S. Harrison (eds), *Governing Medicine: Theory and Practice*. Buckingham: Open University Press. pp. 81–92.

Caccamo, R. (2000) *Back to Middletown: Three Generations of Sociological Reflections: Three Generations of Sociological Reflections*. Stanford, CA: Stanford University Press.

Campbell, D.T. (1988a) '"Degrees of freedom" and the case study', in E.S. Overman (ed.), *Methodology and Epistemology for Social Science: Selected Papers by Donald T. Campbell*. Chicago, IL: University of Chicago Press.

Campbell, D.T. (1988b) *Methodology and Epistemology for Social Science: Selected Papers*, edited by E.S. Overman. Chicago, IL: University of Chicago Press.

Campbell, D.T. (1988c) 'Qualitative knowing in action research', in E.S. Overman (ed.), *Methodology and Epistemology for Social Science: Selected Papers by Donald T. Campbell*. Chicago, IL: University of Chicago Press.

Campbell, D.T. and Stanley, J.C. (1966) *Experimental and Quasi-Experimental Designs for Research*. Chicago, IL: Rand McNally.

Campbell, R., Pound, P., Pope, C., Britten, N., Pill, R., Morgan, M. and Donovan, J. (2003) 'Evaluating meta-ethnography: a synthesis of qualitative research on lay experiences of diabetes and diabetes care', *Social Science and Medicine*, 65: 671–84.

Carr, W. and Kemmis, S. (1986) *Becoming Critical*. Lewes: Falmer.

Cartwright, N. (1989) *Nature's Capacities and Their Measurement*. Oxford: Oxford University Press.

Cartwright, N. (2007) 'Are RCTs the gold standard?' *Biosocieties*, 2: 11–20. Available at http://personal.lse.ac.uk/cartwrig/Papers%20on%20Evidence.htm (accessed 12 March 2009).

Chalmers, A.F. (1999) *What Is This Thing Called Science?*, 3rd edn. Buckingham: Open University Press.

Chalmers, I. (2003) 'Trying to do more good than harm in policy and practice: the role of rigorous, transparent, up-to-date evaluations', *Annals of the American Academy of Political and Social Science*, 589: 22–40.

Chalmers, I. (2005) 'If evidence-informed policy works in practice, does it matter if it doesn't work in theory?', *Evidence and Policy*, 1 (2): 227–42.

Chalmers, I., Hedges, L.V. and Cooper, H. (2002) 'A brief history of research synthesis', *Evaluation and the Health Professions*, 25 (1): 12–37.

Chandler, A. (1977) *The Visible Hand*. Cambridge, MA: Harvard University Press.

Chandler, A. with Takashi Hikino (1990) *Scale and Scope: the Dynamics of Industrial Capitalism*. Cambridge, MA: Harvard University Press.

Charlton, B. (1997) 'Review of Sackett et al. *Evidence-based Medicine*', *Journal of Evaluation in Clinical Practice*, 3 (2): 169–72.

Christie, D. and Pollard, A. (2009) 'Taking stock of educational research and the impact of the UK Teaching and Learning Research Program', in R. St Clair (ed.), *Education Science: Critical Perspectives*. Rotterdam: Sense.

Cicourel, A.V. (1964) *Method and Measurement in Sociology*. New York: Free Press.

Clarke, C. (1998) 'Resurrecting research to raise standards', *Social Sciences: News from the ESRC*, Issue 40, October, p. 2.

Clarke, J. and Newman, J. (1997) *The Managerial State: Power, Politics and Ideology in the Remaking of Social Welfare*. London: Sage.

Clifford, J. (1986) 'On ethnographic allegory', in Clifford, J. and Marcus, G. (eds) *Writing Culture: The Poetics and Politics of Ethnography*. Berkeley CA: University of California Press.

Cochrane, A. (1972) *Effectiveness and Efficiency*. London: Nuffield Provincial Hospitals Trust.

Collier, J. (1945) 'United States Indian administration as a laboratory of ethnic relations', *Social Research*, 12: 275–6.

Collini, S. (2012) *What Are Universities For?* London: Penguin.

Collins, H. and Evans, R. (2007) *Rethinking Expertise*. Chicago, IL: University of Chicago Press.

Cook, T. D. (2001) 'A critical appraisal of the case against using experiments to assess school (or community) effects', *Education Next*. Available online at: http://media.hoover.org/sites/default/files/documents/ednext20013unabridged_cook.pdf (accessed 20 July 2012).

Cooper, B., Glaesser, J., Gomm, R. and Hammersley, M. (2012) *Challenging the Qualitative-Quantitative Divide: Explorations in Case-focused Causal Analysis*. London: Continuum.

Cooper, H. (1984) *The Integrative Research Review*. Beverly Hills, CA: Sage.

Cooper, H. (1998) *Synthesizing Research: A Guide for Literature Reviews*, 3rd edn. Thousand Oaks, CA: Sage.

Cooper, H. (2010) *Research Synthesis and Meta-Analysis*, 4th edn. Los Angeles: Sage.

Cooper, H. and Hedges, L. (1994) 'Research synthesis as a scientific enterprise', in H. Cooper and L. Hedges (eds), *Handbook of Research Synthesis*. New York: Russell Sage.

Cooper, H., Hedges, L. and Valentine, J. (2009) *The Handbook of Research Synthesis and Meta-Analysis*, 2nd edn. New York: Russell Sage.

Cressey, P. (1932) *The Taxi-Dance Hall*. Chicago, IL: University of Chicago Press.

Cronbach, L. (1979) 'Prudent aspirations for social inquiry', in W. Kruskal (ed.), *The Social Sciences: Their Nature and Uses*. Chicago, IL: University of Chicago Press.

Daly, J. (2005) *Evidence-Based Medicine and the Search for a Science of Clincial Care*. Berkeley, CA: University of California Press.

Daston, L. and Garrison, P. (2007) *Objectivity*. New York: Zone Books.

Davies, H.T.O., Nutley, S.M. and Smith, P.C. (eds) (2000) *What Works? Evidence-Based Policy and Practice in the Public Services*. Bristol: Policy Press.

Davies, P. (1999) 'What is evidence-based education?', *British Journal of Educational Studies*, 47 (2): 108–21.

Davies, P. (2000a) 'The relevance of systematic reviews to educational policy and practice', *Oxford Review of Education*, 26 (3/4): 365–78.

Davies, P. (2000b) 'Contributions from qualitative research', in H.T.O. Davies, S.M. Nutley and P.C. Smith (eds), *What Works? Evidence-based Policy and Practice in the Public Services*. Bristol: Policy Press.

Davies, P. (2006) 'What is needed from research synthesis from a policy-making perspective', in J. Popay (ed.), *Moving Beyond Effectiveness in Evidence Synthesisis: Methodological Issues in the Synthesis of Diverse Sources of Evidence*. London: National Institute for Health and Clinical Excellence.

Demeritt, D. (2000) 'The new social contract for science: accountability, relevance and value in US and UK science and research policy', *Antipode*, 32 (3): 308–29.

Denzin, N.K. (1970) *The Research Act: A Theoretical Introduction to Sociological Methods*. Chicago, IL: Aldine.

Denzin, N.K. (1978) *The Research Act*, 2nd edn. New York: McGraw–Hill.

Denzin, N.K. (1992) 'Whose Cornerville is it anyway?', *Journal of Contemporary Ethnography*, 21: 120–32.

Denzin, N.K. and Lincoln, Y.S. (eds) (2000) *Handbook of Qualitative Research*, 2nd edn. Thousand Oaks, CA: Sage.

Denzin, N.K. and Lincoln, Y.S. (eds) (2005) *The Sage Handbook of Qualitative Research*, 3rd edn. Thousand Oaks, CA: Sage.

Denkin, N.K. and Lincoln, Y.S. (2011) *The Sage Handbook of Qualitative Research*, 4th edn. Thousand Oaks, CA: Sage.

Denzin, N. and Giardina, M. (2006) *Qualitative Inquiry and the Conservative Challenge*. Walnut Creek, CA: Left Coast Press.

Department for Education and Skills (2003) *The Future of Higher Education*. London: HMSO.

Deutscher, I. (1973) *What We Say/What We Do: Sentiments and Acts*. Glenview, IL: Scott, Foresman.

Devine, P.J., Lee, N., Jones, R.M. and Tyson, W.J. (1985) *An Introduction to Industrial Economics*. London: Unwin Hyman.

Dewey, J. (1929) *The Quest for Certainty*. New York: Minton, Balch.

Dey, I. (1999) *Grounding Grounded Theory*. San Diego, CA: Academic Press.

Dingwall, R. (1997) 'Accounts, interviews and observations', in G. Miller and R. Dingwall (eds), *Context and Method in Qualitative Research*. London: Sage.

Dixon, D. (1996) 'Unifying concepts in parents' experiences with health care providers', *Journal of Family Nursing*, 2: 111–32.

Dixon-Woods, M. (2011) 'Using framework-based synthesis for conducting reviews of qualitative studies', *BioMed Central Medicine*, 9: 39: 1–2. Available at www.biomedcentral.com/content/pdf/1741-7015-9-39.pdf (accessed 29 March 2012).

Dixon-Woods, M., Agarwal, S., Young, B., Jones, D. and Sutton, A. (2004) *Integrative Approaches to Quantitative and Qualitative Evidence*. London: Health Development

Agency. Available at www.nice.org.uk/niceMedia/pdf/Integrative_approaches_ evidence.pdf (accessed 8 March 2012).

Dixon-Woods, M., Agarwal, S., Jones, D., Young, B. and Sutton, A. (2005) 'Synthesising qualitative and quantitative evidence: a review of possible methods', *Journal of Health Service Research and Policy*, 10 (1): 45–53.

Dixon-Woods, M., Kirk, D., Agarwal, S., Annandale, E., Arthur, T., Harvey, J., Hsu, R., Katbamna, S., Olsen, R., Smith, L., Riley, R. and Sutton, A. (2005) *Vulnerable Groups and Access to Health Care: A Critical Interpretative Synthesis*. A report for the National Co-ordinating Centre for NHS Delivery and Organisation R and D (NCCSDO). Available at http://mighealth.net/uk/images/8/84/Dix1.pdf (accessed 26 March 2012).

Dixon-Woods, M., Bonas, S., Booth, A., Jones, D., Miller, T., Sutton, A., Shaw, R., Smith, J. and Young, B. (2006) 'How can systematic reviews incorporate qualitative evidence?', *Qualitative Research*, 6 (1): 27–44.

Dixon-Woods, M., Cavers, D., Agarwal, S., Annandale, E., Arthur, A., Harvey, J., Hsu, R., Katbamna, S., Olsen, R., Smith, L., Riley, R. and Sutton, A. (2006) 'Conducting critical interpretative synthesis of the literature on access to health care by vulnerable groups', *BioMed Central Research Methodology*, 6: 35.

Dixon-Woods, M., Booth, A. and Sutton, A. (2007) 'Synthesizing qualitative research: a review of published reports', *Qualitative Research*, 7 (3): 375–422.

Donaldson, S., Christie, C., and Mark, M. (eds.) (2009) *What Counts as Credible Evidence in Applied Research and Evaluation Practice*. Thousand Oaks CA: Sage.

Dreyfus, H. and Dreyfus, S. (1986) *Mind Over Machine: The Power of Human Intuition and Expertise in the Era of the Computer*. New York: Free Press.

Dryzek, J. (1990) *Discursive Democracy: Politics, Policy, and Political Science*. Cambridge: Cambridge University Press.

Duncan, O.D. (1984) *Notes on Social Measurement: Historical and Critical*. New York: Russell Sage Foundation.

Dunn, W. (ed.) (1998) *The Experimenting Society: Essays in Honour of Donald T. Campbell*. New Brunswick, NJ: Transaction Books.

Dunne, C. (2011) 'The place of literature review in the grounded theory research', *International Journal of Social Research Methodology*, 14(2): 111–24.

Dunne, J. (1997) *Back to the Rough Ground: Practical Judgment and the Lure of Technique*. Notre Dame, IN: University of Notre Dame Press.

Eisenhart, M. (1998) 'On the subject of interpretive reviews', *Review of Educational Research*, 68 (4): 391–9.

Eisenhart, M. (2006) 'Qualitative science in experimental time', *International Journal of Qualitative Studies in Education*, 19 (6): 697–707.

Eisenhart, M. and Towne, L. (2003) 'Contestation and change in national policy on "scientifically based" education research', *Education Researcher*, 32 (7): 31–8.

Eisner, E. (1992) 'Objectivity in educational research', *Curriculum Inquiry*, 22 (1): 9–15.

Elgin, C. (1996) *Considered Judgment*. Princeton, NJ: Princeton University Press.

Elliott, J. (2001) 'Making evidence-based practice educational', *British Educational Research Journal*, 27 (5): 555–74. (Reprinted in M. Hammersley, *Educational Research and Evidence-Based Practice*. London: Sage, 2007.)

Emmet, D. (1966) *Rules, Roles and Relations*. London: Macmillan.

Erickson, F. and Gutierrez, K. (2002) 'Culture, rigor, and science in educational research', *Educational Researcher*, 31 (8): 21–4.

Etzioni, A. (1969) *The Semi-Professions and their Organization*. New York: Free Press.

Evans, J. (2000) 'Systematic reviews of educational research', *Research Intelligence*, 73: 25–6.

Evans, J. and Benefield, P. (2001) 'Systematic reviews of educational research: Does the medical model fit?', *British Educational Research Journal*, 27: 527–41.

Farrington, D. (1983) 'Randomized experiments on crime and justice', in M. Tonry and N. Morris (eds), *Crime and Justice: An Annual Review of Research*, Volume 4. Chicago, IL: University of Chicago Press.

Farrington, D. and Welsh, B. (2001) 'Preface', *Annals of the American Academy of Political and Social Science*, 578: 8–13.

Feest, U. (2005) 'Operationism in psychology: what the debate is about, what the debate should be about', *Journal of the History of the Behavioral Sciences*, 41 (2): 131–49.

Ferlie, E., Ashburner, L., Fitzgerald, L. and Pettigrew, A. (1996) *The New Public Management in Action*. Oxford: Oxford University Press.

Feuer, M.J., Towne, L. and Shavelson, R.J. (2002) 'Scientific culture and educational research', *Educational Researcher*, 31 (8): 4–14.

Feyerabend, P. (1975) *Against Method*. London: Verso.

Finfgeld D. (1999) 'Courage as a process of pushing beyond the struggle', *Qualitative Health Research*, 9 (6): 803–14.

Finfgeld, D. (2003) 'Metasynthesis: the state of the art – so far', *Qualitative Health Research*, 13 (7): 893–904.

Foster, P. (1999) '"Never mind the quality, feel the impact" A methodological assessment of teacher research sponsored by the Teacher Training Agency', *British Journal of Educational Studies*, 47 (4): 380–98.

Foster, P. and Hammersley, M. (1998) 'A review of reviews: structure and function in reviews of educational research', *British Educational Research Journal*, 24: 609–33.

Foster, P., Gomm, R. and Hammersley, M. (2000) 'Case studies as spurious evaluations: the example of research on educational inequalities', *British Journal of Educational Studies*, 48 (3): 215–30.

Fowler, P.B.S. (1995) Letter. *The Lancet*, 346: 838.

Freeman, D. (1983) *Margaret Mead and Samoa: The Making and Unmaking of an Anthropological Myth*. Cambridge, MA: Harvard University Press.

Freeman, D. (1999) *The Fateful Hoaxing of Margaret Mead: A Historical Analysis of Her Samoan Research*. Boulder, CO: Westview.

Freese, L. (1980) 'The problem of cumulative knowledge', in L. Freese (ed.), *Theoretical Methods in Sociology*. Pittsburgh, PA: University of Pittsburgh Press.

Furlong, J. and Oancea, A. (2005) *Assessing Quality in Applied and Practice-based Educational Research: A Framework for Discussion*. Oxford: Oxford Department of Educational Studies. Available at www.bera.ac.uk/pdfs/Qualitycriteria.pdf (accessed 26 February 2006).

Gage, N. (1991) 'The obviousness of social and educational research results', *Educational Researcher*, 20 (1): 10–16. (Reprinted in Hammersley, M. (ed.), *Educational Research and Evidence-Based Practice*. London: Sage.)

Garland, D. and Sparks, R. (2000) 'Criminology, social theory, and the challenge of our times', in D. Garland and R. Sparks (eds), *Criminology and Social Theory*. Oxford: Oxford University Press.

Gaukroger, S. (2001) *Francis Bacon and the Transformation of Early-Modern Philosophy*. Cambridge: Cambridge University Press.

Geertz, C. (1966) 'Religion as a cultural system', in M. Banton (ed.), *Anthropological Approaches to the Study of Religion*. London: Tavistock.

Geertz, C. (1973) *The Interpretation of Cultures*. New York: Basic Books.

Geuss, R. (2008) *Philosophy and Real Politics*. Princeton, NJ: Princeton University Press.

Gibbons, M. (2000) 'Mode 2 society and the emergence of context-sensitive science', *Science and Public Policy*, 26 (5): 159–63.

Gibbons, M., Limoges, C., Nowotny, H., Schwartzman, S., Scott, P. and Trow, M. (1994) *The New Production of Knowledge: The Dynamics of Science and Research in Contemporary Societies*. London: Sage.

Gillborn, D. (1998) 'Policy and research in "race" and education in the UK: symbiosis or mutual abuse?' Paper given at 14th World Congress of Sociology, Montreal, July 1998.

Gillborn, D. and Gipps, C. (1996) *Recent Research on the Achievements of Ethnic Minority Pupils*. London: Office for Standards in Education/Her Majesty's Stationery Office.

Gillies, D. (1993) *Philosophy of Science in the Twentieth Century*. Oxford: Blackwell.

Glaser, B. (1968) *Organizational Careers: A Sourcebook for Theory*. Chicago, IL: Aldine.

Glaser, B.G. (2003) 'Naturalist inquiry and grounded theory', *Forum: Qualitative Sozialforschung/Forum: Qualitative Social Research*, 5 (1): Art. 7. Available at www.qualitative-research.net/index.php/fqs/article/view/652/1412 (accessed 29 March 2012).

Glaser, B.G. with the assistance of J. Holton (2004) 'Remodeling grounded theory', *Forum Qualitative Sozialforschung/Forum: Qualitative Social Research*, 5 (2): Art. 4, http://nbn-resolving.de/urn:nbn:de:0114-fqs040245.

Glaser, B. and Strauss, A. (1967) *The Discovery of Grounded Theory: Strategies for Qualitative Research*. Chicago, IL: Aldine.

Glaser, B. and Strauss, A. (1971) *Status Passage: A Formal Theory*. Chicago, IL: Aldine.

Glass, G. (1976) 'Primary, secondary, and meta-analysis of research', *Educational Researcher*, 5: 3–8.

Glass, G. (1987) '*What Works*: Politics and research', *Educational Researcher*, 16 (3): 5–10.

Glass, G. (2005) 'Meta-analysis at 25', available at www.gvglass.info/papers/meta25.html (accessed 19 April 2012).

Goertz, G. (2006) *Social Science Concepts: A User's Guide*. Princeton, NJ: Princeton University Press.

Goldthorpe, J.H. (2000) *On Sociology: Numbers, Narratives, and the Integration of Research and Theory*. Oxford: Oxford University Press.

Gordon, B. (1999) 'Who do you believe, me or your eyes? Perceptions and issues in educational research: reviews and the journals that validate them', *Review of Educational Research*, 69 (4): 407–11.

Gough, D. (2007) 'Weight of evidence: a framework for the appraisal of the quality and relevance of evidence', *Research Papers in Education*, 22 (2): 213–28.

Graebner, W. (1986) 'The small group and democratic social engineering, 1900–1950', *Journal of Social Issues*, 42 (1): 137–54.

Graue, E. and Grant, C. (1998) 'What sort of tool is a review? Editors' introduction to companion essays', *Review of Educational Research*, 68 (4): 389.

Graue, E. and Grant,C. (1999) 'What sort of tool is a review? Editors' introduction to companion essays', *Review of Educational Research*, 69 (1): 1.

Gray, J.A.M. (1997) *Evidence-Based Healthcare: How to Make Health Policy and Management Decisions*. London: Churchill Livingstone.

Greenhalgh, T. (1997) *How to Read a Paper: The Basics of Evidence-Based Medicine*. London: BMJ Books.

Greenwood, D. and Levin, M. (1998) *Introduction to Action Research*. Thousand Oaks, CA: Sage.

Greenwood, D. and Levin, M. (2005) 'Reform of the social sciences and of the universities through action research', in Denzin and Lincoln (eds.).

Grice, P. (1991) *Studies in the Way of Words*. Cambridge, MA: Harvard University Press.

Gubrium, J. and Holstein, J. (1990) *What Is Family?* Mountain View, CA: Mayfield.

Gubrium, J. and Holstein, J. (1993) 'Phenomenology, ethnomethodology, and family discourse', in P. Boss, W. Doherty, R. LaRossa, W. Schumm, and S. Steinmetz (eds), *Sourcebook of Family Theories and Methods: A Contextual Approach*. New York: Plenum.

Gueron, J. (2002) 'The politics of random assignment: implementing studies and affecting policy', in F. Mosteller and R. Boruch (eds), *Evidence Matters: Randomized Trials in Education Research*. Washington, DC: Brookings Institution.

Gunz, J. (1996) 'Jacob L. Moreno and the origins of action research', *Educational Action Research*, 4 (1): 145–8.

Guston, D.H. and Keniston, K. (eds) (1994) *The Fragile Contract: University Science and the Federal Government*. Cambridge, MA: MIT Press.

Guthrie, W.K.C. (1971) *The Sophists*. Cambridge: University of Cambridge Press.

Haack, S. (2003) *Defending Science – Within Reason: Between Scientism and Cynicism*. Amherst, NY: Prometheus Books.

Haack, S. (2009) *Evidence and Inquiry*, 2nd end. Amherst, NY: Prometheus Books.

Habermas, J. (1987) *The Philosophical Discourse of Modernity*. Cambridge: Polity Press.

Halfpenny, P. (1982) *Positivism and Sociology*. London: Allen and Unwin.

Hammersley, M. (1985) 'From ethnography to theory: a programme and paradigm in the sociology of education', *Sociology*, 19 (2): 244–59.

Hammersley, M. (1986) 'Measurement in ethnography: the case of Pollard on teaching style', in M. Hammersley (ed.), *Controversies in Classroom Research*. Milton Keynes: Open University Press.

Hammersley, M. (1987) 'Some notes on the terms "validity" and "reliability"', *British Educational Research Journal*, 13 (1): 73–81.

Hammersley, M. (1989a) *The Dilemma of Qualitative Method: Herbert Blumer and the Chicago Tradition*. London: Routledge.

Hammersley, M. (1989b) 'The problem of the concept: Herbert Blumer on the relationship between concepts and data', *Journal of Contemporary Ethnography*, 18 (2): 133–59.

Hammersley, M. (1991) 'A note on Campbell's distinction between internal and external validity', *Quality and Quantity*, 25: 381–7.

Hammersley, M. (1992) *What's Wrong with Ethnography?* London: Routledge.

Hammersley, M. (1993) 'On the teacher as researcher', in M. Hammersley (ed.), *Educational Research: Current Issues*. London: Paul Chapman.

Hammersley, M. (1995) *The Politics of Social Research*. London: Sage.

Hammersley, M. (1997) 'Educational research and teaching: a response to David Hargreaves' TTA lecture', *British Educational Research Journal*, 23 (2): 141–61. (Reprinted in M. Hammersley (ed.), *Educational Research and Evidence-Based Practice*, London: Sage, 2007.)

Hammersley, M. (1998) *Reading Ethnographic Research*, 2nd edn. London: Longman.

Hammersley, M. (1999) 'Sociology, what's it for? A critique of Gouldner', *Sociological Research Online*, 4 (3): September. www.socresonline.org.uk/socresonline/4/3/hammersley.html>

Hammersley, M. (2000a) 'The sky is never blue for modernisers: the threat posed by David Blunkett's offer of "partnership" to social science', *Research Intelligence*, 72 (June).

Hammersley. M. (2000b) *Taking Sides in Social Research: Essays on Partisanship and Bias*. London: Routledge.

Hammersley, M. (2000c) 'Varieties of social research: a typology', *International Journal for Social Research Methodology*, 3 (3): 221–9.

Hammersley, M. (2002) *Educational Research, Policymaking and Practice*. London: Paul Chapman.

Hammersley, M. (2003a) 'Media representation of social and educational research: the case of a review of ethnic minority education', *British Educational Research Journal*, 29 (3): 327–44.

Hammersley, M. (2003b) 'Can and should educational research be educative?', *Oxford Review of Education*, 29 (1): 3–25.

Hammersley, M. (2004) 'Should ethnographers be against inequality? On Becker, value neutrality and researcher partisanship', in B. Jeffrey and G. Walford (eds), *Ethnographies of Educational and Cultural Conflicts: Strategies and Resolutions*. Oxford: Elsevier.

Hammersley, M. (2005a) 'Countering the "new orthodoxy" in educational research: a response to Phil Hodkinson', *British Educational Research Journal*, 31 (2): 139–55.

Hammersley, M. (2005b) 'Is the evidence-based practice movement doing more good than harm?', *Evidence and Policy*, 1 (1): 1–16.

Hammersley, M. (2006) *Media Bias in Reporting Social Research? The Case of Reviewing Ethnic Inequalities in Education*. London: Routledge.

Hammersley, M. (2008a) 'Assessing validity in social research', in P. Alasuutari, L. Bickman and J. Brannen (eds), *Handbook of Social Research Methods*. London: Sage.

Hammersley, M. (2008b) 'Paradigm war revived? On the diagnosis of resistance to randomized controlled trials and systematic review in education', *International Journal of Research and Method in Education*, 31 (1): 3–10.

Hammersley, M. (2008c) *Questioning Qualitative Inquiry*. London: Sage.

Hammersley, M. (2008d) 'Troubles with triangulation', in M. Bergman (ed.), *Advances in Mixed Methods Research*. London: Sage.

Hammersley, M. (2008e) 'Troubling criteria: a critical commentary on Furlong and Oancea's framework for assessing educational research', *British Educational Research Journal*, 34 (6): 747–62.

Hammersley, M. (2009a) 'Challenging relativism: the problem of assessment criteria', *Qualitative Inquiry*, 15 (1): 3–29.

Hammersley, M. (2009b) 'Closing down the conversation? A reply to Smith and Hodkinson', *Qualitative Inquiry*, 15 (1): 40–8.

Hammersley, M. (2010a) 'Can we re-use qualitative data via secondary analysis? Notes on some terminological and substantive issues', *Sociological Research Online*, 15: 1. Available at www.socresonline.org.uk/15/1/5.html

Hammersley, M. (2010b) 'Reproducing or constructing: Some questions about transcription in social research', *Qualitative Research*, 10 (5): 553–69.

Hammersley, M. (2011) 'Objectivity: a reconceptualisation', in M. Williams and P. Vogt (eds), *The Sage Handbook of Methodological Innovation*. London: Sage.

Hammersley, M. (2012a) 'Qualitative causal analysis: Grounded theorizing and the qualitative survey', in B. Cooper, J. Glaesser, R. Gomm and M. Hammersley, *Challenging the Qualitative-Quantitative Divide*. London: Continuum.

Hammersley, M. (2012b) *What is Qualitative Research?* London: Bloomsbury.

Hammersley, M. (2012c) 'Review of Norman Denzin's *The Qualitative Manifesto: A Call to Arms*', *Qualitative Research*, 12, 3: 360–363.

Hammersley, M. and Atkinson, P. (2007) *Ethnography: Principles in Practice*, 3rd edn. London: Routledge.

Hammersley, M. and Gomm, R. (1997) 'Bias in social research', *Sociological Research Online*, 2: 1. www.socresonline.org.uk/socresonline/2/1/2.html (Reprinted in Hammersley 2000c.)

Hammersley, M. and Gomm, R. (2000) 'Case study and generalization', in R. Gomm, M. Hammersley and P. Foster (eds), *Case Study Method*. London: Sage.

Hammersley, M. and Gomm, R. (2008) 'Assessing the radical critique of interviews', in M. Hammersley, *Questioning Qualitative Inquiry*. London: Sage.

Hammersley, M., Scarth, J. and Webb, S. (1985) 'Developing and testing theory: the case of research on pupil learning and examinations', in R.G. Burgess (ed.), *Issues in Educational Research: Qualitative Methods*. Lewes: Falmer Press.

Hammond, K. and Stewart, T. (2001) *The Essential Brunswik*. Oxford: Oxford University Press.

Hampton, J.R. (1997) 'Evidence-based medicine, practice variations and clinical freedom', *Journal of Evaluation in Clinical Practice*, 3 (2): 123–31.

Hand, D.J. (2004) *Measurement Theory and Practice: The World Through Quantification*. London: Arnold.

Hannes, K. and Lockwood, C. (eds) (2012) *Synthesising Qualitative Research*. Oxford: Wiley–Blackwell.

Hardcastle, G.L. (1995) 'S.S. Stevens and the origins of operationism', *Philosophy of Science*, 62 (3): 404–24.

Harden, A. (2006) 'Extending the boundaries of systematic reviews to integrate different types of study: Examples of methods developed within reviews on young people's health', in J. Popay (ed.), *Moving Beyond Effectiveness in Evidence Synthesisis: Methodological Issues in the Synthesis of Diverse Sources of Evidence*. London: National Institute for Health and Clinical Excellence.

Hargreaves, D.H. (1996). 'Teaching as a Research-Based Profession: Possibilities and Prospects' (Annual Lecture). London: Teacher Training Agency. (Reprinted in M. Hammersley (ed.), *Educational Research and Evidence-Based Practice*. London: Sage, 2007.)

Hargreaves, D.H. (1999) 'The knowledge-creating school', *British Journal of Educational Studies*, 47: 122–44.

Hart, C. (1998) *Doing a Literature Review: Releasing the Social Science Research Imagination*. London: Sage.

Heath, A. and Martin, J. (1997) 'Why are there so few formal measuring instruments in social and political research?', in L. Lyberg, P. Biemer, M. Collins, E. de Leeuw, C. Dippo, N. Schwarz and D. Trewin (eds), *Survey Measurement and Process Quality*. New York: Wiley.

Hedges, L. and Olkin, I. (1985) *Statistical Methods for Meta-Analysis*. Orlando, FL: Academic Press.

Heshusius, L. (1994) 'Freeing ourselves from objectivity: managing subjectivity or turning toward a participatory mode of consciousness?', *Educational Researcher*, 23 (3): 15–22.

Hillage, J., Pearson, R. Anderson, A. and Tamkin, P. (1998) *Excellence in Research on Schools*. London: Department for Education and Employment.

Hodkinson, P. (2001) 'Response to the National Strategy Consultation Paper, for the National Educational Research Forum', *Research Intelligence*, 74 (February).

Hodkinson, P. (2004) 'Research as a form of work: expertise, community and methodological objectivity', *British Educational Research Journal*, 30 (1): 9–26.

Hodgkinson, P. (2000) 'Who wants to be a social engineer? A commentary on David Blunkett's speech to the ESRC', *Sociological Research Online*, 5: 1. www.socresearchonline.org.uk/5/1/hodgkinson.html

Holbeche, L. (2012) 'The nature and impact of the "new work culture" on white collar workers in the UK, 1997–2010'. Unpublished PhD thesis, The Open University.

Hollingdale, R.J. (ed.) (1977) *A Nietzsche Reader*. Harmondsworth: Penguin.

Hotopf, M. (2002) 'The pragmatic randomized controlled trial', *Advances in Psychiatric Treatment*, 8: 326–33.

House, E. and Howe, K. (2000) *Values in Evaluation and Social Research*. Thousand Oaks, CA: Sage.

Howell Major, C. and Savin-Baden, M. (2010) *An Introduction to Qualitative Research Synthesis: Managing the Information Explosion in Social Science Research*. London: Routledge.

Hoyningen-Huene, P. (1993) *Reconstructing Scientific Revolutions: Thomas S. Kuhn's Philosophy of Science*. Chicago, IL: University of Chicago Press. (First published in German in 1989.)

Hughes, R. (1991) *The Shock of the New: Art and the Century of Change*. London: Thames and Hudson.

Hunter, J. and Schmidt, F. (2004) *Methods of Meta-Analysis: Correcting Error and Bias in Research Findings*, 2nd edn. Thousand Oaks, CA: Sage.

Jesson, J., Matheson, L. and Lacey, F. (2011) *Doing Your Literature Review: Traditional and Systematic Approaches*. London: Sage.

John, M., Eckhardt, G. and Hiebsch, H. (1989) 'Kurt Lewin's early intentions (dedicated to his 100th birthday)', *European Journal of Social Psychology*, 19: 163–9.

Johnson, H.M. (1936) 'Pseudo-mathematics in the mental and social sciences', *American Journal of Psychology*, 48 (2): 342–51.

Johnson, T., O'Rourke, D., Chavez, N., Sudman, S., Warnecke, R., Lacey, L. and Horm. J. (1997) 'Social cognition and responses to survey questions among culturally diverse populations', in L. Lyberg, P. Biemer, M. Collins, E. de Leeuw, C. Dippo, N. Schwarz and D. Trewin (eds), *Survey Measurement and Process Quality*. New York: Wiley.

Kaplan, A. (1964) *The Conduct of Inquiry: Methodology for Behavioural Science*. New York: Chandler.

Kearney, M. (1988) 'Ready-to-wear: discovering grounded formal theory', *Research in Nursing Health*, 21: 179–86.

Kearney, M. (1998) 'Truthful self-nurturing: a grounded formal theory of women's addiction recovery', *Qualitative Health Research*, 8 (4): 495–512.

Kearney, M. (2001) 'Enduring love: a grounded formal theory of women's experience of domestic violence', *Research in Nursing and Health*, 24: 270–82.

Kelly, A. (1985) 'Action research: what is it and what can it do?', in R.G. Burgess (ed.), *Issues in Educational Research: Qualitative Methods*. London: Falmer.

Kemmis, S. (1982) 'General introduction', in Action Research in Curriculum Course Team (eds), *The Action Research Reader*. Deakin: Deakin University Press.

Kemmis, S. (1988) 'Action research', in J.P. Keeves (ed.), *Educational Research, Methodology, and Measurement: An International Handbook*. Oxford: Pergamon.

Kempf-Leonard, K. (ed.) (2004) *Encyclopedia of Social Measurement*, 3 volumes. Amsterdam: Elsevier Academic Press.

Konnerup, M-K. and Kongsted, H. (2012) 'Do Cochrane reviews provide a good model for social science? The role of observational studies in systematic reviews', *Evidence and Policy*, 8 (1): 79–96.

Kuhn, T.S. (1961) 'The function of measurement in modern physical science', *Isis*, 52: 161–90. (Reprinted in Kuhn 1977.)

Kuhn, T.S. (1970) *The Structure of Scientific Revolutions*, 2nd edn. Chicago, IL: University of Chicago Press.

Kuhn, T.S. (1977) *The Essential Tension*. Chicago, IL: University of Chicago Press.

Kuhn, T.S. (2000) *The Road Since Structure: Philosophical Essays, 1970–1993*. Chicago, IL: University of Chicago Press.

Lakoff, G. and Johnson, M. (1980) *Metaphors We Live By*. Chicago, IL: University of Chicago Press.

Laming, D. (2002) 'A review of *Measurement in Psychology: a critical history of a methodological concept*', *Quarterly Journal of Experimental Psychology A*, 55: 689–92.

Lane. J-E. (2000) *New Public Management.* London: Routledge.

LaPiere, R.T (1934) 'Attitudes versus actions', *Social Forces*, 13 (2): 230–7.

Lather, P. (1993) 'Fertile obsession: validity after poststructuralism', *The Sociological Quarterly*, 34:4: 673–693.

Lather, P. (1999) 'To be of use: the work of reviewing', *Review of Educational Research*, 69 (1): 2–7.

Lather, P. (2004) 'This *IS* your father's paradigm: Government intrusion and the case of qualitative research in education', *Qualitative Inquiry*, 10 (1): 15–34.

Leach, E. (1969) 'Virgin birth', in *Genesis as Myth.* London: Jonathan Cape.

Lear, J. (1988) *Aristotle: The Desire to Understand.* Cambridge: Cambridge University Press.

Letherby, G. (2004) 'Quoting and counting: an autobiographical response to Oakley', *Sociology*, 38 (1): 175–89.

Levy, R. (2010) 'New public management: end of an era?', *Public Policy and Administration*, 25 (2): 234–40.

Lewin, K. (1946) 'Action research and minority problems', *Journal of Social Issues*, 2: 34–46. (Reprinted in K. Lewin, *Resolving Social Conflicts and Field Theory in Social Science.* Washington, DC: American Psychological Association, 1997.)

Lewin, K. (1951) *Field Theory in Social Science: Selected Theoretical Papers* (ed. D. Cartwright). New York: Harper and Row.

Lewin, M. (1987) 'Kurt Lewin and the invisible bird on the flagpole: a reply to Graebner', *Journal of Social Issues*, 43 (3): 123–39.

Light, R.J. and Pillemer, D.B. (1984) *Summing Up: The Science of Reviewing Research.* Cambridge, MA: Harvard University Press.

Lincoln, Y. and Cannella, G. (2004) 'Dangerous discourses: methodological conservatism and governmental regimes of truth', *Qualitative Inquiry*, 10 (1): 5–14.

Lincoln, Y. and Guba, E. (1985) *Naturalistic Inquiry.* Newbury Park, CA: Sage.

Lindblom, C. (1979) 'Still muddling, not yet through', *Public Administration Review*, 39: 517–26.

Lindblom, C.E. and Cohen, D.K. (1979) *Usable Knowledge: Social Science and Social Problem Solving.* New Haven, CT: Yale University Press.

Lippitt, R. (1986) 'The small group and participatory democracy: comment on Graebner', *Journal of Social Issues*, 42 (1): 155–6.

Livingston, G. (1999) 'Beyond watching over established ways: a review as recasting the literature, recasting the lived', *Review of Educational Research*, 69 (1): 9–19.

Loader, I. and Sparks, R. (2010) *Public Criminology?* London: Routledge.

Lobkowicz, N. (1967) *Theory and Practice.* Notre Dame, IN: Notre Dame University Press.

Lobkowicz, N. (1977) 'On the history of theory and *praxis*', in T. Ball (ed.), *Political Theory and Praxis: New Perspectives.* Minneapolis, MN: University of Minnesota Press.

Lofland, J. (1970) 'Analytic interruptus and interactionist imagery', in T. Shibutani (ed.), *Human Nature and Collective Behavior: Papers in Honor of Herbert Blumer.* Englewood Cliffs, NJ: Prentice–Hall.

Lofland, J. (1971) *Analyzing Social Settings.* Belmont, CA: Wadsworth.

Loughlin, M. (2003) 'Ethics and evidence-based medicine: fallibility and responsibility in clinical science [Kenneth Goodman, essay review]', *Journal of Evaluation in Clinical Practice*, 9 (2): 141–4.

Lynch, M. (1993) *Scientific Practice and Ordinary Action*. Cambridge: Cambridge University Press.

Maasen, S. and Weingart, P. (2005) 'What's new in scientific advice to politics?', in S. Maasen and P. Weingart (eds), *Democratization of Expertise?* Dordrecht: Springer.

Macdonald, G. (1996) 'Ice therapy? Why we need randomised controls', in Barnado's *What Works? Effective Social Interventions in Child Welfare*. Ilford: Barnado's.

Macdonald, K. (1995) *The Sociology of the Professions*. London: Sage.

MacIntyre, A. (1985) *After Virtue*, 2nd edn. London: Duckworth.

MacLure, M. (2002) 'Postmodernism: a postscript', in C. Day, J. Elliott, B. Somekh and R. Winter (eds), *Theory and Practice in Action Research*. Oxford: Symposium Books. (First published in *Educational Action Research*, 3 (1): 1995.)

MacLure, M. (2005) 'Clarity bordering on stupidity: where's the quality in systematic review?', *Journal of Education Policy*, 20 (4): 393–416.

Maltby, J. (2008) 'There is no such thing as audit society: a reading of Power on *The Audit Society*'. Available at https://lra.le.ac.uk/handle/2381/3828 (accessed 4 April 2012).

Marks, H.M. (1997) *The Progress of Experiment*. Cambridge: Cambridge University Press.

Marris, P. and Rein, M. (1967) *Dilemmas of Social Reform*, 2nd edn. London: Routledge and Kegan Paul.

Marris, R.L. (1971) 'The economic theory of "managerial" capitalism', in G.C. (ed.), *The Theory of the Firm*. Harmondsworth: Penguin.

Marrow, A. (1969) *The Practical Theorist: The Life and Work of Kurt Lewin*. New York: Teachers College Press.

Matheson, G. (2006) 'Intervals and ratios: the invariantive transformations of Stanley Smith Stevens', *History of the Human Sciences*, 19 (3): 65–81.

Maxwell, J. (2004) 'Reemergent scientism, postmodernism, and dialogue across differences', *Qualitative Inquiry*, 10 (1): 35–41.

Mayne, J. and Zapico-Goni, E. (eds) (1997) *Monitoring Performance in the Public Sector*. New Brunswick, NJ: Transaction Books.

McKinney, J.C. (1954) 'Constructive typology in social research', in J.T. Doby, E.A. Suchman, J.C. McKinney, R.G. Francis and J.P. Dean (eds), *An Introduction to Social Research*. Harrisburg, PA: Stackpole.

McKinney, J.C. (1966) *Constructive Typology and Social Theory*. New York: Appleton–Century–Crofts.

McKinney, J.C. (1970) 'Sociological theory and the process of typification', in J.C. McKinney and E.A. Tiryakian (eds), *Theoretical Sociology: Perspectives and Developments*. New York: Appleton–Century–Crofts.

McNaughton, D. (2000) 'A synthesis of home visiting research', *Public Health Nursing*, 17 (6): 405–14.

McSherry, R., Simmons, M. and Abbott, P. (eds) (2002) *Evidence-Informed Nursing: A Guide for Clinical Nurses*. London: Routledge.

Meacham, S.J. (1998) 'Threads of a new language: a response to Eisenhart's "On the subject of interpretive reviews"', *Review of Educational Research*, 68 (4): 401–7.

Mead, M. (1928) *Coming of Age in Samoa*. New York: HarperCollins.

Merton, R.K. (1973) *The Sociology of Science*. Chicago, IL: University of Chicago Press.

Merton, R.K., Sills, D.L. and Stigler, S.M. (1984) 'The Kelvin dictum and social science; an excursion into the history of an idea', *Journal of the History of the Behavioral Sciences*, 20: 319–31.

Michell, J. (1997) 'Quantitative science and the definition of measurement in psychology', *British Journal of Psychology*, 88: 355–83.

Michell, J. (1999) *Measurement in Psychology: Critical History of a Methodological Concept*. Cambridge: Cambridge University Press.

Michell, J. (2000) 'Normal science, pathological science and psychometrics', *Theory and Psychology*, 10 (5): 639–67.

Michell, J. (2002) 'Stevens's theory of scales of measurement and its place in modern psychology', *Australian Journal of Psychology*, 54 (2): 99–104.

Michell, J. (2007) 'Measurement', in S.P. Turner and M.W. Risjord (eds), *Philosophy of Anthropology and Sociology*. Amsterdam: Elsevier.

Miles, M. and Huberman, M. (1994) *Qualitative Data Analysis*, 2nd edn. London: Sage.

Miller, L. and Whalley, J.B. (2005) 'Stories from the field – "taking the piss": notes on collaborative practice as research', in B. Somekh and C. Lewin (eds), *Research Methods in the Social Sciences*. London: Sage. pp. 313–17.

Moles, J.A. (1977) 'Standardization and measurement in cultural anthropology: a neglected area', *Current Anthropology*, 18 (2): 235–58.

Morgan, D. (1996) *Family Connections: An Introduction to Family Studies*. Cambridge: Polity Press.

Morgan, D. (2011a) 'Locating "family practices"', *Sociological Research Online*, 16 (4): 14. Available at www.socresonline.org.uk/16/4/14.html (accessed 20 December 2011).

Morgan, D. (2011b) *Rethinking Family Practices*. Basingstoke: Palgrave Macmillan.

Mosteller, F. and Boruch, R. (eds) (2002) *Evidence Matters: Randomized Trials in Education Research*. Washington, DC: Brookings Institution.

Mueller, C.W. (2004) 'Conceptualization, operationalization, and measurement', in M.S. Lewis-Beck, A. Bryman and T.F. Lia (eds), *The Sage Encyclopedia of Social Science Research Methods*. Thousand Oaks, CA: Sage.

Murphy, E., Dingwall, R., Greatbatch, D., Parker, S. and Watson, P. (1998) 'Qualitative research methods in health technology assessment: a review of the literature', *Health Technology Assessment,* 2 (16): 1–260. Available at www.hta.nhsweb.nhs.uk/execsumm/summ216.htm (accessed 14 August 2002).

Naroll, R. (1962) *Data Quality Control – A New Research Technique: Prolegomena to a Cross-cultural Study of Culture Stress*. New York: Free Press.

Naroll, R. (ed.) (1973) *A Handbook of Method in Cultural Anthropology*. New York: Columbia University Press.

National Educational Research Forum (2000) *A National Strategy Consultation Paper*. Nottingham: NERF.

National Research Council (NRC) (2002) *Scientific Research in Education* (eds Richard J. Shavelson and Lisa Towne). Washington, DC: National Academies Press.

Naylor, G. (1988) *Mama Day*. New York: Ticknor and Fields.

Needham, R. (1975) 'Polythetic classification: convergence and consequences', *Man* N.S., 10 (3): 349–69.

Newell, R.W. (1986) *Objectivity, Empiricism, and Truth*. London: Routledge and Kegan Paul.

Newman, E.B. (1974) 'On the origin of "scales of measurement"', in H.R. Moskowitz et al. (eds), *Sensation and Measurement: Papers in Honor of S. S. Stevens*. Dordrecht: Reidel.

Nisbet, J. and Broadfoot, P. (1980) *The Impact of Research on Policy and Practice in Education*. Aberdeen: Aberdeen University Press.

Noblit, G.W. and Hare, R.D. (1988) *Meta-Ethnography: Synthesizing Qualitative Studies*. Newbury Park, CA: Sage.

Norris, N. (1990) *Understanding Educational Evaluation*. London: Palgrave Macmillan.

Nove, A. (1980) *The Soviet Economic System*, 2nd edn. London: Allen and Unwin.

Nussbaum, M. (1986) *The Fragility of Goodness*. Cambridge: Cambridge University Press.

Nussbaum, M. (1990) *Love's Knowledge*. Oxford: Oxford University Press.

O'Hear, A. (ed.) (1996) *Verstehen and Humane Understanding*. Cambridge: Cambridge University Press.

Oakeshott, M. (1962) *Rationalism in Politics, and Other Essays*. London: Methuen.

Oakley, A. (1999) 'Paradigm wars: some thoughts on a personal and public trajectory', *International Journal of Social Research Methodology*, 2 (3): 247–54.

Oakley, A. (2000) *Experiments in Knowing: Gender and Method in the Social Sciences*. Cambridge: Polity Press.

Oakley, A. (2006) 'Resistances to "new" technologies of evaluation: education research in the UK as a case study', *Evidence and Policy*, 2 (1): 63–87.

Oakley, A. (2007) 'Evidence-informed policy and practice: challenges for social science', in M. Hammersley (ed.), *Educational Research and Evidence-based Practice*. London: Sage. pp. 91–105. (First published by Manchester Statistical Society, 13 February 2001.)

Oswald, N. and Bateman, H. (2000) 'Treating individuals according to evidence: why do primary care practitioners do what they do?', *Journal of Evaluation in Clinical Practice*, 16 (2): 139–48.

Otto, H-U., Polutta, A. and Ziegler, H. (eds) (2009) *Evidence-Based Practice: Modernising the Knowledge Base of Social Work?* Opladen: Barbara Budrich.

Paddock, J. (1961) 'Oscar Lewis's Mexico', *Anthropological Quarterly*, 34 (3): 129–49.

Paterson, B., Thorne, S., Canam, C. and Jillings, C. (2001) *Meta-Study of Qualitative Health Research: A Practical Guide to Meta-Analysis and Meta-Synthesis*. Thousand Oaks, CA: Sage.

Pawson, R. (2001a) *Evidence Based Policy I. In Search of a Method*. ESRC UK Centre for Evidence Based Policy and Practice: Working Paper 3.

Pawson, R. (2001b) *Evidence Based Policy II. The Promise of 'Realist Synthesis'*, ESRC UK Centre for Evidence Based Policy and Practice: Working Paper 4.

Pawson, R. (2006) *Evidence-based Policy: A Realist Perspective*. London: Sage.

Pawson, R. and Tilley, N. (1997) *Realistic Evaluation*. London: Sage.

Peirce, C. S. (1965) 'The fixation of belief', in C. Hartshorne and P. Weiss (eds), *Collected Papers of Charles Sanders Peirce*, Volume V. Cambridge, MA: Belknap Press. (First published in 1877.)

Pels, D. (2003) *Unhastening Science*. Liverpool: Liverpool University Press.

Peräkylä, A. (1997/2003) 'Validity and reliability in research based on tapes and transcripts', in D. Silverman (ed.), *Qualitative Analysis: Issues of Theory and Method*. London: Sage. pp. 201–20. (Revised edition 2003; reprinted in C. Seale (ed.), *Social Research Methods. A Reader*. London: Routledge, 2003.)

Petticrew, M. and Roberts, H. (2006) *Systematic Reviews in the Social Sciences*. Oxford: Blackwell.

Phillips, D.L. (1971) *Knowledge From What? Theories and Methods in Social Research*. Chicago, IL: Rand McNally.

Polanyi, M. (1958) *Personal Knowledge*. Chicago, IL: University of Chicago Press.

Polanyi, M. (1962) 'The republic of science', *Minerva*, 1 (1): 54–73.

Polanyi, M. (1966) *The Tacit Dimension*. Garden City, NY: Doubleday.

Pollitt, C. (1990) *Managerialism and the Public Services*. Oxford: Blackwell.

Pollitt, C. (1998) 'Managerialism revisited', in B. Peters and D. Savoie (eds), *Taking Stock: Assessing Public Sector Reforms*. Montreal: McGill-Queens University Press.

Polsky, N. (1971, originally published 1967) *Hustlers, Beats and Others*. Harmondsworth: Penguin.

Pólya, G. (1957) *How to Solve It*. Garden City, NY: Doubleday.

Popay, J., Rogers, A. and Williams, G. (1998) 'Rationale and standards for the systematic review of qualitative literature in health services research', *Qualitative Health Research*, 8 (3): 341–51.

Pope, C., Mays, N. and Popay, J. (2007) *Synthesizing Qualitative and Quantitative Health Evidence: A Guide to Methods*. Maidenhead: Open University Press.

Poplewitz, T. (1999) 'Reviewing reviews: "RER", research, and the politics of educational knowledge', *Review of Educational Research*, 69 (4): 397–405.

Popper, K. R. (1957) *The Poverty Of Historicism*. London: Routledge and Kegan Paul.

Popper, K R. (1959) *The Logic of Scientific Discovery*. London: Hutchinson.

Popper, K.R. (1963) *Conjectures and Refutations: The Growth of Scientific Knowledge*. London: Routledge and Kegan Paul.

Potter, J. and Hepburn, A. (2005) 'Qualitative interviews in psychology: problems and possibilities', *Qualitative Research in Psychology*, 2 (4): 281–307.

Pound, P., Britten, N., Morgan, M., Yardley, L., Pope, C., Daker-White, G. and Campbell, R. (2005) 'Resisting medicines: a synthesis of qualitative studies of medicine taking', *Social Science and Medicine*, 61: 133–55.

Power, M. (1997) *The Audit Society: Rituals of Verification*. Oxford: Oxford University Press.

Pring, R. (2000) *Philosophy of Educational Research*. London: Continuum.

Putnam, H. (2002) *The Collapse of the Fact-Value Dichotomy and Other Essays*. Cambridge, MA: Harvard University Press.

Ragin, C. (1987) *The Comparative Method*. Berkeley, CA: University of California Press.

Ragin, C. (2008) *Redesigning Social Inquiry*. Chicago, IL: University of Chicago Press.

Rajchman, J. (1991) *Philosophical Events: Essays of the 80s*. New York: Columbia University Press.

Rapoport, R. (1970) 'Three dilemmas in action research', *Human Relations*, 23 (6): 499–513.

Ravetz, J.R. (1971) *Scientific Knowledge and Its Social Problems*. Oxford: Oxford University Press.

Reason, P. and Bradbury, H. (2001) 'Introduction', in P. Reason and H. Bradbury (eds), *Handbook of Action Research: Participative Inquiry and Practice*. London: Sage.

Reichenbach, H. (1951) *The Rise of Scientific Philosophy*. Berkeley, CA: University of California Press.

Ridley, D. (2008) *The Literature Review: A Step-by-Step Guide for Students*. London: Sage.

Robinson, A. (2007) *The Story of Measurement*. New York: Thames and Hudson.

Robinson, R. (1954) *Definition*. Oxford: Oxford University Press.

Rockefeller, S. (1991) *John Dewey: Religious Faith and Democratic Humanism*. New York: Columbia University Press.

Rogers, C. (1982) *Social Psychology of Schooling*. London: Routledge.

Rosch, E. (1999) 'Reclaiming concepts', in R. Nunez and W.J. Freeman (eds), *Reclaiming Cognition: The Primacy of Action, Intention and Emotion*. Exeter: Imprint Academic. Published simultaneously in *The Journal of Consciousness Studies*, 6 (11–12): 61–77. Also available at http://psychology.berkeley.edu/faculty/profiles/erosch1999.pdf (accessed 19 February 2008).

Rosenblatt, P. (1981) 'Ethnographic case studies', in M. Brewer and B. Collins (eds), *Scientific Inquiry and the Social Sciences*. San Francisco, CA: Jossey–Bass.

Rosenthal, R. (1984) *Meta-Analytic Procedures for Social Research*, Newbury Park, CA: Sage.

Rosnow, R. (1981) *Paradigms in Transition: The Methodology of Social Inquiry*. New York: Oxford University Press.

Rothman, J. and Thomas, E.J. (eds) (1994) *Intervention Research: Design and Development for Human Service*. New York: Haworth Press.

Rule, J. (1997) *Theory and Progress in Social Science*. Cambridge: Cambridge University Press.

Ryan, A. (1995) *John Dewey and the High Tide of American Liberalism*. New York: W.W. Norton.

Ryan, K. and Hood, L. (2004) 'Guarding the castle and opening the gates', *Qualitative Inquiry*, 10 (1): 79–95.

Sackett, D.L., Rosenberg, W., Gray, J.A.M., Haynes, R.B. and Richardson, W. (1996) 'Evidence-based medicine: what it is and what it isn't', *British Medical Journal*, 312: 71–2.

Sackett, D., Straus, S., Richardson, W., Rosenberg, W. and Haynes, R. (2000) *Evidence-Based Medicine: How to Practice and Teach EBM*, 2nd edn. New York: Churchill Livingstone.

Sandelowski, M. and Barroso, J. (2007) *Handbook for Synthesizing Qualitative Research*. New York: Springer.

Sanford, N. (1970) 'Whatever happened to action research?', *Journal of Social Issues*, 26 (4): 3–23.

Sargant, N. (1995) 'Consumer power as a pillar of democracy', in G. Dench, T. Flower and K. Gavron (eds), *Young at Eighty: The Prolific Public life of Michael Young*. Manchester: Carcanet Press.

Sartori, G. (ed.) (1984) *Social Science Concepts: A Systematic Analysis*. Beverly Hills, CA: Sage.

Sartori, G., Riggs, F.W. and Teune, H. (1975) *Tower of Babel: On the Definition and Analysis of Concepts in the Social Sciences*. Occasional Paper No. 6. Pittsburgh, PA: International Studies Association.

Scharff, R.C. (1995) *Comte After Positivism*. Cambridge: Cambridge University Press.

Schegloff, E.A. (1971) 'Notes on a conversational practice: formulating place', in D. Sudnow (ed.), *Studies in Social Interaction*. New York: Free Press.

Scheurich, J.J. (1997) *Research Method in the Postmodern*. London: The Falmer Press.

Schofield, J. (1990) 'Increasing the generalizability of qualitative research', in E. Eisner and A. Peshkin (eds), *Qualitative Inquiry in Education*. New York: Teachers College Press.

Schön, D. (1983) *The Reflective Practitioner*. London: Temple Smith.

Schön, D. (1987) *Educating the Reflective Practitioner*. San Francisco, CA: Jossey–Bass.

Schütz, A. (1962) *Collected Papers*, Volume 1. The Hague: Martinus Nijhoff.

Schütz, A. (1970) *Reflections on the Problem of Relevance*. New Haven, CT: Yale University Press.

Schwandt, T. (1996) 'Farewell to criteriology', *Qualitative Inquiry*, 2 (1): 58–72.

Schwandt, T.A. (1998) 'The interpretive review of educational matters: is there any other kind?', *Review of Educational Research*, 68 (4): 409–12.

Schwandt, T.A. (2002) *Evaluation Practice Reconsidered*. New York: Peter Lang.

Scriven, M. (2009) 'Demythologizing causation and evidence', in Donaldson, S., Christie, C., and Mark, M. (eds.) (2009) *What Counts as Credible Evidence in Applied Research and Evaluation Practice*. Thousand Oaks CA: Sage.

Shadish, W.R., Cook, T.D. and Leviton, L.C. (1991) *Foundations of Program Evaluation: Theories of Practice*. Newbury Park, CA: Sage.

Shahar, E. (1997) 'A Popperian view of "evidence-based medicine"', *Journal of Evaluation in Clinical Practice*, 3 (2): 109–16.

Sharrock, R. and Read, R. (2002) *Kuhn: Philosopher of Scientific Revolution*. Cambridge: Polity Press.

Shaw, I.F. (1999) *Qualitative Evaluation*. London: Sage.

Sherman, L., Farrington, D., Welsh, B. and MacKenzie, D. (2002) *Evidence-Based Crime Prevention*, 2nd edn. London: Routledge.

Silverman, D. (ed.) (1997) *Qualitative Research: Theory, Method and Practice*. London: Sage.

Slavin, R. (1986) 'Best-evidence synthesis: an alternative to meta-analysis and traditional reviews', *Educational Researcher*, 15 (9): 5–11.

Slavin, R.E. (1995) 'Best evidence synthesis: an intelligent alternative to meta-analysis', *Journal of Clinical Epidemiology*, 48 (1): 9–18.

Slavin, R.E. (2002) 'Evidence-based education policies: transforming educational practice and research', *Educational Researcher*, 31 (7): 15–21.

Slavin, R.E. (2004) 'Education research can and must address "what works" questions', *Educational Researcher*, 33 (1): 27–8.

Smith, G. (2000) 'Research and Inspection: HMI and OFSTED, 1981–1996 – a commentary', *Oxford Review of Education*, 26 (3&4): 333–52.

Smith, J.K. (1984) 'The problem of criteria for judging interpretive inquiry', *Educational Evaluation and Policy Analysis*, 6 (4): 379–91.

Smith, J.K. (1989) *The Nature of Social and Educational Inquiry: Empiricism Versus Interpretation*. Norwood, NJ: Ablex.

Smith, J.K. and Deemer, D.K. (2000) 'The problem of criteria in the age of relativism', in N.K. Denzin and Y.S. Lincoln (eds), *Handbook of Qualitative Research*, 2nd edn. Thousand Oaks, CA: Sage.

Smith, J.K. and Hodkinson, P. (2005) 'Relativism, criteria, and politics', in N. Denzin and Y. Lincoln (eds), *The Sage Handbook of Qualitative Research*, 3rd edn. Thousand Oaks, CA: Sage. pp. 915–32.

Smith, J.K. and Hodkinson, P. (2009) 'Challenging neorealism: a response to Hammersley', *Qualitative Inquiry*, 15: 30–9.

Smith, M. and Glass, G. (1977) 'Meta-analysis of psychotherapy outcome studies', *American Psychologist*, 32: 752–60.

Sohn, D. (1996) 'Meta-analysis and science', *Theory and Psychology*, 6 (2): 229–46.

Spencer, L., Richie, J., Lewis, J. and Dillon, L. (2003) *Quality in Qualitative Evaluation: A Framework for Assessing Research Evidence*. Prepared by the National Centre for Social Research on behalf of the Cabinet Office.

Sperber, D. and Wilson, D. (1986) *Relevance, Communication and Cognition*. Oxford: Blackwell.

St Clair, R. (ed.) (2009) *Education Science: Critical Perspectives*. Rotterdam: Sense.

St Pierre, E. (2002) '"Science" rejects postmodernism', *Educational Researcher*, 31 (8): 25–7.

St Pierre, E. (2006) 'Scientifically based research in education: Epistemology and ethics', *Adult Education Quarterly*, 56 (4): 239–66.

Stacey, M., Batstone, W., Bell, C. and Murcott, A. (1975) *Power, Persistence and Change: A Second Study of Banbury*. London: Routledge and Kegan Paul.

Stake, R. (1978) 'The case-study method in social inquiry', *Educational Researcher*, 7: 7–8.

Stake, R. (1995) *The Art of Case Study Research*. Thousand Oaks, CA: Sage.

Steger, M. and Roy, R. (2010) *Neoliberalism: A Very Short Introduction*. Oxford: Oxford University Press.

Stenhouse, L. (1975) *An Introduction to Curriculum Research and Development*. London: Heinemann.

Stevens, S.S. (1946) 'On the theory of scales of measurement', *Science*, 103: 677–80.

Stokes, D. (1997) *Pasteur's Quadrant: Basic Science and Technological Innovation*. Washington, DC: Brookings Institution Press.

Stove, D. (1982) *Popper and After*. Oxford: Pergamon Press.

Strauss, A. (1970) 'Discovering new theory from previous theory', in T. Shibutani (ed.), *Human Nature and Collective Behavior*. Englewood Cliffs, NJ: Prentice–Hall.

Strauss, A. (1976) *Images of the American City*. New Brunswick, NJ: Transaction Books.

Strauss, A. (1978) *Negotiations: Varieties, Contexts, Processes, and Social Order*. San Francisco, CA: Jossey–Bass.

Strauss, A. (1987) *Qualitative Analysis for Social Scientists*. Cambridge: Cambridge University Press.

Strauss, A.L. and Corbin, J.M. (1998) *Basics of Qualitative Research*, 2nd edn. Thousand Oaks, CA: Sage.

Strike, K. and Posner, G. (1983) 'Types of synthesis and their criteria', in S.A. Ward and L.J. Reed (eds), *Knowledge Structure and Use: Implications for Synthesis and Interpretation*. Philadelphia, PA: Temple University Press.

Swift, A. and White, S. (2008) 'Political theory, social science, and real politics', in D. Leopold and M. Stears (eds), *Political Theory: Methods and Approaches*. Oxford: Oxford University Press.

Taylor, J.R. (2001) 'Linguistics: prototype theory', in N.J. Smelser and P.B. Baltes (eds), *International Encyclopedia of the Social and Behavioral Sciences*. Amsterdam: Elsevier.

Taylor, J.R. (2003) *Linguistic Categorization*. Oxford: Oxford University Press.

Thomson, Sir William (Lord Kelvin) (1889) *Popular Lectures and Addresses*, Volume 1. London: Macmillan.

Thorne, S., Jenson, L., Kearney, M.H., Noblit, G. and Sandelowski, M. (2004) 'Qualitative metasynthesis: reflections on methodological orientation and ideological agenda', *Qualitative Health Research*, 14: 1342–65.

Tiryakian, E.A. (1968) 'Typologies', in D.L. Sills (ed.), *International Encyclopedia of the Social Sciences*. New York: Free Press.

Tooley, J. with Darby, D. (1998) *Educational Research: A Critique*. London: Ofsted.

Torgerson, C., Brooks, G. and Hall, J. (2006) *A Systematic Review of the Research Literature on the Use of Phonics in the Teaching of Reading and Spelling*. London: Department for Education and Skills. Available at http://collection.europarchive. org/tna/20060731065549/http://www.dcsf.gov.uk/research/data/uploadfiles/ RR711_.pdf (accessed 3 April 2012).

Torgerson, W. (1958) *Theory and Method of Scaling*. New York: Wiley.

Trinder, L. with Reynolds, S. (eds) (2000) *Evidence-Based Practice: A Critical Appraisal*. Oxford: Blackwell Science.

Truzzi, M. (ed.) (1974) *Verstehen: Subjective Understanding in the Social Sciences*. Reading, MA: Addison-Wesley.

Turner, S.P. (1980) *Sociological Explanation as Translation*. Cambridge: Cambridge University Press.

Turner, S.P. (2005) 'Expertise and political responsibility: the *Columbia* shuttle catastrophe', in S. Maasen and P. Weingart (eds), *Democratization of Expertise?* Dordrecht: Springer.

van Elteren, M. (1992) 'Karl Korsch and Lewinian social psychology: failure of a project', *History of the Human Sciences*, 5 (2): 33–61.

van Inwagen, P. (2007) 'Metaphysics', in *Stanford Encyclopedia of Philosophy*. Available at http://plato.stanford.edu/entries/metaphysics/ (accessed 8 March 2012).

Vellemann, P.F. and Wilkinson, L. (1993) 'Nominal, ordinal, interval, and ratio scale typologies are misleading', *American Statistician*, 47: 65–72.

Vietor, R.H.K. (1994) *Contrived Competition: Regulation and Deregulation in America*. Cambridge, MA: Harvard University Press.

Viswanathan, M. (2005) *Measurement Error and Research Design*. Thousand Oaks, CA: Sage.

Walker, R. (1995) 'The dynamics of poverty and social exclusion', in G. Room (ed.), *Beyond the Threshold: The Measurement and Analysis of Social Exclusion*. Bristol: Policy Press.

Wallace, M. (1986) 'A historical review of action research: some implications for the education of teachers in their managerial role', *Journal of Education for Teaching*, 13 (2): 97–115.

Weiss, C. (1977) 'Research for policy's sake: the enlightenment function of social science research', *Policy Analysis*, 3 (4): 531–45.

Weiss, C. (1979) 'The many meanings of research utilisation', *Public Administration Review*, 39: 426–31.

Weiss, C. with Bucuvalas, M. (1980) *Social Science Research and Decision Making*. New York: Columbia University Press.

Weiss, C. (1983) 'Ideology, interests, and information', in D. Callahan and B. Jennings (eds), *Ethics, The Social Sciences, and Policy Analysis*. New York: Plenum Press.

Welsh, B. and Farrington, D. (2001) 'Toward an evidence-based approach to preventing crime', *The Annals of the American Academy of Social and Political Science*, 578: 158–73.

Westbrook, R. (1991) *John Dewey and American Democracy*. Ithaca, NY: Cornell University Press.

Westmarland, N. (2001) 'The quantitative/qualitative debate and feminist research: a subjective view of objectivity', *Forum Qualitative Sozialforschung/Forum: Qualitative Social Research*, 2 (1), Art. 13. http://nbn-resolving.de/urn:nbn:de:0114-fqs0101135 Available at www.qualitative-research.net/index.php/fqs/article/view/974 (accessed June 2012).

Wilks, S.S. (1961) 'Some aspects of quantification in science', in H. Woolf (ed.), *Quantification: A History of the Meaning of Measurement in the Natural and Social Sciences*. Indianapolis, IN: Bobbs–Merrill.

Willer, D. and Willer, J. (1973) *Systematic Empiricism: Critique of a Pseudoscience*. Englewood Cliffs, NJ: Prentice–Hall.

Williams, Michael (2001) *Problems of Knowledge: A Critical Introduction to Epistemology*. Oxford: Oxford University Press.

Williams, Malcolm (2001) 'Complexity, probability and causation: implications for homelessness research'. Available at www.whb.co.uk/socialissues/mw.htm (accessed 11 March 2008).

Williamson, T. (1994) *Vagueness*. London: Routledge.

Winch, P. (1958) *The Idea of a Social Science*. London: Routledge and Kegan Paul.

Wirth, L. (ed.) (1940) *Eleven Twenty-Six: A Decade of Social Science Research*. Chicago, IL: University of Chicago Press.

Wolf, A. (2002) *Does Education Matter? Myths about Education and Economic Growth*. Harmondsworth: Penguin.

Woolf, H. (ed.) (1961) *Quantification: A History of the Meaning of Measurement in the Natural and Social Sciences*. Indianapolis, IN: Bobbs–Merrill.

Woolgar, S. (1988a) *Science: The Very Idea*. London: Routledge.

Woolgar, S. (ed.) (1988b) *Knowledge and Reflexivity*. London: Sage.

Worrall, J. (2002) 'What evidence in evidence-based medicine?', *Philosophy of Science*, 69: S316–S330.

Yin, R. and Heald, K. (1975) 'Using the case survey method to analyze policy studies', *Administrative Science Quarterly*, 20: 371–81.

Zeller, R.A. and Carmines, E.G. (1980) *Measurement in the Social Sciences*. Cambridge: Cambridge University Press.

Ziman, J. (2000) *Real Science*. Cambridge: Cambridge University Press.

Zimmerman, D.H. and Pollner, M. (1971) 'The everyday world as a phenomenon', in J.D. Douglas (ed.), *Understanding Everyday Life*. London: Routledge.

Zuckert, C. (2002) 'Hermeneutics in practice: Gadamer on ancient philosophy', in R.J. Dostal (ed.), *The Cambridge Companion to Gadamer*. Cambridge: Cambridge University Press.

NAME INDEX

SUBJECT INDEX